The publisher gratefully acknowledges the generous support of the Ahmanson Foundation Humanities Endowment Fund of the University of California Press Foundation.

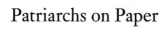

Patriarchs on Paper

Patriarchs on Paper

*A Critical History of Medieval
Chan Literature*

Alan Cole

UNIVERSITY OF CALIFORNIA PRESS

University of California Press, one of the most
distinguished university presses in the United States,
enriches lives around the world by advancing scholarship
in the humanities, social sciences, and natural sciences. Its
activities are supported by the UC Press Foundation and
by philanthropic contributions from individuals and
institutions. For more information, visit www.ucpress.edu.

University of California Press
Oakland, California

© 2016 by The Regents of the University of California

Library of Congress Cataloging-in-Publication Data

Names: Cole, Alan, author.
Title: Patriarchs on paper : a critical history of medieval
    Chan literature / Alan Cole.
Description: Oakland, California : University of
    California Press, [2016] | Includes bibliographical
    references and index.
Identifiers: LCCN 2016021494 (print) | LCCN 2016023440
    (ebook) | ISBN 9780520284067 (cloth : alk. paper) |
    ISBN 9780520284074 (pbk. : alk. paper) | ISBN
    9780520959750 ()
Subjects: LCSH: Zen literature, Chinese—China—
    History and criticism. | Zen Buddhism—History of
    doctrines—Middle Ages, 600–1500.
Classification: LCC BQ9264.4.C62 C65 2016 (print) |
    LCC BQ9264.4.C62 (ebook) | DDC 294.3/9270951—dc23
LC record available at https://lccn.loc.gov/2016021494

Manufactured in the United States of America

25 24 23 22 21 20 19 18 17 16
10 9 8 7 6 5 4 3 2 1

If I were to define the Chan/Zen tradition as a single, unambiguous object of historical research, I would present it as a discourse—a set of ideas and tropes.

T. Griffith Foulk, 2007

CONTENTS

PREFACE

Many things, even supposedly simple things, turn out to be hard to understand. In fact, there is little about being human that is easily understood. For example, how should we understand language? While most of us naturally learn to speak at a very early age, it is far from certain that we have any idea what we are doing when we so incessantly make these chirping noises to one another. Sometimes this chirping makes us happy, at other times angry; sometimes it fills us with awe and fear, at other times it bends us over in laughter—and despite its monumental presence and power in our lives, most of the time we pay no attention it. The oddness and opacity of language doubles or triples when we try to understand writing. How is it that scribbles on paper or parchment turn so naturally into the sound of someone talking to us? And then stepping up another level of complexity, what to make of the way that various religious traditions have, in the past two or three millennia, written out different kinds of "final language"—language that claims to perfectly describe the nature of reality and our place in it?[1] This gets extra tricky when it becomes clear that this kind of written

1. My ideas about "final language" are indebted to Richard Rorty's discussion of "final vocabularies" in his *Contingency, Irony, and Solidarity* (New York: Cambridge University Press, 1989), esp. chaps. 3 and 4.

religious language often pretends to have been oral to begin with. Chan, better known in English as "Zen," is just such a literary tradition: one that developed several kinds of final language that supposedly originated in spontaneous orality but, on closer inspection, reflect the growing ability in medieval China to present literary *images* of spoken truth, images that were engaging, inspiring, and, in many ways, beautiful. *Patriarchs on Paper* attempts to trace how and why this new "zenny" kind of literature emerged.

Focusing on Chan as language and literature doesn't mean, however, that we won't be trying to understand Chan as a way of being in the world—we will! It just turns out that the Chan way of being in the world is much more involved with language, literature, and aesthetics than most people realize. And here retelling a well-known joke might be useful: two young fish are chatting with each other when an older fish swims by and says, "How's the water today, fellas?" They nod politely, but after the older fish has passed by, one of the young fish looks at the other and says, "What's water?"[2] The gist of the joke seems to be this: like the young fish, we normally live in habitats—linguistic, social, historical, physical, and so on—that are so immediate we can't recognize them or name them. The joke, then, is a gentle reminder of the depth of our everyday blindness to our surroundings and, at the same time, suggests that we *could* get around to noticing prominent aspects of our lived realities, while also developing a vocabulary for this world of ours, as the old fish clearly has. In this way, the fish-in-water joke serves as a decent analogy for what this book seeks to do as it pieces together a history of Chan literature: it casts Chan as a kind of habitat, one that gradually emerged and allowed a group of people to "swim" around in a certain kind of water, as it were. And, as in the joke, some of the swimmers were more aware of the water than others, and even had, as the older fish does, a language to articulate that quality of being-in-water.

2. David Foster Wallace opened his 2005 Commencement speech at Kenyon College, Ohio, with this joke, but I believe it has been around for a very long time.

Taking Chan to be an emerging habitat of sorts works well for several reasons, but it has to be understood at the outset that Chan's discourse actually has two habitats built into it. There is, on the one hand, the everyday world of language, culture, history, and so on, that, according to the enlightened masters, is painful, confusing, out-of-control, and essentially hellish—it's the one we non-masters live in day to day, and in which, according to standard Buddhist cosmology, we are destined to remain trapped, birth after birth. Then, on the other hand, there is this other unthinkable world of enlightenment, a place that is the special purview of the masters, where one realizes that self and reality are really one entity, and where there is no desire, no karma, no retribution, no hell, and even no Buddhism. Much of Chan literature is dedicated to presenting this split-screen perspective on reality for readers, while also tempting them with the possibility that *they themselves* could acquire the vision of the masters in which everything resolves into a natural, innate nirvana that preexists the split between nirvana and samsara. Evoking the reality of this naturally present nirvana, while also condemning the world of ordinary language and "normal" Buddhism that fails to appreciate this "everyday nirvana," is what Chan literature is largely all about.

Of course, the situation is more than a little ironic since it was only in Chan's various forms of literature that a nirvanic, language-free world was conjured up, just as it was only with complicated histories that the masters' total freedom from time, history, and samsara was confirmed. This doesn't mean that Chan is just a language game. It isn't. And yet it is also true that the construction of the Chan tradition, *and* its daily practice, relies on the mastery of complex forms of language and historical thinking, even as both language and history are regularly disparaged in Chan literature. Exploring how all this works is what this book is about.

Since many of the ideas from Chan and Zen, and in particular that promise of a language-free form of human perfection, have become part of modern "Western" cultural traditions, it seems fair to say that this book is also about the kind of water we swim in. And here things become a little less funny, since I have to admit that the arguments in this book undermine most of what is taken to be common knowledge about Chan and Zen. Worse, it is my experience that these arguments can leave readers feeling perplexed, anxious, and, most of all, annoyed. This kind of reader, I presume, would prefer to swim in the sea of Chan and Zen literature without reckoning it to be a kind of "water." For some, this denial may be a fine and healthy choice, and yet I am hoping that other readers—those more curious by nature or, at least, more flexible in their thinking—will enjoy getting a better understanding of how things got to be the way they are in Chan and Zen, even if that means challenging some comforting assumptions about how the traditions were put together.

Given this critical approach, readers might want to know something about my relationship to Chan and the Buddhist tradition. While I don't think it is necessarily a good idea to present autobiographic details in a preface, here it might be useful, just so that no one thinks that I am a crypto-Christian or, more likely, a malicious Marxist out to destroy Chan. So here is a very brief history of my relationship to Buddhism that will reveal something about my choices in sculpting this history of Chan literature. In my late teens I got very interested in Buddhist ideas and practices; I would even say I became obsessed with them. I switched my college major from physics to religious studies, worked hard at learning classical Tibetan with Donald S. Lopez Jr. at Middlebury College (in Vermont), and was a participant in Antioch University's Buddhist Studies in India program during my senior year, 1984. I continued with these interests after college and lived for several months at the Tibetan Buddhist Learning Center in Washington, New Jersey. During this time, I did a lot of meditation, a lot of "Buddhist thinking," and had a very positive view of Buddhism in general, although I never accepted some of the basic doctrines, such as reincarnation and karma.

My struggles with the Buddhist tradition intensified when, after a year and a half of graduate work in Tibetan Buddhist Studies with

Jeffrey Hopkins at the University of Virginia, I spent the summer of 1987 in Tibet. During that summer, when I spoke a decent modern Tibetan, I concluded that most Western notions of Buddhism—my notions, that is—were noticeably at odds with what we might call "Buddhism on the ground." That realization prompted me to leave the UVA program—well known, then, for its pro-Buddhist orientation—in order to join the Buddhist Studies program at the University of Michigan, one committed to a more critical approach. There, I studied Chinese and Japanese, and worked with Luis O. Gómez and T. Griffith Foulk on various topics related to the development of the Chinese Buddhist tradition. Foulk's research on the history of Chan Buddhism was particularly influential on me since in his 1987 dissertation and in other publications, he called attention to the *production* of Chan literature in order to ask whether or not the historians of the masters might have been more important than the masters in the invention of Chan and Zen. Foulk's arguments helped generate an important paradigm shift in the field of Chan studies, and this book is, in part, an effort to think through those insights and put them before a wider public.[3]

After two years at the University of Michigan, it was another stay in a country deeply influenced by Buddhism—this time Taiwan—that led me again to reconsider Western notions of Buddhism. Following eight months of research in Taiwan, I came back to Michigan in the spring of 1992 convinced that Buddhist authors were a whole lot more complicated in the ways that they lived in the water-of-tradition. In short, I had become persuaded that many Buddhist writers felt justified in subtle (and not so subtle) acts of puppeteering, whereby they took hold of the cherished figures of authority in tradition in order to make them speak new truths that these latter-day authors wished to put before the public.

3. For a slightly earlier overview of the problem of history and Chan, see John C. Maraldo, "Is There Historical Consciousness in Ch'an?" *Japanese Journal of Religious Studies*, 12, nos. 2–3 (1985): 141–72.

In this way I came to focus on *the art of rewriting tradition,* a perspective that shaped my dissertation on the invention of Buddhist family values in medieval China, which was later published in 1998 as *Mothers and Sons in Chinese Buddhism.* A similar style of investigation informed my next book, which focused on the writing of early Mahāyāna sutras in India, *Text as Father: Paternal Seductions in Early Mahāyāna Buddhist Literature* (2005), as well as my third book, which explored the production of the early Chan texts: *Fathering Your Father: The Zen of Fabrication in Tang Buddhism* (2009). I then tried to expand these reading strategies by comparing the reinvention of tradition in Buddhism with the case of early Christianity; that project resulted in *Fetishizing Tradition: Desire and Reinvention in Buddhist and Christian Narratives* (2015).

Patriarchs on Paper follows in the footsteps of these earlier works but aims at a more comprehensive account of Chan writing, one that covers both the Tang and the Song dynasties and tries thereby to explain the emergence of some fairly stable writing strategies in the development of Chan and its various visions of the past. I should add that, given my limitations, this book's arguments are focused exclusively on Chan in China and regrettably leave developments in Korea, Japan, Tibet, and Vietnam out of the picture. I think telling the basic "story" of Chan literature still works within these limits, but I expect that my colleagues with wider-ranging expertise can improve this narrative, and I can only hope that they will find things here that will be useful to their own projects.

While on the topic of limitations, I should add that this book was conceived as an introductory overview of Chan literature and the "state of the field," one designed for upper-level undergraduates, but also for the general reading public. Consequently, I have tried to keep my analyses brief, jargon-free, and accessible to the nonspecialist. Likewise, I have minimized debates with my colleagues over various points of interpretation, debates which might distract less involved readers and would take up a great deal of space that I hadn't, in fact, been allotted. Finally, an earlier version of this book had a large number of Chinese characters set in the text to justify translation choices and to clarify

Chan authors' terminology. Regrettably, the University of California Press decided that inputting the characters would be too costly, and so I have removed them, leaving only a few phrases and terms in *pinyin*. Happily, most of the texts that I draw on are digitized and interested readers can thus easily consult them online at the Chinese Buddhist Electronic Text Association (CBETA), www.cbeta.org.

ACKNOWLEDGMENTS

Many thanks, first, to my wife, Jennie Tsen, who "looked after me," as she likes to say, as I struggled to finish this book over the past two years. I hope she sees reflected here at least a glimmer of the charm and wit she's brought into my life. Then, as just mentioned, I owe much to T. Griffith Foulk (now at Sarah Lawrence College) for helping me rethink the history of Chan. Even in the years since grad school, when we rarely see each other, his creative perspectives and clear writing have been a steady inspiration for me. This book has also benefitted from some twenty-five years of conversations with Brook Ziporyn (now at the University of Chicago's Divinity School). We might not agree on the nature of Chan and its literature, but, as usual, I learned much from the debates. Here in Portland, Oregon, my life has been enriched by years of camaraderie (and music) with Kurt Fosso, professor of English at Lewis & Clark College; it is hard to believe that I've had the good fortune to host our weekly sessions now for two decades. And, as always, Stuart Lachs has been a first-rate friend and email-buddy—I don't know anyone with a better sense of humor, especially about the tough stuff in life.

At the University of California Press, Eric Schmidt helpfully guided me through the writing process, and Maeve Cornell-Taylor solved a number of problems alone the way. Max Moerman of Columbia University wrote an encouraging review of an early draft of the book, which inspired me in the final phases of writing. When it came to editing, Peter Dreyer did a remarkable job sorting out my idiosyncratic prose style, and Cindy Fulton painstakingly finalized *all those edits!*

Finally, I would like to acknowledge the influence of my father, Robert C. Cole, professor of English and journalism at the College of New Jersey, who did much to shape my thinking on language, politics, and art. Unfortunately, he passed away in August 2015 and didn't get to see the book in print; but at least he knew of the title and, even in the haze of his Parkinson's, seemed to enjoy the double entendre.

A NOTE ON REFERENCES TO
THE CHINESE BUDDHIST CANON

The most commonly referenced version of the Chinese Buddhist canon, the *Taishō shinshū daizōkyo*, 100 vols., edited by Takakusa Junjirō and Watanabe Kaigyoku (Tokyo: Taishō issaikyō kankōkai, 1924–32), is cited in the notes as *T,* followed by the "*Taishō* serial number" in parentheses, then the volume, page, register (a, b, c), and then line number, e.g., *T* (no. 1911), 46.1b.15. When a text is contained in what is known as the supplement to the *Taishō*, the *Dai Nippon zokuzōkyo,* I will refer to the Chinese reprint of that collection called the *Xuzang jing.* Citations to this version of the collection follow the same protocol as the *Taishō*, except that instead of "*T*" at the front of the reference, there will be a "*X*". Both collections are available on line through the Chinese Buddhist Electronic Text Association (CBETA), www.cbeta.org.

Introduction

Chan—What Is *It?*

BODHIDHARMA'S FAMILY

Like many cultural inventions—such as, say, capitalism or country music—it is impossible to offer an air-tight definition of Chan or, for that matter, to determine when exactly it came into being. The problem is that, like a tropical storm turning into a typhoon, Chan's characteristic elements only *gradually* assumed a form that was relatively stable and self-sustaining. Despite these problems of definition and origin, it still seems wise to start our history of Chan literature in the late seventh century when a cycle of narratives appeared asking readers to believe that a perfect and final understanding of Buddhism had been brought to China by an Indian monk named Bodhidharma (n.d.). These narratives also explained how Bodhidharma, once in China, installed this wisdom, suddenly and totally, in a Chinese monk named Huike (n.d.), who then transmitted it to his disciple Sengcan (n.d.) in a similarly miraculous manner, and Sengcan in turn transmitted it to his disciple Daoxin (d. 651), and so on, thereby generating a continuous track of perfectly realized Chinese masters, all of whom supposedly gained the same enlightenment that the Buddha had won back in India some 1,000 years earlier. It is this complex historical claim, slowly pieced together by mid-Tang authors, that has been essential to Chan ideology down to the present.

By the mid-eighth century, the story of Bodhidharma and his spiritual heirs had been recycled several times by high-profile authors, and the imperial court had endorsed it in various ways, as well. The growing acceptability of this basic genealogical framework did not, however, preclude authors from shifting around various parts of the story. Thus, Bodhidharma appeared to have different Indian ancestors depending on who was telling the story, just as his supposed Chinese heirs were also regularly redefined. Oddly enough, then, those authors most interested in promoting the story appear to have been those most willing to change it—an ironic fact that Chan studies has, in general, not handled very well. Of course, part of the motivation for rewriting the Bodhidharma narrative derived from the simple need to keep the story up to date so that more recent figures could claim to have inherited this form of perfect Buddhism. In fact, it wasn't long before some authors who updated the Bodhidharma story also claimed that they themselves were the most recent heirs in the lineage of truth. At least in some cases, then, the historians of the Chinese buddhas turned themselves into Chinese buddhas.

When found in obscure texts from Tang-era China, these curious stories that celebrate certain men as Chinese buddhas perhaps seem suitably mysterious and medieval, and therefore unremarkable, but consider the oddness of such claims when they are placed in a modern setting. Imagine walking into a pub in Portland, Oregon, and someone says to you, "Yesterday, John received perfect enlightenment from a Chan master and is now a recognized member of the Bodhidharma family." And you think, "The John I know? Enlightened? Really? How? What Bodhidharma family? Why are you even telling me this?" If there is a pause in the conversation, more questions might come piling in, such as: "Wait, isn't enlightenment basically an Asian thing? This John, if I'm remembering correctly, is from Eugene, Oregon, right? Isn't he twenty-eight years old, regularly out of work, and well known as a confused hipster?" And so on. Facing up to the awkwardness involved in this modern moment when the arrival of total truth is publicly announced gives some sense of how many doubts have to be pushed aside to make such a radical claim about someone's ownership of truth and tradition appear plausible.[1]

Now drawing a parallel between the genesis of Chan Buddhism in medieval China and some random claims about a modern fellow like John-from-Eugene might seem annoying and unwarranted at first, especially given the way most of us prefer to imagine the past as a romantic place, free of such moments of invention and self-aggrandizement. And, yet, with Buddhist India at a great distance from the China, Chan authors had the same practical problems that American Buddhists have when they try to present American men and women as perfect masters of Buddhist truth—it simply is rather difficult to convince anyone that a perfect version of tradition has arrived from so far away and from so long ago. In thinking through this comparison, the challenge is to let go of one's nostalgia long enough to consider that past figures in tradition surely had to fight their own battles for legitimacy, just as those of today do.[2]

Another way to get at this problem of nostalgia is to remember that the earliest Japanese masters, such as Eisai (1141–1215) and Dogen (1200–1253), felt obliged to prove their *Chinese* credentials to their Japanese audiences. Consequently, they embarked on dangerous trips to China to receive the formal approval of various Chan masters. For the founders of Japanese Zen, then, the only good Zen was found on the other side of the Sea of Japan. Noting how similar situations developed in other times and places, it would seem accurate to say that there is a well-established cycle of nostalgia within the history of Buddhism such

1. Various scenes in Martin Scorsese's *The Last Temptation of Christ* (1988) where William Dafoe, as Jesus, publicly announces that he is the Son of God can give one a clear sense of the problems involved in linking the arrival of universal truth with the history of a particular man, in a particular town, with a particular hair style, and so on.

2. For insightful reflections on the dynamics at work in canonizing modern masters, see Sor-Ching Low, "Seung Sahn: The Makeover of a Modern Zen Patriarch," in *Zen Masters*, eds. Steven Heine and Dale S. Wright (New York: Oxford University Press, 2010), 267–85; see also Dale S. Wright's essay, "Humanizing the Image of a Zen Master: Taizan Maezumi Roshi," ibid., 239-65.

that at each historical juncture when Buddhism was imported from one culture to another, the importer cannot see that the previous owners of tradition also had their very own sense of inadequacy vis-à-vis those sources that *they* took to be the founts of tradition. Hence, modern Chan enthusiasts in American and Europe long for the natural authenticity that Japanese Zen masters supposedly had, just as the Japanese masters longed for the authenticity that the Chinese masters supposedly had, and so on. Actually, even back in India, authors felt that it was necessary that the Buddha himself should have legitimizing ancestors, and thus a very distant lineage of buddhas was invented to endorse the Buddha of our epoch. In short, Buddhist authority regularly remains one step away from where it is actually needed.

It is also true that in China those who wished to identify this or that figure as a member of the Bodhidharma lineage regularly appealed to the state—the imperial court, that is—to ratify their claims. On this front, religious authority again remains "one step away" in the sense that Buddhist masters needed leading political powers to secure their claims to religious perfection. In the first half of the eighth century, claims to be a Chinese buddha were relatively few and were often recognized by the throne with the bestowal of the magnificent title "Teacher of the Nation" (*guoshi*). Soon, though, with the breakdown of Tang imperial control, the situation became chaotic, with more and more claimants asserting their place in the Bodhidharma family, based on political support from local officials. This continued on for some two hundred years, until the beginning of the Song dynasty, when, with the return of robust state control, the divergent lineages from the Tang were suppressed, forgotten, or rewritten such that there was only one large, extended Chan family of masters, all of whom were supposedly directly related to the Indian Buddha.

As we try to piece together a history of these "histories," we need to remember that most of these genealogies from the Tang era would have never come to our attention had they not been hastily tucked in a cave outside a Silk Road town called Dunhuang, in the eleventh century, and then forgotten.[3] In fact, it was only in 1900 that a Daoist priest named Wang Yuanlu noticed a hidden doorway into this cave and thereby rediscovered this vast collection of texts, documents, art work, and much more. Over the next ten years he sold much of the collection to Western and Japanese explorers for relatively small sums of money. As modern scholars sifted through these texts, it became clear that during the Tang dynasty, the figure of Bodhidharma had been the focus of some ten conflicting "genealogies of truth." This was particularly surprising given the fact that the surviving Chan and Zen traditions had presented the Tang era as Chan's heyday, a time treasured for its supposed simplicity and freedom from religious politics. So, with this tangle of antagonistic genealogies suggesting a past quite at odds with tradition's account of itself, modern scholars began trying to give a more critical account of how and why Chan Buddhism was invented. This book is an effort to synthesize those findings and reflect on them in new ways.

CRITICAL THINKING VERSUS THE TYRANNY OF NOSTALGIA

Writing a critical account of Chan's development isn't simply a matter of rejecting the nostalgic assumptions that structured earlier discussions of Chan. Thus, it isn't enough to say, "Well, yes, it is obvious that the whole idea of instantly transmitting enlightenment is mythical, just as it is clear that all the stories that slotted Chinese men into the Bodhidharma family were made up, and so on." Getting those facts and perspectives in view is a good place to start, but a more comprehensive history would also ask *why* Chan's literary adventures took the form they did.

Why, for instance, did Chan authors rely on the model of the patriarchal family to explain the presence of buddhas in China? Was it simply

3. For a useful discussion of Buddhism at Dunhuang, see Henrik H. Sørensen, "Perspectives on Buddhism in Dunhuang during the Tang and Five Dynasties Period," in *The Silk Roads: Highways of Culture and Commerce*, ed. Vadime Elisseeff (New York: Berghahn Books, 2000), 27–48.

that by organizing Buddhist authority in this manner Chan advocates hoped to make Buddhism—or at least its leaders—look a bit like the traditional Confucian family, and, to a certain extent, the royal family? Or, was it that Buddhist genealogists took their cue from Daoist authors who had, in the centuries that preceded Chan writing, relied on secret lineages to explain the transmission of esoteric Daoist wisdom? Although these two types of families—Confucian and Daoist—appear to have influenced the construction of the Bodhidharma lineages, a fuller explanation of the "why" question would focus on the way that the family of Chinese buddhas was designed to solve the vexing problem of how to interpret the ocean of Buddhist sutras that had been pouring into China. With the final truth of Buddhism installed in this or that master, in a secure and familiar father-to-son manner, the daunting task of interpreting Buddhist literature was finally over because, in effect, the newly minted Chinese buddhas could be trusted to interpret Buddhism as well as their Indian forefathers had. Thus, in a gesture that promised to make the past present, inventing the clan of Chinese truth-fathers went a long way towards solving the problem of China's distance from Indian Buddhism's origins: once Chan masters appeared as buddha equivalents, India, with all its saints and sutras, gradually became of secondary importance.

Put that way we can see that this hereditary model for owning and transmitting truth addressed a range of problems regarding the establishment of final forms of Buddhist authority in China. Consequently, the invention of Chan lineages appears as a good case of *religion being about itself.* Thus, it wasn't that there was some unique new Chan content that authors thought to put in these patriarchal conduits for safekeeping; rather, Chan content was the very invention of those conduits and all the security and perfection that they promised. The circularity of religious doctrines creating and securing the authority of the religious leaders who espouse them might appear a little baffling at first, but it will become clearer as we work through the details.

Setting up new forms of Buddhist authority in China also required making these new forms look natural and therefore unassailable. One way this was accomplished was by developing stories about how masters got Buddhist enlightenment *from life itself* and not from Buddhist books and practices. Thus, we get down-home, work-loving buddhas—like Hongren or Huineng—who supposedly relished all things simple, and gained their enlightenments naturally, in the fields or in the mountains. Of course, establishing nature—in the broadest sense of the term—as the origin of their authority hardly prevented their historians from also explaining how these rustic buddhas went on to become authority figures at the peak of Buddhist culture, where they supposedly *spoke* spontaneously and unerringly about the final meaning of the imported Buddhist literature. In short, from the earliest phases of Chan writing, Chan authors produced literature that celebrated figures who, with an uncanny and unschooled ability, *naturally* came to dominate the literary tradition that they lived in. Publicly circulating literature that championed these lovable anti-literature buddhas naturally enhanced the appeal and authority of living monks who claimed to be related to them, even as it also laid the foundation for a world of fantasy regarding the perfect and natural mastery of Buddhist truth and tradition, a floating world of desire and longing that would be essential to Chan's future.

With these perspectives in view, it becomes clear that the basic problem with popular accounts of Chan (and Zen) is that they take these stories about all-natural buddhas as factual, uninvented, and definitely uninvolved with Buddhist politics in China, when, of course, nothing could be further from the truth. Moreover, many casual readers of Chan literature overlook the fact that such stories belong within a highly developed literary culture, which, even before Buddhism showed up, delighted in just this kind of story—presented in elegant and erudite Chinese—that exalted the value and power of all things beyond language and culture. Now, a hundred years or so into Chan studies, it is clear that reading Chan texts without this literary, historical, and political context in mind is a lot like looking at Chinese nature paintings and thinking that they reflect real mountains and rivers, when in fact they were more often than not painted from other paintings, in comfortable urban studios.

Although medieval Chan emerged *gradually* as a set of discourse strategies for celebrating the perfect masters of the past, modern nostalgia for Chan came into being in a much more sudden fashion. And here we need to turn to the curious and influential figure of D.T. Suzuki (1870-1966). Suzuki published widely on Zen—which he casually lumped together with Chan—and other Buddhist topics, but several of his books, such as *An Introduction to Zen Buddhism*, were particularly influential. *An Introduction*, which first came out in 1934, presents Zen (and Chan) as a wonderfully unthinkable way of being in the world, free of myth, ritual, rules, institutions, hierarchy, language, logic, and so on—Zen was put forward as "the whole mind" and "the spirit of all religions and philosophies."[4] This utopian vision of Zen as pure spirit seems to have fired up English readers considerably, and was a key node in the development of some very misguided ideas about Zen and Chan.

To begin to understand how this Zen for moderns was invented we would do well to situate Suzuki's quirky discourse in its historical context. As Robert Sharf notes in his classic 1993 essay "The Zen of Nationalism," Suzuki was never a Zen monk; he had only brief training at a Zen monastery as a college kid in the 1890s, and his master, Shaku Sōen, was an avant-garde figure, trained in Western thought and dedicated to reforming Zen after the Meiji Restoration (1864–68) had nearly eradicated traditional Zen.[5] Equally important to know is that Suzuki spent some eleven years (beginning in 1897) in LaSalle, Illinois, studying and living with Paul Carus, a German American theologian who was intent on developing what he called the "religion of science." It was under Carus's tutelage that Suzuki seems to have found what he wanted: a thoroughly modern vision of religion that claimed that the essence of religion

4. D. T. Suzuki, *An Introduction to Zen Buddhism* (1934; New York: Grove Press, 1964), 38, 44. For more on Suzuki's reinvention of Chan and Zen, see Bernard Faure, *Chan: Insights and Oversights: An Epistemological Critique of the Chan Tradition* (Princeton, NJ: Princeton University Press, 1993), chap. 2.

5. See Robert H. Sharf, "The Zen of Nationalism," *History of Religions* 33, no. 1 (1993), pp. 1–43; and id., "D. T. Suzuki," in the *Encyclopedia of Religion*, 2nd ed. (Detroit: Macmillan Reference USA, 2005), 13: 8884–87.

(Zen included) was to be found, not in traditional rituals and institutional realities, but instead in a kind of transcendental spiritual perception that was fully in accord with science and, better still, could escape critiques from modern Western philosophy. And so it was that under the influence of Paul Carus's teachings, Suzuki went on to create a thoroughly modernized form of Zen that, no surprise, appealed to many twentieth-century readers.

Although the details of Suzuki's reinvention of tradition don't make for very uplifting reading, we can nonetheless see in the Suzuki affair a useful example of how Chan/Zen rhetoric works. First, while universalizing Zen as the ineffable spiritual Thing that stands at the base of all religious traditions, Suzuki was also quite clear about the fact that Zen is something that only the Japanese have direct access to. Thus, there is an fundamental tease at work in Suzuki's presentation: Zen is purportedly the spiritual essence of man and all religious traditions, and yet Suzuki claimed that it was not available to Westerners, whom he characterized as overly rational and too restless to grasp the profound subtleties of Zen.[6] Then, along with privatizing truth, authenticity, and authority in this manner, Suzuki also makes pronouncements such as "Coal is not black" and "Zen is the ocean, Zen is the air, Zen is the mountain,"[7] giving readers the impression that these statements came from a master who, *uniquely*, had access to transcendental truths that, although found on the other side of the fog bank of mundane thinking, are still completely relevant to all humans.

In short, while Suzuki was obviously privatizing truth in a very Chan/Zen manner, his readers could feel satisfied knowing that at least *somebody* knew what was going on with life and humanity. Moreover, in accepting Suzuki's claims to have mastered the meaning of being human, we gain a way to relate to truth in a new and invigorating manner: we

---

6. For this assessment of the West, see Suzuki, *An Introduction to Zen Buddhism*, 35–36; for more details on Suzuki's claims regarding Zen and the uniqueness of the Japanese people, see Sharf, "Zen of Nationalism," 25–29.

7. Suzuki, *Introduction to Zen Buddhism*, 33, 45.

can buy Zen books, discuss their contents, practice meditation after school or after work, and, of course, appear much cooler than our friends who aren't up on their Zen. Consequently, the whole arrangement can appear rather inspiring. Now one might see our delight in Suzuki's discourse as yet more proof of our troubling affection for authority, but for the purposes of this book, it is more important to focus on this dialectic in which one gives someone the right to own total truth in the hopes of getting some of it back, even if one never gets to be equal to the truth holder. This dialectic is, as I hope to show, key to understanding Chan's success.

With some general sense for what Chan was in the medieval period, and how D. T. Suzuki and others reinvented it in the twentieth century, let's turn to consider several theoretical issues regarding writing, history, and art that will help us build a more balanced account of Chan and its literature.

Making History: Chan as an Art Form

OVERVIEW: HISTORY VERSUS LIFE

Making history was, from the beginning, essential to the emergence of Chan, and thus it is worth clarifying several important elements at work in the process of writing (and reading) history. The first thing to see is that writing history represents a doubling of reality: in addition to the everyday world that we live in, where our senses are engaged in a fluid and continuous manner, the writer of history works to evoke scenes and events that, though invisible, can be made to appear to the reader as integral parts of reality, albeit in the past. In this overlay of the past onto the present, the way we get back to those past events is via imagination and fantasy. In the writing of history, then, there is a kind of alchemy at work in which words disappear as they magically turn into quasi-visible events, and these events then are given various meanings that can be shaped for the audience's instruction and entertainment. In short, however fictional or factual a history might be, it is born of imagination—the author's and the reader's.

Put this way, we can begin to see how much intelligence, self-control, and linguistic dexterity is involved in producing a captivating history of an event or figure. Better still, we can appreciate how the skills needed to write history reflect the growing human ability to *artify the world*, that talent to remake the given-of-the-world in new and dramatic ways, and to then hand those complex art fantasies over to others.[1] Why this matters for understanding Chan literature is that one wouldn't be far wrong in describing Chan as a gradually solidifying set of literary gestures designed to enhance—and organize—the present, by carefully designing and curating images of an imaginary past.

Although it is relatively easy to see that the early accounts of Chan in the West were largely off mark because they took the literature evoking the past patriarchs and their teachings to be a clear window into the reality of the Chan tradition, it takes a bit more wherewithal to appreciate the craft and intelligence of these authors who so painstakingly composed that literature for their sophisticated and well-read audiences. Perhaps this oversight is to be expected since, after all, Chan literature was designed such that the art of writing history would disappear as the reader peered *through* the carefully constructed narratives, thinking he could thereby see into a departed, but still visible, world where the patriarchs spoke and acted in tantalizing ways that gave the impression that they were totally free of the Buddhist literary traditions, even though it was only in literature that they could behave like this.

ASSUMPTIONS TO AVOID

Taking Chan texts as artful reconstructions of the past means stepping away from a number of assumptions that have shaped past discussions. The first assumption to avoid is that Chan is best defined as the "school of meditation." Now it is true that the Chinese character for "Chan" means meditation—since it is a shortening of *chan na*, which was used as a sound-translation of the Sanskrit word for meditation, *dhyāna*—and yet in the mid-Tang the word *chan* shifted from meaning "meditation"

---

1. Here I have been much influenced by Jean-Paul Sartre's *What Is Literature?* (1948; 3rd ed., Cambridge, MA: Harvard University Press, 1988), esp. chap. 2, "Why Write?"

to signifying something more like "perfect" or "enlightened."[2] Thus, up until the mid-seventh century, a chan master (*chanshi*) was a monk who focused on meditation, instead of, for instance, focusing on sutra exegesis, or magic, or monastic discipline (*vinaya*). Then, in 690, in a biographic stele cut at Shaolin Monastery for a certain monk named Faru, we find previously unrelated masters linked together in a lineage of truth-fathers who supposedly descended from Bodhidharma and, ultimately, from the Indian Buddha. In this genealogy, which arguably is the first "Chan" lineage, we can see that the term "chan master" has shifted from "meditation master" to that fuller sense of "perfect master," one who has inherited a perfect form of Buddhism from Bodhidharma. Thus, somewhat ironically, what came to be known as the "Chan tradition" (*chanzong*) only emerges when *chan* stopped meaning meditation and took on this sense of "perfect."

Another assumption to sidestep is that medieval Chan texts are simple, uninflected statements of truth offered, cost-free, to anyone who can read them. While a small number of Chan texts can be read in this manner, most Chan texts present complicated agendas that require the reader to involve himself in various kinds of ideological and partisan thinking. Hence, it seems unwise to read Chan texts simply for their "philosophic" import without considering other things that might be going on in the text, things that might rather shift what one takes to be the "philosophy" of the text. Likewise, to start off by assigning pure and simple motives to the Chan authors is to ignore how history writing in China, even back in the earliest sources from the Warring States era, was so often a highly politicized project.[3] To assume that Chan histories

2. For an insightful discussion of this shift in the meaning of *chan*, see Eric Greene, "Another Look at Early 'Chan': Daoxuan, Bodhidharma, and the Three Levels Movement," *T'oung Pao* 94 (2008): 49–114, esp. 50–51. See also Robert H. Sharf's discussion of this problem in "Mindfulness and Mindlessness in Early Chan," *Philosophy East & West* 64, no. 4 (Oct. 2014): 933–64, esp. 937ff.

3. For reflections on the politics of writing history in the earliest Chinese sources, see David Schaberg's *A Patterned Past: Form and Thought in Early Chinese Historiography* (Cambridge, MA: Harvard University Press, 2002). Mark Edward Lewis argues in a

were somehow separate from the wider Chinese culture of artfully shaping the past to improve the present seems unjustifiable.

Third, and in a more nuts-and-bolts manner, we ought to avoid accepting information from later sources that isn't findable in earlier sources. This is because, as mentioned, it is clear that Chan authors regularly rewrote the past. Thus, if the earliest accounts of Bodhidharma don't mention that he belonged in a lineage of truth-fathers, we shouldn't believe later accounts that put him in that role, especially when we see that the newer versions of the story also keep changing, getting richer and more beguiling with each retelling. In line with this issue, we should be wary of accepting claims that attach a text to a long-dead figure. Thus, if the only evidence that person x authored text y shows up several decades, or several centuries, after the person's death, chances are the attribution is unreliable. Actually, attributing texts to long-dead cultural heroes was a very standard practice in the centuries before Buddhism arrived in China and thus it was that so many of the Chinese classics got attributed to Confucius. Similar forces seem at work in the Chan tradition: in some cases it appears as though someone thought that an important master would look better if he had a text attached to him; in other cases someone thought a favored text would look better if it was attached to an esteemed patriarch.

The fourth assumption to dodge is essentially a version of the myth of the Fall in which one imagines that Chan started off innocently enough as a loose set of practical teaching and techniques that meditation masters used to enlighten their disciples, and only later got entangled in politics, ancestor-thieving, and the textual production of bogus historical claims. In this approach, it is taken for granted that Chan texts, regardless of how convoluted they might appear, still have to be imagined to have emerged from real communities of dedicated Chan "practitioners"

---

similar vein in his *Writing and Authority in Early China* (Albany: State University of New York Press, 1999); see, esp., chap. 2, "Writing the Masters."

and the experiences that they had.[4] Although this framing of Chan's origins certainly appeals to modern forms of nostalgia, it seems much more likely that Chan began as an expanding swirl of literary claims in which narratives about perfect masters produced more narratives about perfect masters, with little to suggest that these newly produced sketches of the masters had much to do with them or their pasts. Likewise, it is far from clear how much impact these stories had on the day-to-day practice of more solidly established forms of Chinese Buddhism.

Approaching Chan with an emphasis on its creative writing helps us face another problem: as the recent scholarship by Mario Poceski and Albert Welter makes clear (see chapter 8), the most typically zenny elements of the Chan masters' biographies were, by and large, added in long after their deaths. Obviously this means that it was the historians who were inventing the masters and their exciting antinomian ways. This is particularly interesting when, as mentioned above, we see that the new content for the masters' profile makes them look less and less like they belonged to the literary tradition—the very tradition that was, of course, writing them into existence. Apparently, then, the latter-day authors invented their spiritual ancestors as their opposites, and they no doubt knew the value and charm of such an inversion. In short, generation after generation, Chan authors fed a literary tradition that prided itself on staging scenes of its absence.

A final assumption to avoid is the idea that Chan developed in a vacuum. As is well known, the various forms of Chan writing that emerged in the Tang and Song eras relied heavily on Daoism and Confucianism for language, style, logic, institutional arrangements and much more. While acknowledging these tangled borrowings is essential to writing a

4. Except for T. Griffith Foulk's work, recent discussions of Chan—however critical they might be of other aspects of Chan's history—still regularly assume that the "Chan movement" began as a meditation community practicing under Hongren (601–74) on East Mountain, in Huangmei, and only later moved to the capital, where it became corrupted by court intrigue. In *Fathering Your Father: The Zen of Fabrication in Tang Buddhism* (Berkeley: University of California Press, 2009), I point out several good reasons for not accepting this mythic origin for Chan.

good history of Chan literature, it also opens up several problems. First, though it makes sense to use these terms "Daoist" and "Confucian" in a loose way, it is difficult to precisely define the ideas, commitments, and practices that were characteristic of these groups, especially over their many centuries of change and development. Thus one has to be content with weak claims such as, "Well, yes, notions of spontaneity and non-action (*wuwei*) regularly appear in texts associated with Daoism, but the ideas are found in other places as well." The key is simply to appreciate how fluid boundaries were and how often important language was recycled from one zone to another, even though certain linguistic associations and patterns of partisanship were maintained over the centuries.

This issue of recycled material becomes more problematic when we recognize that, to varying degrees, Daoism and Confucianism were shaped by Buddhism and by each other. Naturally, this kind of multidirectional influence can be hard to keep track of. At any rate, one can't simply claim that Daoist thought and literature influenced Chan writing in the Tang when, in fact, the Daoism of that era was already heavily influenced by centuries of borrowing from Buddhist sources and thus was hardly a "pure" Daoism at all. Nonetheless, within these rounds of exchange, I use "Daoism" (or "Daoist") as shorthand for a set of ideas and perspectives that celebrates a powerful and comforting wholeness in the universe, a wholeness that Daoist thinkers thought they could rejoin and even, to some extent, control. In the earliest phases of Daoist writing, such a project of cosmic reunification might be set within the context of more efficacious ruling strategies, as in the *Daode jïng,* or in more relaxed lifestyle choices, as found in the *Zhuangzi.* In either case, these pre-Han cosmologies lacked notions of rebirth, karma, and hell and were, by and large, rather optimistic about the universe and our place in it. It is just this confidence regarding a reunion with a perfect, original wholeness that I take to be central to the category "Daoist," even though Daoism was soon combined with many Buddhist ideas and practices, along with a host of other practices of unknown or unclear origins, such as fasting, sexual yoga, alchemy, exorcism, and so on.

The term "Confucianism" is only slightly easier to work with. I use the term to refer to ideas, texts, and practices that took their inspiration from Confucius and his numerous commentators, and claim an unbroken connection with the glories of China's past, however that past might be construed. Central Confucian concerns had to do with effective governance, terminological exactness, orderly patriarchal reproduction of families—elite and common—and proper ancestor worship. Confucians also, at times, gave voice to confidence in a cosmic totality, as did the Daoists, but never let that vision of the whole overshadow more pressing concerns regarding the maintenance of the literary and ritual traditions that flowed from Confucius and other like-minded "sages" of the past. Chan authors borrowed much from the Confucians in terms of strategies for inheriting the value of the past, but it is also true that by the Song, self-styled Confucian thinkers had absorbed significant ideas from Chan, and in particular adopted a version of the Chan claim that tradition could be passed down through the ages in a perfect manner.

Tracing out these borrowings will be, for some, a satisfying pursuit—it certainly confirms how organic cultural inventions tend to be. However, for others, acknowledging all this borrowing and reborrowing ruins the fantasy that Chan was something pure, simple, and untarnished by sectarian competition and the politics of mimicry and reappropriation. The problem here isn't just that Chan is a thoroughly syncretic cultural invention, but also that Chan's gestures for claiming to be the unique source of truth were themselves borrowed and developed from non-Chan sources. That is, in trying to set up the image of a conduit running from the perfect past of India to the present of Tang and Song China, Chan writers made use of all sorts of local "building material" taken from their Daoist, Confucian, and poetic contemporaries. Of course, once one has become taken with the idea that perfect enlightenment was delivered into the present via a lineage of perfect masters stretching back to the Buddha, it becomes a whole lot harder to think about where the elements of this story really came from.

CHAN AND UNTHINKABILITY

There is one last problem to address before we consider the details of Chan's development, and it has to do with unthinkability. Though it is a modern conceit that everything can be known, and known fast—people tend to forget that *wiki* means "fast" in Hawaiian—the fact of the matter is that, as mentioned in the Preface, we know next to nothing about anything. How does one's nose work, for instance? In our daily experiences, we don't have a clue about how this thing—in league with the brain—detects, registers, and identifies odors. A similar unthinkability confronts us when we consider our stomachs, ears, and so on. Clearly, these zones where reality impinges on our bodily consciousness are simply unavailable for us to reflect on.

Now consider where thoughts come from: How in the world is it that we think? No one knows. Why does a thought or dream or melody or memory suddenly appear? And where was it in the preceding moment? The interface between zones of consciousness seems as mysterious as that between our noses and the mini-particles in the air, with the difference being that with thought it all happens "inside," on our home turf, so to speak. Of course, too, no one really knows what a thought is made of, or if it might not be that we think only one thin side of a thought, while much more of its heft drifts by, mostly concealed from us like an iceberg, but still present and active in determining what is thought next. And then there's the real nightmare question: how is it that *I* think a thought? Put that way it seems that there are three things: a thought, thinking, and the I that thinks. Now while it often does *feel* like that, what if it isn't like that at all? The commonsense notion that static thoughts are called forth by an equally static subject is surely wrongheaded, and yet that dualistic way of thinking about thinking gives us a useful sense of self and control, even when under investigation the realities of thinking seem fluid and altogether ungraspable.

Mentioning the mysterious nature of thought and self-recognition is important here at the beginning because these are topics that have been well considered in the Buddhist tradition, and in Chan in particular. Thus, trying to make sense of Buddhist thought in China naturally involves trying to come up to their level of sensitivity vis-à-vis these rather intractable problems regarding reality, self, and truth. Surely one can hardly make sense of a tradition that claims that selves don't exist if one hasn't come to realize that defining self, experiencing self, reckoning self, and so on, are real problems for any human who has ever stopped to think about it. Thus, while I am interested in being as clear and reasonable about Chan's literary history as I can, I also need to warn the reader here at the outset that we are dealing with traditions—in India and China—that are quite used to dealing with unthinkability and, perhaps, even got quite good at *benefitting* from the many open-ended problems that swirl around language, thought, and identity. In fact, as the chapters to follow suggest, it would seem that Chan literature is largely devoted to chronicling the special "selves" of those who had supposedly mastered no-self. I mention all this here simply to prepare the reader for the paradoxes and contradictions to come.

With a sense for these complex forces shaping Chan's development, let's turn to start piecing together the important prototypes of Chan writing that first appeared in the late sixth century.

2

Plans for the Past

Early Accounts of How Perfect Truth Came to China

To get a sense for how Buddhist genealogical writing took form in China, this chapter compares the oldest surviving accounts of Bodhidharma to slightly earlier narratives that sought to explain how the essence of Buddhism moved from India into the possession of certain Chinese men.[1] Thus, the first part of this chapter looks at how two late-sixth-century masters—Zhiyi (532–597) and Xinxing (540–594)—were presented as perfect receptacles of truth; the second part then covers the earliest accounts of Bodhidharma and his teachings. The final section of chapter looks closely at Huike, the supposed disciple of Bodhidharma, to try to make sense of the way his biography in Daoxuan's *Continued Biographies of Eminent Monks (Xu gaoseng zhuan)* was rewritten so that he appears to stand at the head of a lineage that passes on the essence of Buddhist truth in a man-to-man manner.

1. Elizabeth Morrison presents a useful survey of the earliest lineages in India and China in her *The Power of Patriarchs: Qisong and Lineage in Chinese Buddhism* (Leiden: Brill, 2010), chap. 1.

ZHIYI, GUANDING, AND VARIOUS
ENDORSEMENT STRATEGIES

Zhiyi is one of the most famous Buddhist monks of all time and is justly revered for his creative and intensely scholarly attempts to explain Buddhism to his Chinese compatriots. In the years after his death he came to be regarded as a founding patriarch in what would be known as the Tiantai school of Buddhism. The Tiantai school, with its emphasis on sutra exegesis and carefully reasoned arguments, would, on and off, be Chan's rival and represents an important side of Chinese Buddhism that is often overlooked, especially by those drawn to Chan literature.[2] Exploring the Chan-Tiantai rivalry would be worthwhile for several reasons, but for our purposes what matters is the way that one of Zhiyi's students—Guanding (561–632)—tried to shape Zhiyi's legacy in several contradictory narratives.

For Guanding's first account of Zhiyi's past, we can turn to a set of letters that Guanding compiled after Zhiyi died in 597.[3] In some of the later letters we find brief reports of how Zhiyi had turned into a ghost who regularly haunted a certain monastery that the Prince of Jin had built in Zhiyi's honor, shortly after Zhiyi's death. In the years before and after the monastery was finished in 601, Guanding regularly delivered these accounts to the newly established Sui court, promoting the idea that Zhiyi was a reliable ghost who could, in different and mysterious ways, offer his endorsement of the Sui dynasty. The Prince of Jin, newly installed as Emperor Sui Yangdi in 604, was apparently very impressed by these stories and visited the monastery in 605—or, rather, he visited

2. For an overview of the Tiantai school, see Brook Ziporyn, "Tiantai Buddhism" in the *Encyclopedia of Buddhism*, ed. Robert E. Buswell Jr. (Detroit: Macmillan Reference USA, 2003), 845–51; and id., "Tiantai Buddhism," in The Stanford Encyclopedia of Philosophy Archive (Winter 2014 ed.), ed. Edward N. Zalta, http://plato.stanford.edu /archives/win2014/entries/buddhism-tiantai.

3. These letters were included in what came to be known as *One Hundred Documents from Nation Purified [Monastery]* (*Guoqing bailu*).

the area—in order to bestow on the monastery its formal name, *Guoqing si,* which means "Nation Purified Monastery."

Within this economy of patronage and endorsement, the throne gave Zhiyi's community a monastery and other boons, along with the right to treat their deceased master as a still-present spirit, provided that this spiritual legacy be directed toward supporting and legitimizing the Sui dynasty. What is particularly important here is that in this exchange, Guanding had good reasons to amplify Zhiyi's stature such that, though dead, he could be presented as the most important Buddhist leader in China and, in some sense, a religious figure equal to the Buddha in India. The logic here was simply that the more important Zhiyi appeared, the more the throne would want to hear from him. In effect, then, Zhiyi got virtually buddhafied because he was being constructed as the "Big Other" to the throne.[4] So just as the emperor was, by definition, the sole ruler of China, so too was it that Zhiyi got turned into the singular authority of Chinese Buddhism in order that their "conversation" about China's future could be conducted on more equal footing.

In 605, in conjunction with his visit, Emperor Sui Yangdi called for a biography of Zhiyi to be drawn up. It seems that Guanding then produced a biography in which, not surprisingly, Zhiyi's life appears as a mirror reflecting the legitimacy and power of the Sui dynasty.[5] To

4. I am using the Lacanian term "Big Other" in a slightly idiosyncratic fashion here. For my purposes, it refers to a figure of authority and legitimacy, such as Zhiyi's ghost, who is set up to ratify the "self" that someone wants to be. The "Big" in "Big Other" signifies that this chosen other is imagined to be self-made—like God in Judeo-Christian traditions—and thus somehow outside the politics and constraints of self-other recognitions. As we will see, the entire cycle of Bodhidharma genealogies can be read as a series of attempts to work up more appealing and believable Big Others for various Chinese Buddhist leaders.

5. Zhiyi's cosmic vision regarding the promise of the new Sui dynasty—one that Guanding seems to have invented and then injected into Zhiyi's profile—had to be completely abandoned when the Sui dynasty collapsed in 618 after the emperor Sui Yangdi ran the country into the ground with massive work projects and endless wars of expansion.

build up Zhiyi's profile, Guanding claimed that Zhiyi and his master Huisi (515–577) had, in their previous lives, been with the Buddha in India on the day that the Buddha preached the *Lotus Sūtra*, a sutra much admired in China.[6] With this mini-history, Guanding made it appear that Zhiyi was unusually close to the Buddha and could, based on that unique proximity, better serve as a guarantor for the Sui dynasty.[7]

Sometime later, presumably after the Sui dynasty fell in 618, Guanding crafted what would become the final account of Zhiyi's past. In this version of events, discussion of Zhiyi's intimate involvement with the fortunes of the Sui dynasty disappears and we find instead the simple phrase, "the Chen and Sui states esteemed him and gave him the title 'Teacher of the Nation.'"[8] Likewise, there is no mention of Guoqing monastery, presumably because its close association with the Sui rulers could hardly have been an advantage under the new Tang dynasty. Putting aside these earlier, Sui-related concerns, Guanding's new lineage for Zhiyi was designed to promote a book, the *Great Calming and Contemplation* (*Mohe zhiguan*), that Guanding put together from Zhiyi's lectures. It was in the preface to this book that Guanding attached Zhiyi to a genealogy of twenty-four Indian masters who supposedly descended from the Buddha in order to support the claim that this book would deliver the full truth of Indian Buddhism to Chinese readers.[9]

6. For a collection of recent essays on the *Lotus Sūtra*, see *Readings of the Lotus Sūtra*, eds. Stephen F. Teiser and Jacqueline I. Stone (New York: Columbia University Press, 2009); for an analysis of the *Lotus Sūtra's* history of itself, and its other narrative strategies, see my *Text as Father: Paternal Seductions in Early Mahāyāna Buddhist Literature* (Berkeley: University of California Press, 2005), chaps. 2 and 3.

7. For more discussion of this biography, see Kōichi Shinohara, "Guanding's Biography of Zhiyi, the Fourth Chinese Patriarch of the Tiantai Tradition," in *Speaking of Monks: Religious Biography in India and China,* eds. Phyllis Granoff and Kōichi Shinohara (Oakville, Ont.: Mosaic Press, 1992), 98–232; for Guanding's claim about Zhiyi and Huisi hearing the *Lotus Sūtra* preached by the Buddha, see 119.

8. *T* (no. 1911), 46.1b.15. For a translation of this passage, see Neal Donner and Daniel Stevenson, *The Great Calming and Contemplation* (Honolulu: University of Hawai'i Press, 1993), 105.

9. *T* (no. 1911), 46.1a–3b.10. For a translation of Guanding's preface, see Donner and Stevenson, *Great Calming*, 99–127.

Now this list of twenty-four Indian sages had already appeared in the *History of the Transmission of the Dharma-Treasury* (*Fu fazang yinyuan zhuan*),[10] a text that was forged in China sometime in the fifth or sixth century and originally had nothing to do with Zhiyi. In order to make use of this older genealogy, Guanding claimed that the thirteenth master in the Indian lineage, Nāgārjuna, had written a certain enormous book—the *Mahāprajñāpāramitā śāstra* (*Commentary on the Perfection of Wisdom*)[11]—that supposedly carried the essence of this lineage (and the essence of Buddhism) to China where it was received by a certain scholar named Huiwen (n.d.) who, when he read the book, became enlightened. Huiwen then passed this enlightenment on to Huisi, who then gave it to Zhiyi. Thus when Zhiyi "spoke" the *Great Calming and Contemplation,* it was as though his speech was the direct continuation of this lineage of truth-and-tradition deriving from the Buddha.

That Guanding, in this third version of Zhiyi's past, attached Zhiyi to this list of twenty-four Indian sages is important for several reasons. First, it gives us a sense of the fanciful and self-serving manner in which lineages were appropriated and recycled in the seventh century; second, roughly one hundred and fifty years later, this same list of twenty-four sages would, with slight modifications, be drawn on to glorify and legitimize late-eighth-century Chan masters. The list, once lengthened from twenty-four sages to twenty-eight, would then become part of the basic Chan "history" that survives to this day.

In sum, with Guanding we have a good example of a Buddhist "historian" planning out various accounts of the past in accord with his shifting

10. For more discussion of this text, see Stuart Young, *Conceiving the Indian Buddhist Patriarchs in China* (Honolulu: University of Hawai'i Press, 2015), chaps. 2 and 3; see also Wendi L. Adamek, *The Mystique of Transmission: On an Early Chan History and Its Contents* (New York: Columbia University Press, 2007), 101–10.

11. This book is, in fact, a Mahāyāna-focused encyclopedia, likely put together in China sometime in the early fifth century. For a French translation of a portion of the text, see Nāgārjuna, *Le traité de la grande vertu de sagesse = Mahāprajñāpāramitāśāstra*, trans. and ed. Étienne Lamotte (Louvain, Belgium: Institut orientaliste, Bibliothèque de l'Université, 1966–).

needs. What is unique about the case of Guanding is that his contradictory efforts survive and reveal the politics of his history writing. Thus, if we take Guanding to be the "father" of Buddhist genealogies in China, as Linda Penkower suggests we should, then we ought to see, too, that he produced the earliest exemplars of this genre with a certain combination of ambition, calculation, and disregard for facts and previous statements.[12]

XINXING, THE ABSOLUTE MASTER

Roughly contemporaneous with Zhiyi, we find another nationally famous master, Xinxing, who was at the center of an attempt to recast Chinese Buddhism's relationship to India—and all the imported sutras—by concentrating the totality of tradition in his own person.[13] Thus, Xinxing, with startling levels of success, assumed the identity of a uniquely gifted Buddhist sage, who declared that no other Chinese Buddhist had the right to read or interpret Buddhist scripture and that, instead, Chinese Buddhists ought to focus on silent regimes of meditation and repentance, while also accepting as definitive Xinxing's own idiosyncratic interpretation of tradition. Thus, though Xinxing and his followers, who went under the banner of the Teachings of the Three Levels (*Sanjie jiao*), would be formally banned as heretics several times during the seventh and eighth centuries, the structuring of Xinxing's identity seems to have important resonances with early Chan writing, especially in terms of centralizing tradition into a single man and then slotting followers into subservient roles defined by meditation and repentance.[14]

12. For this assessment of Guanding's role in the invention of Buddhist genealogy, see Linda Penkower, "In the Beginning ... Guanding (561—632) and the Creation of Early Tiantai," *Journal of the International Association of Buddhist Studies* 23, no. 2 (2000): 245–96, esp. 246–48.

13. The following four paragraphs on Xinxing are taken, with changes, from my *Fathering Your Father: The Zen of Fabrication in Tang Buddhism* (Berkeley: University of California Press, 2009), 31–34.

14. For more reflections on Xinxing and his movement's importance in seventh-century discussions of Chan, see Eric Greene, "Another Look at Early 'Chan': Daoxuan, Bodhidharma, and the Three Levels Movement," *T'oung Pao* 94 (2008): 49–114.

There are several other notable things about Xinxing and his agenda that make him relevant to the story of how Chan came to be. First, his legacy was strong enough that his biography was included in the "meditation masters" section of Daoxuan's *Continued Biographies of Eminent Monks*.[15] Thus, a reader leafing through this section of Daoxuan's encyclopedia would have seen the entry for Xinxing sitting not too far from Bodhidharma's, and thus would have had reason to consider Xinxing and his teaching as potentially useful for new history writing. Second, some decades after his death, a certain Tanglin (600–?) wrote the *Record of Miraculous Retribution* (*Mingbao ji*) in which he presented a brief lineage for Xinxing, thereby linking Xinxing's singular identity with the genealogical model for explaining Buddhist authority.[16] Then, in more general terms, the best reason for including Xinxing in a history of Chan is Xinxing's radical reconstruction of Chinese Buddhism around himself. Thus, the case of Xinxing is a good example of creating an "absolute master" who supposedly held the totality of Buddhist tradition in his own person. In short, for his followers, Xinxing *the man* was more important than all other Chinese monks and, equally stunning, more important than all the imported Buddhist literature. And, finally, even though Xinxing insisted on an unbridgeable gulf between himself and his followers, he also preached a seductive ideology in which his followers were consoled in their permanent secondary status by an emphasis on their inherent buddhahood. For these reasons it makes good sense to see in Xinxing an important precedent for the figure of the Chan master that took form in the following centuries.

Equally interesting, and again presaging later developments in Chan literature, Xinxing's mastery of tradition was underscored when, in

15. For discussion of Daoxuan's entry for Xinxing and his sources, see Jamie Hubbard, *Absolute Delusion, Perfect Buddhahood: The Rise and Fall of a Chinese Heresy* (Honolulu: University of Hawai'i Press, 2001), 4–5; for Daoxuan's biography of Xinxing, see *T* (no. 2060), 50.559c.18–560b.10.

16. *T* (no. 2082), 51.788a.29. For a translation, see Donald Gjerston, *Miraculous Retribution: A Study and Translation of T'anglin's Ming pao chi* (Berkeley, CA: Center for South and Southeast Asia Studies, 1989), 157–60.

the middle of his career, he supposedly renounced his robes and monk status, making clear that his authority was no longer dependent on the legitimizing functions normally provided by official Buddhist structures. When we learn that Xinxing also took up manual labor, his independence from the official hierarchies of tradition seems reinforced, even as he now appears humble and close to the earth and the peasants.[17] Arguably, then, Xinxing's perfection was constructed in a way that conjoined the top and the bottom of the symbolic order, just as the biographies of the Chan masters Hongren, Huineng, and others would be in the eighth century. In each of these cases, the master is both the king of Buddhism *and* one of the most lowly laborers, a combination that had lasting appeal for the Chinese. In short, given the fruitful life that parallel rhetorical strategies would have in the centuries to come, excluding Xinxing from the history of Chan would be a big mistake.

With a sense of the work that went into creating the images of Zhiyi and Xinxing, let's turn to the earliest accounts of Bodhidharma. These accounts, too, involve themselves rather obviously in strategies of endorsement, while also working to solve the daunting problem of owning perfect Buddhism in China.

THE EARLIEST MENTION OF BODHIDHARMA

As is widely admitted in Chan studies, it isn't clear that a person named Bodhidharma ever existed. And, even if there was such a person with this name, it is altogether unlikely that he performed the various tasks that Chan narratives assign to him. In the oldest text that mentions him, the *Record of the Buddhist Monasteries of Luoyang* (*Luoyang qielan ji,* written in 547 by Yang Xuanzhi), Bodhidharma is presented as a wandering Buddhist monk, and in this role he has nothing to

---

17. For the context of this gesture, see Hubbard, *Absolute Delusion, Perfect Buddhahood,* 8; and, for more reflections on Xinxing's efforts to demonstrate his humbleness, ibid., 24–27.

do with the transmission of total truth from India to China. According to this text:[18]

> At that time there was a monk of the Western Region named Bodhidharma, a foreigner from Persia (*Bosi guo*), who traveled from the wild borderlands to China. Seeing the golden disks [on the pole on top of Yongning's stupa] reflecting in the sun, the rays of light illuminating the surface of the clouds, the jewel-bells on the stupa blowing in the wind, the echoes reverberating beyond the heavens, he sang its praises. He exclaimed: "Truly this is the work of spirits." He said: "I am 150 years old, and I have passed through numerous countries. There is no country that I have not visited and yet nowhere on earth has a monastery this beautiful." He chanted *Namo* and placed his palms together in salutation for days on end.

In this passage the emphasis is on making Bodhidharma appear as an international art critic qualified to judge the merits of this Chinese pagoda. Thus, as Bodhidharma, the epic world-traveler, enthuses for days over the beauty of this pagoda, the reader can be sure that this temple really was a world-class beauty. And, let's not overlook that it is the beauty of the pagoda that matters in the story, not Bodhidharma.

BODHIDHARMA ENDORSES THE *TREATISE ON THE TWO ENTRANCES AND FOUR PRACTICES*

Bodhidharma next appears in a very different text—the *Treatise on the Two Entrances and Four Practices* (*Erru sixing lun*—hereafter referred to as "the *Two Entrances*"). Here, instead of endorsing Chinese Buddhist architectural achievements, he is endorsing a somewhat bizarre summary of Buddhist thought and practice that was anonymously composed in China, sometime in the early seventh century. In the preface to this text Bodhidharma, identified as the third son of a south Indian king, appears

18. Translation from Jeffrey Broughton, *The Bodhidharma Anthology: The Earliest Records of Zen* (Berkeley: University of California Press, 1999), 54–55, with changes; see also John R. McRae's translation in *The Northern School and the Formation of Early Ch'an Buddhism* (Honolulu: University of Hawai'i Press, 1986), p. 17; *T* (no. 2092), 51.1000b.19.

as a wonderful sage who long ago understood Buddhist and non-Buddhist teachings, and who also happened to be aware, even back in India, of the decline of the dharma in China. Feeling bad about this, Bodhidharma decided to come to China to introduce the "true teachings." Once in China, he found two promising students: Huike and Daoyu. They impressed him with their devotion and intelligence, and he gave them this text, the *Two Entrances*. In short, the preface presents the *Two Entrances* as a perfect summation of Buddhism, transmitted by an incomparably wise Indian master who sought to correct China's supposedly decadent approach to Buddhism. To read this story well, we need to see that Bodhidharma is again being set up as an international expert who can be taken as a final authority on a Chinese Buddhist product. The preface, which becomes notably chaotic by its end, explains:

> The dharma master [Bodhidharma] was from a country in south India, in the western region, the third son of a great Brahmin king. He was naturally brilliant and understood everything he heard. His aspirations were for the path of the Mahāyāna, so he discarded the white [garb of a layman] and assumed the black [robes of a Buddhist monk] in order to continue and develop the sagely seed. His mysterious mind empty and quiescent (*mingxin xuji*), he had a penetrating understanding of the affairs of the world. Wise in both the internal and external, his virtue exceeded the standard of the age. Feeling sad and regretful about the decline of the true teaching in this obscure corner [of the world], he crossed the mountains and oceans to convert those in the far-off land of the Han and Wei (China).
>
> Among those who could overcome their own minds, there wasn't one who did not fail to place their faith in [Bodhidharma]; but those who grasped at appearances and held [incorrect] views reviled him. At the time Daoyu and Huike were his only [students]. These two monks, having lofty aspirations that belied their youth, had the good fortune to meet the dharma master and served him for several years. They reverentially asked to be instructed, and perceived well the master's intention. The dharma master responded to their perfect sincerity (*jingcheng*) by teaching them the true path (*zhendao*), saying: "Such is the pacification of the mind, such is the generation of practice, such is accordance with convention, such are

expedient means. This is the teaching of the pacification of mind in the Mahāyāna—make certain [that it is understood] without error."

Such is the pacification of the mind—wall-contemplation; such is the generation of practice—the four practices; such is accordance with convention—defense against calumnification; such are expedient means—the avoidance of attachment to those [means]. The above is a brief summary of the origins of the ideas expressed in the text that follows.[19]

While the author of this preface somehow knows a good bit more about Bodhidharma, there are no dates or places for any of the events in his life in China, making these claims look dubious. In fact, there are good reasons for thinking that this enhanced, but still very vague, account of Bodhidharma drew on details found in the biography of the Indian master Buddhabhadra (*fotuo*), who appears to have been a real historical figure and who, once in China, founded Shaolin monastery in 495.[20]

Leaving aside questions surrounding the origins of this enhanced biography for Bodhidharma, let's turn to the *Two Entrances* itself. The first thing to say is that the two ways of "entering the Dao" are rather

19. This translation is taken from McRae's *Northern School*, 102–3, with changes; a version of the text, with a different title, can handily be found in the *Xuzang jing*, X (no. 1217), www.cbeta.org/result/normal/X63/1217_001.htm. The *Two Entrances* and its preface were also included in chap. 30 of the eleventh-century *Jingde chuandeng lu*, T (no. 2076), 51.458b.7. McRae took it as fact that Tanlin (506–74) composed this preface (*Northern School*, 101), but this claim only appeared later in Jingjue's notably inventive *History of the Teachers and Students of the Laṅkāvatāra Sūtra*, composed more than one hundred years later. For a translation of this passage that mentions Tanlin as the author of the preface, see J. C. Cleary's *Zen Dawn: Early Zen Texts from Tun Huang* (Boston: Shambhala, 1991), 32, or Bernard Faure, *Le bouddhisme Chan en mal d'histoire: Genèse d'une tradition religieuse dans le Chine des T'ang* (Paris: École française d'Extrême-Orient, 1989), 116. For more details on Dunhuang versions of the *Two Entrances* and for references to relevant Japanese scholarship, see Broughton, *Bodhidharma Anthology*, 121n12; for Broughton's translation of the *Two Entrances*, see ibid., 8–12.

20. For Daoxuan's biography of Buddhabhadra, see T (no. 2060), 50.551a.21; for a French translation, see Paul Pelliot's "Notes sur quelques artistes des Six Dynasties et des T'ang," *T'oung Pao* 22 (1923): 215–91, esp. 245–50. Faure also suspected that the accounts of Buddhabhadra and Bodhidharma were related; see his entry for "Bodhidharma," in the *Encyclopedia of Religion*, 1st ed., 2: 263–65 (Detroit: Macmillan Reference USA, 1986), and his original and influential essay "Bodhidharma as Textual and Religious Paradigm," *History of Religions* 25, no. 3 (1986): 187–98.

different. As we will see below, the First Entrance appears somewhat Daoist in terms of focus, vocabulary, and logic: thus, with no particular practice or teaching mentioned, one simply "returns to the real" (*guizhen*), thereby recovering a quiescence defined as non-action (*wuwei*), with the whole project characterized as "mysteriously tallying with the principle," an altogether Daoist-sounding phrase. The Second Entrance, also mentions Daoist-sounding terms to characterize successful practice, but those terms are used within the context of fairly traditional advice on practicing Buddhism, advice that relies on standard Buddhist ideas regarding karma, and rebirth, supported with sutra quotations. To get a better sense of the difference between these two styles of Buddhism, consider the mysterious monism of the First Entrance:

> Entering by principle (*ruli*) means that one awakens to the essence [of tradition] by relying on the teachings (*jijiao wuzong*). [In particular,] one must deeply believe that all living beings have the same true nature (*shenxin hansheng tongyi zhenxing*). [Normally,] this true nature is not revealed simply because the external "dusts" of mistaken thought cover it up. If one rejects mistaken [thinking] and returns to the true (*shewang guizhen*), fixedly abiding in wall-contemplation (*ningzhu biguan*), then self and other, common man and sage, are [understood to be] identical; firmly abiding without shifting, and without relying on written teachings (*geng bu suiyu wenjiao*)— this is mysteriously tallying with the principle (*yuli mingfu*), and it is without discrimination: quiescent and without action (*wuyou fenbie jiran wuwei*). Just this is called entrance by principle.[21]

Challenging the reader to awaken to the essence [of tradition] in the recognition that "all living beings have the same true nature" might have appeared bewildering to many readers, but what to make of the even more difficult term "wall-contemplation" (*biguan*) that seems part of this final vision of truth? Some have assumed that it refers to a form of meditation, and yet normal Chinese word-order is verb-object, so it can't really mean "contemplating the wall," even if some later Tang commentators

---

21. This translation is indebted to McRae's translation in *Northern School*, 102–5, and Broughton's in *Bodhidharma Anthology*, 9.

parsed it that way. As we saw above, the preface to the *Two Entrances* glosses "wall-contemplation" as "the pacification of mind," but unfortunately "pacification of mind" is a fairly vague term that doesn't do much to clarify the meaning of "wall-contemplation." In fact, it may be that the author of the preface, himself, wasn't sure what to make of "wall-contemplation" since in that final section of the preface where he mentions the term, his otherwise careful prose suddenly gets jumbled and uninformative.[22]

Ambiguity surrounding the term "wall-contemplation" increases when we note that the Two Entrances were discussed elsewhere in seventh-century literature, and in these other passages, the character "wall" is replaced with "awakening," shifting the above phrase from "fixedly abiding in wall-contemplation" to "fixedly abiding in awakening and contemplation" (*ningzhu jueguan*).[23] This phrasing makes more sense grammatically and, equally important, respects the logic of the text, since why should there be the *practice* of "wall-contemplation" in the First Entrance when that entrance was defined as entering the Dao through *principle?* Actual practices, such as meditation, should have, by definition, been consigned to the Second Entrance, and yet there too there is no mention of meditation.[24] In short, it is far from clear what "wall-contemplation" was, or whether or not it was connected with a particular style of meditation.[25]

22. Although some modern readers might assume that "pacification of mind" referred to a type of meditation, other Tang texts treat it as an esoteric state altogether different from the actual practice of meditation. See, for instance, Jingjue's account of Guṇabhadra's teaching, an account that he seems to have invented in the early eighth century and set in his *History of the Teachers and Students of the Laṅkāvatāra Sūtra* (*T* no. 2837, 85.1284a.24; trans. Cleary, *Zen Dawn*, 27–28; Faure, *Bouddhisme Chan*, 105).

23. McRae points out in *Northern School*, 118 and 308n27, that the apocryphal *Vajrasamādhi Sūtra*, chap. 5, depicts the Buddha explaining the Two Entrances in a manner that parallels this passage in the *Two Entrances*, but "fixedly abiding in wall-contemplation" is replaced with "fixedly abiding in awakening and contemplation" (*T* no. 273, 9.369c.7).

24. Adamek, *Mystique of Transmission*, 141, suggests that the Two Entrances are to be practiced in series. However, there is no evidence for this in the text and the entrance by principle doesn't seem preparatory for any other kind of practice.

25. This passage from the *Two Entrances* was translated into Tibetan on several occasions with no mention of wall-contemplation. The phrase in question is, in one

Leaving aside the problem of "wall-contemplation," we can still see that in the First Entrance, the emphasis is on awakening to the reality of a deep pervading sameness that, among other things, levels out the most basic divide in Buddhism: the difference between sages and commoners. Promoting a vision that erases this difference might not seem too striking at first, but it implies that perfect wisdom is presented here as a self-reflexive understanding *regarding those with and without wisdom.* Thus, according to this definition, real sages know that sages aren't ultimately different from commoners, and yet it is this very realization that makes them sages, and therefore totally different from commoners. Put in a manner that reflects the full circularity of the situation: final wisdom culminates in the recognition of the impossibility of the wisdom-program— Buddhism, that is—and yet just this realization is what consummates (and perpetuates) the wisdom-program, since such a realization makes one a sage. Versions of just this Daoist-sounding paradox in which the sage happily discovers that there was, in fact, nothing to discover would become normal in many later Chan discourses.

To get clearer about the Daoist resonances of the First Entrance, let's consider the following three items. First, there is an emphasis on the *return to truth,* a perspective that echoes the trope of returning to the One, or the Dao, that is basic to Daoist thought, and the *Daode jing,* in particular. Likewise, the phrase "mysteriously tallying with the principle" carries Daoist connotations, not simply because anything "mysterious" in Chinese philosophy is often associated with Daoist thinking,

---

case, rendered as *rtogs pa spangs te / lham mer gnas na*: "with thoughts abandoned, abiding in luminosity" which is much closer to the line in the *Vajrasamādhi Sūtra* than to the *Two Entrances'* version. See Broughton, *Bodhidharma Anthology,* 67-68, for more discussion and a slightly different translation of the Tibetan. McRae, *Northern School,* 112–15, surveys various attempts—medieval and modern—to make sense of the term "wall-contemplation." For another discussion of the problem, see Carmen Meinert, "The Conjunction of Chinese Chan and Tibetan *Rdzogs chen* Thought: Reflections on the Tibetan Dunhuang Manuscripts IOL Tib J 689–1 and PT 699," in *Contributions to the Cultural History of Early Tibet,* eds. Matthew Kapstein and Brandon Dotson (Leiden: Brill, 2007), 239–301, esp. 253ff.

but also because tallies (*fu*) figure prominently in various Daoist discussions.[26] And, finally, the description of Bodhidharma in the preface makes him sound like a Daoist sage with "his mysterious mind, empty and quiescent." Taken together, the First Entrance appears rather perplexing since it offers the reader, in terms and phrases that sound distinctly Daoist, the possibility that perfect Buddhist awakening can be won without relying on any kind of specific practice and "without relying on written teachings." In this unthinkable awakening, the final wholeness of the universe can be regained by "mysteriously tallying with the principle"—an offer that appears to have much more to do with Daoist thinking than with the Buddhism imported from India.

The Second Entrance is a good bit longer and more Buddhist-looking since the primary topics discussed are karma, past lives, suffering, and emptiness/selflessness—topics, we should note, that were completely absent from the First Entrance. In the first three of the four practices covered in the Second Entrance, readers are instructed, first, how to understand misfortune as karmic payback, then how to realize that life in cyclic existence is unacceptable, and, finally, how to distrust worldly advancements. In detailing these practices, unnamed sutras are cited to shore up the points, and standard Buddhist ideas and idioms are drawn on to flesh out what is, again, a decidedly Buddhist-looking program of practice. The fourth practice, "in accord with the dharma" briefly defines how one should practice in the recognition that nothing really exists, since all things are void; a short line from the *Vimalakīrti* is

---

26. The character for "tally" (*fu*) is also translated as "seal" in other situations. In ancient China, contracts of various kinds were concluded with a seal or tally that was broken in two, with each party to the bargain keeping half of the original whole. Consequently, "to tally" with something or someone implies not only returning to reconstitute an original whole, but also to fulfill a fundamental relationship and/or understanding. For an account of the role that tallies played in various situations, see Stephan Peter Bumbacher's *Empowered Writing: Exorcistic and Apotropaic Rituals in Medieval China* (Magdalena, NM: Three Pines Press, 2012), 13–82; see also the entry for *fu* by Stephen Bokenkamp in *The Encyclopedia of Taoism*, vol. 1, ed. Fabrizio Pregadio (London: Routledge, 2004), 35–38; and, Mark Edward Lewis's discussion of seals in his *Writing and Authority in Early China* (Albany: State University of New York Press, 1999), 28–34.

cited to support this claim, but the source isn't named. The final phase of this section of the text, while including the line that "yet there is nothing that is practiced,"[27] doesn't veer off to attack the ontological basis of Buddhism itself—as the First Entrance arguably does—nor does this passage, or the Second Entrance in general, engage in discussions of the sameness shared by sages and commoners, a topic that was front and center in the First Entrance. In fact, the third practice of the Second Entrance explicitly relies on there being a clear divide between covetous "worldly people" (*shiren*) and a "person of insight" (*zhizhe*) who "awakens to reality."[28]

That the *Two Entrances* presents these two very different ways of being Buddhist raises some interesting questions. How is one to pick between the two?—no advice is given. The little that we can surmise is that these two entrances seem distinguished in terms of master and novice, since the Second Entrance clearly speaks of practical problems that beginners might have in dealing with misfortune, while the First Entrance, with its mysterious monism and lack of practical advice, would seem aimed at a more refined and advanced reader, one more like Bodhidharma, who, as we just saw, was graced with "a mysterious mind, empty and quiescent." Of course, that these two styles of Buddhism sit so comfortably next to each other might suggest that the reader *isn't* supposed to chose between them and that a new, hybrid kind of Buddhism is being offered, one in which everyone practices a basic form of Buddhism, more or less in accord with the Second Entrance, while knowing about the mysterious, Daoist-sounding Buddhism of the First Entrance that appears largely free of Buddhist concerns. Of course, as just seen above, Xinxing's style of Buddhism, which was wildly popular just when the *Two Entrances* was written, was also built on a similarly bifurcated model of Buddhist practice—one model for masters and one for everyone else—making clear that just such an arrangement was far from being unusual at the time.

27. Broughton, *Bodhidharma Anthology*, 12; McRae, *Northern School*, 105.
28. Broughton, *Bodhidharma Anthology*, 10; McRae, *Northern School*, 104.

Though we might never know why the author of the *Two Entrances* presented these two different styles of Buddhism, it is true that slightly later Chan texts also worked at producing a vision of high and low forms of Buddhism and *bringing them together* to form one coherent gestalt that was to be appreciated by the reader. In fact, one wouldn't be far wrong in thinking that generating just such a vision of a two-tiered Buddhism—sometimes identified as sudden and gradual teachings—is at the heart of most Chan writing. What's most intriguing, and more than a little ironic, is that in doubling Buddhism in this way, it is the elite form of "practice" that appears more Daoist in style, whereas the plebian version remains traditionally Buddhist in form, content, and literary references. In fact, as we will see in the chapters ahead, Chan rhetoric regularly casts the masters as those who are Daoist about being Buddhist, and it is because of *that* that they are to be recognized as the leaders of Buddhism.

Thinking about Chan rhetoric in this manner ought to remind us of the way early Daoist writing offered elites the fantasy of escaping their Confucian obligations—familial and governmental—while nonetheless miraculously getting all cultural tasks done in a fine and blameless fashion. Thus, in the *Daode jing* or in the *Zhuangzi,* and then again in the *Liezi,* the master is the happy (and rare) sage who recognizes his innate oneness with the Dao and, as a consequence, easily rises above the anxieties of the Confucian tradition, even though he still functions perfectly within that system.[29] In short, these Daoist texts offer readers an experience of wholeness that enables one to live the demands of normal Confucian tradition in an ironic, and yet productive, manner. A similar logic seems to be at work organizing the *Two Entrances* since the First

29. For a reading of the *Daode jing* that emphasizes this kind of dialectical relation with the Confucian tradition, see my "Simplicity for the Sophisticated: Rereading the *Daode jing* for the Polemics of Ease and Innocence," *History of Religions* 46 (2006): 1–49. Also, in thinking about precedents for this rhetoric of sameness, it is important to note that Mencius claimed that "The Sage and I are of the same kind." (*Mencius,* 6A.7); see D.C. Lau trans., *Mencius,* London: Penguin Books, 1970), 164. For more discussion of how the sameness between sages and commoners was discussed in the Tang, see Timothy Barrett, *Li Ao: Buddhist, Taoist, or Neo-Confucian?* (Oxford University Press, 1992), 99ff.

Entrance evokes a Daoist-flavored version of final wisdom that recognizes a deep sameness in all creatures, and grants one the confidence to disregard the practical forms of Buddhism—along with those anxiety-producing discourses on karma and rebirth—even though, inexplicably, the final goals of the Buddhist tradition are all achieved.

Once we see several more examples of this setup, it will be worth considering that Chan rhetoric established a position vis-à-vis the wider Buddhist tradition in a manner that parallels how Daoist authors promised a more complete, and definitely more relaxed, way of being Confucian—one in which one mysteriously "practices" non-action while still effortlessly getting everything done. The key here isn't just that the patterns are alike, it's also that Chan authors used the very same terminology that Daoist authors used in announcing their own carefree, and clearly ironic, mastery of the Buddhist system. To argue in this way is simply to accept it as probable that Chan authors recognized how Daoist, Confucian, and Buddhist rhetorical programs worked *as rhetoric,* and then moved between them, mixing and matching strategies to produce new and attractive combinations. And, knowing how much Daoist and Chan literature was produced through forgery—playfully at times and more seriously in other instances—we have even more reason to assume that many Chinese authors received texts and traditions in a decidedly ironic manner, and therefore felt confident refiguring and restaging the truths of these traditions as they liked. In sum, an ironic attitude towards received tradition appears as both the cause and the effect of these views of wholeness and completion, and, as I hope to show, this very traditional irony towards tradition appears essential for understanding the production of Chan literature.

However we decide to imagine the cultural forces that likely shaped Chan's presentation of truth and sagehood, it is essential to see that Chan texts aren't just dedicated to promoting the masters' Daoist-sounding version of Buddhism; instead, they work to present a vision of both high and low styles of Buddhist understanding, presumably within the expectation that everyone should continue with their standard

Buddhist practices, even as they would be impressed (and excited) by this new Daoist-looking way of being Buddhist that, though technically reserved for the masters, was regularly spoken of and written about for the public's delight and edification. Given how prominent these two forms of Chinese Buddhism appear in later Chan writing, the *Two Entrances* likely qualifies as an important first step in establishing this split-level template of desire and hierarchy that appears so essential to Chan.

BODHIDHARMA IN DAOXUAN'S *CONTINUED BIOGRAPHIES OF EMINENT MONKS*

After serving as a shadowy but fully qualified spokesperson endorsing the *Two Entrances,* we next find Bodhidharma in Daoxuan's *Continued Biographies of Eminent Monks.* In this huge and very influential work published at the capital, Luoyang, in 645, Bodhidharma's biography is the fifth one presented in the first of two chapters devoted to meditation masters. Daoxuan doesn't mention his sources, but his account of Bodhidharma's life seems to be based on the preface to the *Two Entrances* that we just considered. In fact, Daoxuan seems to have done little more than inject some new "facts" into that story, while also including the detail that Bodhidharma lived for 150 years, a detail that he presumably took from the *Records of Luoyang.*

That Daoxuan had so little material to work with is, on its own, telling. It means that in the middle of the seventh century, all that Daoxuan— the most celebrated Buddhist historian of his era—had to draw on in writing up Bodhidharma's biography were the two short blurbs treated above, and neither of these sources appears particularly reliable, nor do these two texts suggest that anything like a Chan movement was taking form. In short, though Bodhidharma as a *literary* figure had been set up as the final voice of authority in two fairly out-of-the-way textual statements, that profile-of-authority had not yet gained much traction within the wider world of Chinese Buddhism. However, once

Daoxuan brought this early version of Bodhidharma to the attention of the nation—by including him in his encyclopedia—Bodhidharma would soon attract a lot of interest as a means of solving other problems of final authority. In sum, the fictive figure of Bodhidharma, so casually created back in the sixth and early seventh centuries as a "final art/lit critic," would, as he was passed around from one text to another, become increasingly important precisely because other authors saw how his voice of authority could be used to support different causes.

HUIKE IN DAOXUAN'S *CONTINUED* *BIOGRAPHIES OF EMINENT MONKS*

The entry for Huike in Daoxuan's *Encyclopedia* follows right after Bodhidharma's and has clearly been tampered with. The first half of Huike's biography, which seems to be the section that Daoxuan wrote before 645, presents a version of Huike that revolves around his relationship with Bodhidharma. The second section presents a very different Huike, one who supposedly stood at the head of a lineage of masters who transmitted the *Laṅkāvatāra Sūtra* in a man-to-man manner.[30] This second version of Huike opens up into a loose narrative regarding two other figures—Chan master Na (*chanshi Na*) and master Huiman—who both supposedly inherited a special way of reading the *Laṅkāvatāra Sūtra* from Huike. This final section also mentions that readers should consult another entry on the topic of Huike's lineage, and such an entry does in fact exist in the form of a biography for master Fachong (flourished mid-seventh century) that is tucked into an epilogue chapter on

---

30. The *Laṅkāvatāra Sūtra* appears to have been composed in India in the early fourth century. Among the various topics covered, there are three main philosophic ideas: (1) everything we experience is mind-made (*cittamātra*); (2) in reality, there is no duality between subject and object, and all such impressions of duality and distinction are false; and (3) there is a nascent buddha, or *tathāgatagarbha*, at the base of the consciousness of all sentient beings. Though the text is chaotic and repetitive, it nonetheless provided early Chan writers with a substantial part of their philosophic outlook.

"Miracle Workers."[31] In that entry we find a story of Huike's lineage that mirrors, in a basic way, the one that seems to have been hastily wedged into the second part of Huike's biography. So, as Hu Shih argued almost a century ago, it appears undeniable that sometime after 645 someone altered Huike's biography and, in effect, inserted this lineage story into the Huike entry and then dovetailed it with the Fachong entry in order to give the impression that Huike was the first in a series of Chinese masters who taught that the essence of Buddhism was to be found in the *Laṅkāvatāra Sūtra,* with Fachong then positioned as Huike's most recent descendant in the lineage of masters-of-the-*Laṅkāvatāra Sūtra.*[32]

As for the details: in the first part of Huike's biography several things stand out. First, Daoxuan presents a mini-story in which Huike was supposedly criticized by other Buddhists for not having a master; this criticism is resolved in a just-so manner when Huike meets Bodhidharma and takes him as his master. We learn that: "In a single glance Bodhidharma was pleased with him, and he [Huike] came to serve Bodhidharma as his master."[33] With this moment of sudden recognition demonstrating their natural affinity, this version seems to intensify the Bodhidharma-Huike connection. This special connection also works to privilege Huike over Daoyu, who, though presented as Huike's equal in the preface to the *Two Entrances,* now has disappeared, and certainly doesn't have his own biographic entry.[34]

Further into Huike's biography, Daoxuan introduces information about Bodhidharma's death, and adds that because Bodhidharma was

31. *T* (no. 2060), 50.666a.3.

32. For Hu Shih's discussion, see "Leng-ch'ieh tsung k'ao," in *Hu Shih wen-ts'un,* 3: 194–244 (Taipei: Yuan-t'ung t'u shu kung-szu, 1953), repr. in *Ko Teki zengakuan,* ed. Yanagida Seizan, 154–95 (Kyoto: Chūbun shuppan sha, 1975).

33. Broughton, *Bodhidharma Anthology,* 58; *T* (no. 2060), 50.552a.4.

34. In the various rewritings of Bodhidharma's life in China in the following centuries, Daoyu on and off reappears in the story, but even when he is mentioned, he is always presented as a secondary figure, much in the shadow of the Bodhidharma-Huike connection.

quite famous, there was an imperial proclamation put out after he died. However, Daoxuan doesn't cite any corroborating evidence for either of these claims—and the imperial proclamation seems particularly vague with no date or content given. A parallel tendency to exaggerate is seen in the section that follows, where we learn that Huike drew the ire of a famous Chan master, Daoheng (n.d.), who claimed that Huike's teachings were evil. While at first this sounds like a negative element in an otherwise flattering account of Huike, in fact, this story is dedicated to showing how Huike triumphed over Daoheng and his various murderous plots. Thus when Daoheng sent out a series of his disciples to silence Huike, they all ended up converting to Huike's version of Buddhism. Then, in a particularly unlikely section of the narrative, Daoxuan claims that when Daoheng hired a "common imperial guard" to assassinate Huike, this too failed since even the hired assassin fell under the charms of Huike's sagely manner. Despite these rather impressive additions to Huike's profile, Daoxuan ends this section of the entry declaring that "Therefore, in the end, his undertaking came to a close *without producing any illustrious successors* ... "[35] Without a doubt, then, Daoxuan closes out his account of Huike making clear that Huike had nothing to do with the *Laṅkāvatāra Sūtra*, had no disciples of note, and certainly did not establish a lineage.

This image of Huike is completely overturned in the second part of Huike's biography. Here, rather awkwardly, there are several other masters introduced into the story, and they are, save for the first— layman Xiang (*xiang jushi*)—allied in their commitment to transmitting the *Laṅkāvatāra Sūtra*. Layman Xiang, for his part, appears to have other roles in the story. First, he is a figure who lived close to nature since he "hid away in the forests and fields, and ate off the trees."[36] And, then, in addition to his taste for all things natural, he appears obsessed with the final truth of reality and, based on that obsession, writes Huike a letter.

35. Broughton, *Bodhidharma Anthology,* 59; *T* (no. 2060), 50.552a.27.
36. Ibid., 60; *T* (no. 2060), 50.552a.27.

In this philosophic note we see that strain of Chinese thought in which final wisdom is marked by a leveling of sages and commoners, along with Daoist-sounding accounts of reality and truth such as: "In principlelessness they create principles, and because of these principles, disputations arise."[37] Though there is some Buddhist vocabulary along the way—nirvana, buddhahood, and awakening are all mentioned—the letter appears fairly Daoist in tone and sentiment.

Huike's letter back to Xiang follows suit since we get more Daoist-sounding riffs on the "true, hidden principle" (*zhen youli*), along with that standard claim that buddhas and commoners are fundamentally the same.[38] The narrator adds that Huike wrote "these truthful words without resorting to erasure or rewrites,"[39] giving the sense that Huike's wisdom was natural and spontaneously perfect. Of course, the entire letter-writing gambit appears as an excellent way to introduce new material into the Huike story, thereby fleshing out Huike's persona, while also using his growing celebrity to ratify this position regarding the deep sameness between buddhas and the rest of us, a sameness that calls normal Buddhist practice into question, as do other passages from both letters. Huike's letter appears to have circulated on its own, and it would, in time, along with several other letters, be appended to the *Two Entrances*.[40] In short, we are witnessing an interesting dialectic whereby the profiles of select masters were plumped up with new doctrines, and new doctrines were then pumped up by being associated with these masters.

Continuing in this second half of the biography, the narrative turns to explain how Huike's form of wisdom was based on the *Laṅkāvatāra Sūtra*—a totally new claim contradicting what was said in the first part of Huike's biography, and of course also contradicting what was said

---

37. Ibid., 61; *T* (no. 2060), 50.552b.4.

38. Ibid.; *T* (no. 2060), 50.552b.8.

39. Ibid., with a slight change; *T* (no. 2060), 50.552b.13.

40. For translation of these letters, see Broughton, *Bodhidharma Anthology*, 12–14, and McRae, *Northern School*, 105–6.

about him in the preface to the *Two Entrances*. Here, we learn that Bodhidharma had given Huike the *Laṅkāvatāra Sūtra,* saying, "When I examine the land of China, it is clear that this is the only sutra [that matters]. If you rely on it to practice, you will be able to cross over the world [and go to nirvana]."[41] With this two-sentence conversation, Bodhidharma's power-of-endorsement—as it had been detailed in his own entry—shifts from the *Two Entrances* to the *Laṅkāvatāra Sūtra*. The story then moves to compare Huike with a certain scholar named Tanlin, identified as an expert in the *Śrīmālādevī Sūtra,* another Mahāyāna work with an emphasis on the internal buddha. Tanlin seems to have been brought into the story at this point to demonstrate how stoic Huike was. Thus, instead of discussing the relative merits of the men and their preferred sutras, the narrative veers off into an account of how each master handled having his arm cut off by bandits. Supposedly, Huike calmly cauterized his wound, bandaged it up, and went out for his normal begging rounds. Tanlin, the fall guy in the story, wept all night long and then became angry with Huike for not helping him eat.

To get at the logic of this gruesome mini-narrative, it helps to know that Tanlin appears to have been a real historical person who flourished circa 600 and who, in various texts, was noted as a scholar of the *Śrīmālādevī Sūtra*. And, since he is also referred to as "One Arm-Lin," we can assume that he was indeed an amputee.[42] In short, the handicapped Tanlin was introduced into the narrative to serve as a foil for Huike: they both have their choice sutras, and they both lose their arms, but since Huike so outperforms Tanlin in terms of handling the pain of amputation, we are presumably being asked to conclude that the *Laṅkāvatāra Sūtra* really is the better sutra. After all, why would a master with Huike's unflinching fortitude chose a second-rate sutra? And, anyway, at the top of the little vignette, Bodhidharma—in his

41. Broughton, *Bodhidharma Anthology,* 62; *T* (no. 2060), 50.552b.21.

42. For more details on Tanlin and his activities in the sixth and seventh centuries, see ibid., 143n24. Broughton also supplies pre-Daoxuan sources for Tanlin's other moniker "Armless Tan" (ibid., 144n26).

standard role of the Big Other Who Knows What's Best for China—
was made to say that it was the *Laṅkāvatāra Sūtra* that was the ultimate
teaching for China, so the whole mini-story of their arm amputations
appears set here to underwrite that initial claim. Those modern readers
who know of the account of Huike cutting off his own arm and offering
it to Bodhidharma—in return for the dharma—may be surprised to
see how Huike's arm loss first entered the swirl of early Chan writing.
Here, obviously, the author has invented Huike's arm loss to help convince the reader that the *Laṅkāvatāra Sūtra* is really better than the
Śrīmālādevī Sūtra, just as the stoic Huike is superior to the well-
educated, but weak, Tanlin.

Mixing accounts of physical fortitude with the putative supremacy
of the *Laṅkāvatāra Sūtra* continues in the next two mini-narratives,
where we learn of the exploits of the two other supposed inheritors of
the *Laṅkāvatāra Sūtra,* Chan master Na and Huiman. Na was purportedly famous for practicing asceticism, since he wore but one robe, ate
but one meal a day, and so on. Travelling about to "four hundred
locales," Na shunned towns and residences, and he also didn't write or
read conventional books. Instead, he promoted only the *Laṅkāvatāra
Sūtra,* and, when he bumped into Huiman, gave him a dharma discourse based on the *Laṅkāvatāra Sūtra* that so moved Huiman that he
became a monk and took up an arduous ascetic lifestyle like Na's. In
particular, we learn of the night on Mount Song (*Song shan,* the general
locale of Shaolin monastery some twenty miles south of Luoyang)
when Huiman stood in a snowstorm, even though the snow piled up
"five feet deep on all sides" of him.[43]

Just after this story, which will be rewritten in the next century so
that it is Huike and not Huiman braving the snow, the author turns to
wrap things up, stressing that the *Laṅkāvatāra Sūtra* is the best sutra and
that it has been supported by a lineage of indomitable masters who
hand it down, one master to the next:

43. Ibid., 63; *T* (no. 2060), 50.552c.15.

Therefore the masters Na and Huiman always handed over the four-roll *Laṅkāvatāra Sūtra* and took it as the essence of mind (*yiwei xinyao*). Whether preaching or practicing, they did not fail to hand it down. Later, in Luoyang, without illness, Huiman died seated in a cross-legged posture. He was about seventy. These followers, Na and Huiman, were both in the lineage of Huike.... [44]

Here, in complete contradiction with what had been written about Bodhidharma and Huike in the two earlier texts, and in contradiction even with what was presented in the front part of Huike's biographic entry, we see a lineage taking form. Apparently someone hijacked the Bodhidharma-Huike connection, itself surely a fiction, in order to explain how a perfect form of Buddhism based on the *Laṅkāvatāra Sūtra* was transmitted, relay-style, down this lineage of tough and fearless men—such as masters Na and Huiman—who apparently lived free of the trappings of normal culture.

In trying to make sense of this new material in the Huike biography, we should first note that there are two gestures of overcoming at work here. First, the *Laṅkāvatāra Sūtra* is being defined as the textual container for the essence of Buddhism, thus naturally rendering all the other sutras *and practices* superfluous. Second, though the essence of Buddhism is said to be in the *Laṅkāvatāra Sūtra,* normal readings of the text are inadequate since one needs to receive a special kind of teaching from a master in the Huike lineage, making it clear that these masters must also be seen as containers of the essence of tradition. Hence, tradition has two sources and, like double-tube epoxy glue, one needs the contents of both tubes to produce the magical bonding. This implies that one really shouldn't bother reading sutras without a master of the lineage on hand, since the masters supply the essential supplement that makes a final reading of tradition possible.

The passage also makes clear that receiving the *Laṅkāvatāra Sūtra* from a member of Huike's lineage renders other kinds of literary engagements meaningless. Thus, after Na met with Huike and received

44. Ibid., with slight changes; *T* (no. 2060), 50.552c.21.

from him the *Laṅkāvatāra Sūtra,* he "no longer took up the writing brush and conventional books."[45] Likewise, the reader would assume that Huiman, who never stayed anywhere for longer than a day, wasn't carrying much of a library around with him. This renunciation of literary pursuits is amplified by describing how the masters so impressively handled pain and deprivation (Huike's arm loss and Huiman standing in the snow), with Huiman also showing his mastery over the body inasmuch as he supposedly died seated in meditation, not to mention that the narrative adds that: "When he arrived at a monastery, he chopped firewood and made sandals. He always attended to his begging rounds."[46] In sum, these masters of the *Laṅkāvatāra Sūtra* appear as no-nonsense monks who have total Buddhist wisdom *and* the most unflinching contact with the pedestrian stuff of life—a combination that will be essential to later depictions of Chan masters.

The man-to-man transmission of the *Laṅkāvatāra Sūtra* is emphasized more clearly in Fachong's biography. The passage reads:

> He [Fachong] met Master Huike's later descendants, among whom there was a thriving practice of this sutra. Fachong then trained with their master but frequently attacked the important points in that master's approach to the *Laṅkāvatāra Sūtra.* That master then gave up his group and entrusted the work of spreading the *Laṅkāvatāra Sūtra* to Fachong. He [Fachong] then lectured on the *Laṅkāvatāra Sūtra* thirty consecutive times. He also met someone who had personally received a transmission [of the *Laṅkāvatāra Sūtra*] from Huike. Fachong then lectured on it one hundred more times in reliance on the essence of the One Vehicle of south India.[47]

Here transmission of the *Laṅkāvatāra Sūtra* seems to function a bit like a magical zap that needs to be received from someone who himself was

45. Ibid., 62; *T* (no. 2060), 50.552c.5.
46. Ibid., 63; *T* (no. 2060), 50.552c.11.
47. Ibid., 64, with changes; *T* (no. 2060), 50.666b.2. Mention of "South India" in this final line is presumably intended to link these claims of scriptural authority to Bodhidharma, who, according to Daoxuan's encyclopedia and the preface to the *Two Entrances,* supposedly came from south India.

zapped by a master, and so on, back up the line to Huike and Bodhidharma. Obvious, too, is the close connection between receiving this kind of private initiation and being fully qualified to lecture on the text in public.

Fachong's story then opens up into a brief history of how this special lineage based on the *Laṅkāvatāra Sūtra* supposedly got started with Bodhidharma. Here it seems that the basic trope of using Bodhidharma to endorse certain Buddhist items in China—seen first in the *Records of Luoyang* and the preface to the *Two Entrances*—is simply getting redefined yet again. That another author appears to have enlisted the image of Bodhidharma for a new endorsement job leaves little doubt about the level of awareness and craft at work here since clearly seventh-century authors had learned how to appropriate prior claims to authority and reapply them to their own projects. As for the *Laṅkāvatāra Sūtra*, Fachong's biography explains:

> This sutra was translated into Chinese by Tripiṭaka master Guṇabhadra of the Liu Song era (420–479) and copied down by dharma master Huiguan. Its wording and principles are in harmony; its practice and substance are linked. Its sole focus is on a type of insight that does not lie in the spoken word. Later Chan master Bodhidharma transmitted it to the south and the north. Forgetting words, forgetting thoughts, with nothing attained, correct insight was the essential [teaching] (*wangyan wangnian wude zhengguan weizong*). Later this was practiced on the Central Plain of the north. Chan master Huike was the first to apprehend the key point of this teaching. Many of the literati of the Wei region could not sink their teeth into it, but those who received this essential teaching and understood the meaning, attained awakening immediately. Because that generation is becoming ever more distant from us, later trainees have been led into error. A separate biographical entry for Huike gives a summary of the particulars. Now I will relate what the master [Fachong] acknowledged as the succession. There is evidence for every detail of what I learned. After Chan master Bodhidharma, there were the two, Huike and Huiyu [Daoyu]. Master [Dao]Yu received awakening in his mind but never spoke of it. After Chan master Huike [came]:

Chan master Can
Chan master Hui
Chan master Sheng
Old master Na
Chan master Duan
Tripiṭaka master Chang
Chan master Chen
Chan master Yu

The above all spoke of the mysterious principle (*xuanli*) but did not produce written records.[48]

The above passage from Fachong's biography warrants careful reflection
since, with even more clarity than the second half of Huike's biography, a
veritable lineage of Chinese masters is sketched out. What this lineage
promises to provide is a crucial supplement to an otherwise publicly
available statement of truth—the *Laṅkāvatāra Sūtra*. Looked at this way,
we can see an interesting tension between the man-to-man transmission
of the text, which is characterized as "forgetting words, forgetting
thoughts," and the sutra itself which, of course, is all about words and
thoughts. So, in essence, the passage presents a circle of authority between
the *Laṅkāvatāra Sūtra* and the masters: the masters have that extra Something that they can give to another reader of the text, a Something that
allows the reader to be enlightened to the text and, of course, to then be
ready to pass this extra Something on to the next reader.

Within this effort to create a crucial supplement to reading, we
shouldn't miss that this lineage was also designed to overcome the Chinese Buddhist literati, since, supposedly, "Many of the literati of the Wei
region could not sink their teeth into it [the *Laṅkāvatāra Sūtra*]." Thus,
this author, like others to follow, has figured out that setting up priva-
tized ways of passing on perfect Buddhist truth required belittling

48. Ibid., 65, with changes; *T* (no. 2060), 50.666b.6. For another discussion of Fachong
and the *Laṅkāvatāra Sūtra*, see Bernard Faure, *The Will to Orthodoxy: A Critical Genealogy
of Northern Chan Buddhism*, trans. Phyllis Brooks (Stanford, CA: Stanford University
Press, 1997), 145–50.

others who also might claim to have access to the heart of tradition. Of course, disenfranchising those outside the lineage made its appearance back in the preface to the *Two Entrances,* when we learned that it was precisely because China had a second-rate form of the dharma that Bodhidharma supposedly felt compelled to travel to China in order to deliver a perfect form of Buddhism—at least, that is, to Huike and Daoyu.

Though Fachong isn't directly named as the final inheritor of this lineage based on the *Laṅkāvatāra Sūtra,* this is surely implied insofar as the passage above insists that "Fachong acknowledged" the succession, leaving little doubt that he is in charge of the story and, after all, this lineage is presented inside Fachong's biography. In sum, at this point in the second half of the seventh century, the elements of the narrative that will turn into the basic "Chan history of truth" are coming into view, since Bodhidharma is now set up as the truth-origin, and a lineage of Chinese masters is identified as a conduit through which the final truths of Buddhism flow, even if the masters' primary role is to provide final commentary on the *Laṅkāvatāra Sūtra.* Thus, the story is no longer simply about a chosen text like the *Two Entrances* that would then be endorsed for the Chinese reader; instead, we now have a living lineage of sorts, with a chosen *man*—Fachong—identified as the current holder of tradition. Or rather, we have a chosen man with the key to opening up the chosen text that was taken to be the essence of tradition—the *Laṅkāvatāra Sūtra.*

Standing back from these late additions to Daoxuan's *Continued Biographies of Eminent Monks,* we can see a basic tension between literature and "natural wisdom" in the presentation of the masters of the *Laṅkāvatāra Sūtra.* Thus, though we hear about the masters of the *Laṅkāvatāra Sūtra* living exceedingly simple lives and performing astounding feats of renunciation and asceticism, this narrative itself resulted from a careful and determined *literary effort* to slide this macho form of natural Buddhism into Daoxuan's scholarly encyclopedia. Consequently, once one gained sufficient mastery of the literary tradition, one could read about these most excellent masters who didn't rely on the literary tradition to find their way into the heart of tradition, just as one was also invited into a fantasy about a certain kind of supplement to reading that can only be found outside of literature—in the form of that newly minted family of tough-guy masters. This after all is the logic of the lineage: through some kind of physical contact, these men supposedly passed on the very Thing necessary for a full *reading* of the *Laṅkāvatāra Sūtra,* and, since this sutra is supposedly the essence of tradition, a full reading of Buddhist truth. In a few decades, authors would claim that pure truth was passed on man-to-man, with no talismanic sutra needed, but for the moment we see an awkward combination in which the sutra needs the lineage as much as the lineage needs the sutra.

This tension between a ruggedly simplistic Buddhism and the literature it lives in has within it another tension, one that revolves around trying to persuade people of the grandeur of the masters of the *Laṅkāvatāra Sūtra* when these masters, themselves, supposedly lived "off-grid," in humble obscurity. Thus, while the men in the lineage seem completely uninterested in self-promotion or public recognition, the author of this lineage is the opposite because he clearly went to some lengths developing stories designed to get the public to accept these claims about the wonders of this newly invented lineage. More exactly, it would seem that when the author read the original version of Huike's life in the *Continued Biographies,* he saw that he could open up Huike's entry and hook his stories into the core of the now-famous Huike, with the logic being: if you think Huike is wonderful—and you should think this, given what Daoxuan is saying about him in this very famous book—then you are surely going to carry that enthusiasm over to these new figures that I am now quietly tucking into the story.

One more tension needs to be pointed out: as just mentioned, the person who invented this lineage has been reading texts, and in particular those texts that had mentioned Bodhidharma and Huike. And thus, the lineage, with its supposed independence from literature and culture, is being invented by someone very much involved in the literary tradition. In short, it would seem that it was *because* our author was well aware of the public-relation strategies at play in the earlier

Bodhidharma-Huike texts that he decided to take the project to another level. Hence within the very literature dedicated to presenting impressive masters supposedly free of literature, we catch sight of another, undeclared lineage, one based on reading and writing, in which each new author set himself in that series of authors who had read the previous material that presented Bodhidharma as a final spokesman for the tradition, and then adopted those elements useful for their own public-relations purposes.

In sum, as the Bodhidharma lineage is getting pieced together, we see a packet of five items moving forward in time: (1) a growing body of historical claims about certain masters—especially Bodhidharma and Huike—which developed as they were recycled from one text to the next; (2) literary strategies of endorsement that were apparently recognized for what they were and then reassigned to new tasks; (3) certain favored texts, such as the *Two Entrances* or the *Laṅkāvatāra Sūtra*, that now are handed down relay-style, with the promise that they hold all of tradition; (4) confidence in a private and secret form of truth that is passed down through a lineage of men and used to verify the full presence of the Buddhist tradition in China; and, finally, (5) an invisible, but sought after, public that is getting accustomed to reading about these figures in the hope of extracting a final truth about Buddhism, or at least delighting in the knowledge of someone else's knowledge of the final truth of Buddhism. Getting a sense of these five items is crucial since, arguably, this packet represents the matrix for later Chan writing. Though some of the later genealogies will drop item 3—the assumption that a particular text has to be transmitted—the other four items will continue to structure the ongoing development of the lineage stories and the claims they make about owning tradition.

CONCLUSION

With this seventh-century material in view, we would do well to sum up what we have and have not seen thus far. First, we have good evidence that Chinese authors were inventing the truth-fathers that they needed. Certainly, Guanding was engaged in this work of ancestor invention, and the same seems true of the earliest Bodhidharma stories. In both cases, the particular ancestors themselves aren't that important—they can be swapped in or out as needed. What is important is the role they play in public-relations efforts, efforts that work at condensing authority in the past and then delivering it into the present. Thus, for instance, whether Zhiyi's ancestors were built out of story *x* or *y* doesn't seem to have mattered to Guanding, just as Huike was suddenly given a whole roster of descendants, even when the prior record said he had none.

Likewise, the *content* of the ancestors' truth can be shifted as required. Thus Guanding could pick up that lineage of twenty-four Indian masters and confidently claim that their transmitted wisdom essentially popped out of the lineage in the form of the *Mahāprajñāpāramitā śāstra* and then in time reappeared in Zhiyi's text, the *Great Calming and Contemplation*. Similarly, that Bodhidharma was once supposedly the purveyor of the *Two Entrances* hardly matters, since he could just as easily be made to endorse the *Laṅkāvatāra Sūtra*, if that is what the historian wished. Authorial power over the ancestors made itself even clearer in the case of Huike's arm loss—somebody thought that to make Huike look really impressive, it would be a good idea to set him up next to one-armed Tanlin so that Huike, now missing an arm too, could be shown to be the obvious winner of the pain contest. And, of course, other kinds of heroism were also being developed and applied in these proto-lineage stories: master Na and Huiman both appeared as particularly rugged Buddhist monks, and that ruggedness seems emphasized in stories that work to show how deserving they were as holders of truth and how utterly impressive they were.

In presenting figures who supposedly had mastered the (ordinary) Buddhist tradition, we see these authors recycling Daoist language and tropes that had, in other contexts, signaled similar kinds of mastery of Confucianism. The proto-Chan master, then, wasn't just Daoist-looking in some superficial or cosmetic way; rather, he was Daoist-looking in a functional manner since he stood over and against an established public tradition, endowed as he was with an esoteric wisdom that reconnected him to the Dao, the infinitely "deep," prehistoric source of culture, meaning, and tradition. Moreover, we should also remember that Daoism, from the fourth century on, often emphasized a private rite of initiation in which the master would bestow a Daoist text on his chosen disciple, while also providing an esoteric commentary on the text that was supposedly indispensable for correctly reading and interpreting it—just as we see here in the construction of the lineage for transmitting the *Laṅkāvatāra Sūtra*.[49] Thus, next to the adoption of Daoist literary flourishes to enhance the allure of Buddhist masters, it would seem that early Chan writers also mimicked well-established Daoist ritual templates for organizing and controlling the transmission of especially valued texts. The key here is that the form and content of these claims to own the totality of tradition were themselves borrowed from older literary templates, so that it was by carefully recycling material from *outside* Buddhism that authors could give readers the impression that these masters had penetrated into the heart of the Buddhist tradition. Ironically, then, Chan writing resulted, in part, from the growing ability to select and employ older literature—both Buddhist and non-Buddhist—in order to give the reader the sense that the masters really had gotten beyond the literature of traditional Buddhism.

Next to these points about the form and content of early Chan writing, we need to be very clear about what isn't in view. First, there seems to be no new form of Buddhist practice that could be associated with a community or a particular place. Instead these stories about the masters and their special texts are floating around in a kind of literary

49. For discussion of secret textual transmissions evident in Daoism by the fourth century, see Livia Kohn, "Medieval Daoist Ordination," *Acta Orientalia Academiae Scientiarum Hungaricae* 56, nos. 2–4 (2003): 379–98, esp. 381ff. One of her earliest sources is Ge Hong's *The Book of the Master Who Embraces Simplicity* (*Baopuzi*); for a translation of this work, see James R. Ware, *Alchemy, Medicine and Religion in the China of A.D. 320: The Nei Pien of Ko Hung* (1967; New York: Dover, 1981), esp. 70–75, and for mention of the secret transmission of religious texts, 91. See also Bumbacher, *Empowered Writing*, 158–61.

whirlwind. The people in most of these stories likely never existed— how could one have much faith in Bodhidharma or Huike as historical figures? Likewise, the lives of master Na and Huiman seem vague, rather extreme, unknown in any source other than the amended section of Huike's biography, and produced by a secretive author who, given other aspects of his rewriting of Huike's biography, has clearly proven his disregard for prior statements in the textual record.

Most important, though, is that these stories don't seem attached to any institutional setting. There is no evidence of a Bodhidharma school taking form; instead he appears as an useful literary figure put to work endorsing this or that new element in the Chinese Buddhist tradition. Likewise, Huike is long dead (if he ever existed) before he gets credited with passing on an esoteric understanding of the *Laṅkāvatāra Sūtra*, just as he was only depicted as the first Chinese patriarch of a budding lineage because the editor of his biography wanted to capitalize on his supposed relationship to Bodhidharma. In short, while we don't have any institutional realities associated with these various lineage claims regarding Bodhidharma and his descendants, we have something like a *brand name* emerging: Bodhidharma and his supposed "clan" are starting to appear as a reliable source for endorsing national claims about religious authority in Chinese Buddhism.

Precisely these patterns of writing and posturing will become significantly more involved when in 690 the Bodhidharma brand name was put to work endorsing a new item, and this time it would have institutional realities attached to it. For this development, we need to turn to Shaolin Monastery and its story of master Faru.

3

Portable Ancestors

Bodhidharma Gets Two New Families

In the decades after someone wrote up the lineage for Fachong and smuggled it into Daoxuan's *Continued Biographies,* several other authors used Bodhidharma and his growing family to advance a variety of agendas. Having looked, in the previous chapter, at the three earliest Bodhidharma stories, it isn't hard to see that these newer versions of the Bodhidharma family—two covered in this chapter and two in the next—belong within this same category of texts that work up endorsement strategies based on Bodhidharma's growing prestige. What stands out in this phase of writing is that instead of endorsing a pagoda in Luoyang or a text (the *Two Entrances*) or a sutra (the *Laṅkāvatāra Sūtra*), Bodhidharma and his flexible family are now harnessed to the careers of several high-profile Buddhist monks, in particular, Faru (d. 689), Shenxiu (d. 706), Puji (d. 739), Jingjue (683–ca. 750), and Shenhui (d. 758). Putting these new versions of the Bodhidharma family in the context of the three preceding Bodhidharma narratives, and the many that follow, leaves little doubt that these authors saw how the prior Bodhidharma stories functioned and then redesigned them for their own purposes. In short, as suggested at the end of the previous chapter, the Bodhidharma family became something of a brand name that could be put to work in various public-relations projects.

To build up useful perspectives for the coming discussion, it is worth taking a moment to consider modern strategies for recycling brand names. For instance, for some time now American companies have recognized that once an ad campaign successfully implants brand recognition in public memory, that brand recognition has a life of its own and can continue to exist long after the product has been discontinued. Moreover, the enduring power of the brand to elicit positive associations—even in the absence of a real product—can be treated as a kind of "equity," and thus bought and sold. As the *New York Times* explained in 2008:

> Marketers like to talk about something called brand "equity," a combination of familiarity and positive associations that clearly has some sort of value, even if it's impossible to measure in a convincing empirical way. Exploiting the equity of dead or dying brands—sometimes called ghost brands, orphan brands or zombie brands—is a topic many consumer-products firms, large and small, have wrestled with for years.... "In most cases we're dealing with a brand that only exists as intellectual property," says Paul Earle, River West's founder. "There's no retail presence, no product, no distribution, no trucks, no plants. Nothing. *All that exists is memory. We're taking consumers' memories and starting entire businesses.*"[1]

At first this is a little mind-boggling—Why would anyone want to buy a dead brand name?—but with a little more reflection it seems sensible enough: "brand equity" is just a fancy way to talk about chunks of public memory that, once stamped with a certain icon, retain that mark and its various associations for some time, regardless of the presence or absence of the product itself. And, naturally, that set of associations has a certain potential value for future marketing projects.

Although I'm not claiming that medieval Chinese authors were buying and selling (dead) brand names as entrepreneurs are in modern America, it turns out that treating the Bodhidharma lineage as an icon

---

1. Rob Walker, "Can a Dead Brand Live Again?" *New York Times Magazine*, May 18, 2008; emphasis added.

loaded with "brand equity" will work well in trying to understand how it was that the Bodhidharma lineage *as logo* was so regularly reassigned to promote new products, and, in particular, to support monks angling for leadership roles. I am aware that such a theoretical perspective will seem unlikely, or perhaps even outrageous, to my more conservative readers. I only ask that they stay with the argument long enough to see how these texts actually work before they dismiss this point of view.

FARU'S BRAND NEW ANCESTORS

In 690, the monks at Shaolin Monastery carved into stone a biography for the recently deceased Chan master Faru. But, instead of simply explaining his life and works, as a normal funerary biography would, the narrative opens up into a much longer history detailing how an esoteric form of perfect Buddhism was secretly transmitted man-to-man, beginning with the Indian Buddha and ending up with Faru, who is presented as the undisputed leader of Chinese Buddhism. In short, the Faru biography represents a significant development in Tang genealogical writing and thus, though the text is complex, it warrants careful consideration.

The Faru biography claims that perfect Buddhist truth flowed through a lineage of five masters that ran from Bodhidharma to Huike to Sengcan to Daoxin to Hongren and then, finally, to Faru. The first three members of that list are, as we saw in the previous chapter, part of the Fachong narrative in Daoxuan's *Continued Biographies,* but the two final figures—Daoxin and Hongren—aren't mentioned in that context. These two figures are, however, findable in another section of Daoxuan's *Continued Biographies* where Daoxin is given an entry that presents him as a monk who lived, for the final thirty years of his life, on Twin Peaks Mountain (*shuang feng,* later referred to as "East Mountain") in Huangmei, in the mid-seventh century.[2] Hongren appears as one of

2. For more details, see John R. McRae, *The Northern School and the Formation of Early Ch'an Buddhism* (Honolulu: University of Hawai'i Press, 1986), 31–33.

Daoxin's chief disciples since Daoxin, just before dying, asked Hongren to prepare a stupa for him.[3] What's crucial to notice is that Daoxin's biography contains no mention that he engaged in any Chan-related practice or rhetoric, or that he had any connection with Bodhidharma, Huike or the *Laṅkāvatāra Sūtra,* or that he gave Hongren any special transmission of truth. In fact, just before he died, when asked if he was going to give a special entrustment (*fuzhu*) of his teachings to someone, he replied that he had already done so many times in his life, and then passed away. Given Daoxin's evident uninvolvement with the key elements of proto-Chan, we might speculate that the Shaolin authors pulled him and Hongren into their new version of Bodhidharma's family simply because Daoxin's biography *hints* at a special master-disciple succession when Daoxin asks Hongren to build him a stupa. Of course, it also helped that Daoxin and Hongren had lived and died in the decades before 690, so that they could be plausibly identified as Faru's spiritual predecessors.

While current Chan studies accepts, *in a general way,* that Chan lineage claims are largely fabricated, it still is often believed that parts of Chan stories can be taken as reliable history. Faru's stele is a case in point since the assumption remains that his life story, despite containing some fictive elements, is still basically factual, and thus we should accept that there really was an early school of Chan developing on Twin Peaks Mountain where Daoxin trained his numerous disciples, including Hongren, and that Faru then studied there with Hongren, received his teachings, and brought them to Shaolin Monastery. In this view, one doesn't worry that these claims from Faru's biography contradict the statements in Daoxuan's *Continued Biographies* that make clear that Daoxin had no connection with anything related to Chan, just as one doesn't bother to sort through the complicated political situation at Shaolin that was developing just when the story was written, or how specific aspects of the Faru's biography reveal it to be a very improbable

3. Ibid., 32; *T* (no. 2060), 50.606b.20.

account of Faru's supposed domination of the world of Chinese Buddhism. Once we take stock of these matters, most readers will likely agree that we should abandon the theory that Chan started at Twin Peaks Mountain, with Daoxin and Hongren, and then moved to Shaolin and the capital.

BUDDHIST POLITICS, SHAOLIN-STYLE

Shaolin Monastery is located some thirty-five miles southeast of the capital city, Luoyang, and had close connections with the imperial court throughout the seventh century. In 621, when the Sui Dynasty was collapsing, it seems that Shaolin monks took up arms and fought in support of the incoming Tang forces. The monks of Shaolin even managed to retake a fortified farm complex called the Baigu Estate (*Baigu zhuang*) that had once belonged to them and that had been occupied by a Sui general during the war. In so doing, they also kidnapped the general's nephew. Later, after Tang forces won the war, the Prince of Qin who was in charge of capturing Luoyang, and was soon to become the second Tang emperor, Taizong (r. 626–49), formally returned the Baigu Estate to Shaolin Monastery and praised the monks for the military service they had rendered. We know all this because, circa 690, the Shaolin monks cut a stele reproducing the Prince of Qin's 621 account of these events, as found in the "The Prince of Qin's Instruction to the Chief of Shaolin Monastery."[4] (In 728, the Shaolin monks again cut this document into what is called the "Shaolin Stele," a stele that was well known throughout the medieval and pre-modern eras.)

4. For this letter from the Prince of Qin, see Tonami Mamoru, *The Shaolin Monastery Stele on Mount Song*, trans. and annotated by P.A. Herbert, ed. Antonino Forte (Kyoto: Italian School of East Asian Studies, 1990), 10–14. For more discussion of these events, see Meir Shahar, *The Shaolin Monastery: History, Religion, and the Chinese Martial Arts* (Honolulu: University of Hawai'i Press, 2008), chap. 2, and id., "Epigraphy, Buddhist Historiography, and Fighting Monks: The Case of Shaolin Monastery," *Asia Major*, 3rd ser., vol. 13.2 (2000), 15–36, esp. 21–27.

Although it might take modern readers a moment to get used to the idea of Chinese monks engaging in successful military action, the key question for our purposes is: Why was this letter from the Prince of Qin cut in stone around 690 just when the Faru story was created? Was that a coincidence, or was something rather complicated going on? The key here is to factor in some basic court history. In 683, the third Tang emperor, Gaozong (r. 649–83) died, and his former concubine-wife Wu Zetian became the de facto Tang ruler; then, in 690 she declared herself empress of a new dynasty, the Zhou. Though Empress Wu was known to be pro-Buddhist in her outlook, dynastic shifts were nevertheless particularly anxious times for Buddhist monasteries since Buddhist rights to land were often redefined by the new ruler. By carving in stone this account of how they had reacquired the Baigu Estate from the Prince of Qin, the Shaolin monks no doubt hoped to remind the new secular powers of the promises that had been made to them at the beginning of the Tang.

In addition to this agenda, we also need to factor in the way that Shaolin had, for some time, been presenting itself as the leading monastery in the empire. Thus, in the mid-seventh century, it had developed a close dialogue with the throne in which Emperor Gaozong and Wu Zetian looked to Shaolin for help working out their religious and political agendas. In short, just as Guanding worked to offer up Zhiyi's postmortem aura of legitimacy to the new Sui dynasty, here Shaolin monastery seems to have been a key player in various efforts to use Buddhism to promote the Tang dynasty. To this end, the imperial couple visited the monastery (or at least got close to it) and supplied funds for several building projects, including a ten-story pagoda built to commemorate the death of Wu Zetian's mother.[5]

In short, even though Shaolin monastery had been famous since its founding in the 490s, it had, throughout the course of the seventh century, increasingly involved itself with the imperial court. These

5. Shahar, *Shaolin Monastery*, 18.

complex conversations with the throne seem to have come to a head in 690 when Wu Zetian crowned herself empress and Shaolin came up with this story explaining how a Chinese buddha had just recently lived at their monastery. The timing of course was impeccable: Faru conveniently died in 689 so that in 690 the monastery was able to publicize a history that made Shaolin look like the leading monastery in the nation and *for religious reasons, not political ones.* When the Faru biography mentions that a picture of the Indian Buddha was placed on Faru's grave site, we get a clear sense for how the story was, in effect, saying: "Shaolin monastery is the one place in China that recently had a buddha for a leader, and we want you, the public and the government, to know and respect that."

With a sense for the politics of the moment, let's consider how the Faru biography works as literature. In a sparse opening, we learn how Faru first encountered Buddhism, and then, advised by a certain master Ming, went off to study meditation (*samādhi, sanwei*) under Hongren. However, *studying* Buddhism was not to be an option for Faru since at their first meeting, Hongren simply transmitted the totality of tradition to him:

> [Upon meeting Hongren,] when Faru was done bowing and asking [for teachings], the patriarch (*zushi*) didn't say anything, as there was a prior karmic connection [between them]. [Instead,] he just transmitted his Dao to him (*jishou qidao*). So with the secret meaning of the Buddha opened, Faru suddenly entered into the One Vehicle. And, of all causes and noncauses, both were finalized, and he went to the pond of pure peace, and entered into the empty dwelling of nirvana. One could say that it was a case of not moving from the final limit of truth, and yet knowing all things.[6]

In establishing this momentous encounter, the narrative, often presented in elegant four-character lines, demonstrates that the essence of

---

6. This translation was produced with important assistance from Brook Ziporyn and Chen Jinhua. Yanagida Seizan's edited text of the stele and his copious notes were also indispensable; see his *Shoki Zenshū shisho no kenkyū* (Kyoto: Hōzōkan, 1967), 487–96.

tradition was transmitted to Faru, fully and absolutely, through some unexplained action on Hongren's part. Of course, Faru appears to have done nothing in order to receive it. Instead, the narrative makes clear that the power to give tradition was in the hands of Hongren, who, without words or deeds, simply bestowed "his Dao" on Faru, and this effected all sorts of perfections in Faru. Hongren, in effect, buddhafied Faru, in the first minute of their first meeting.

This is, of course, a monumental claim. And while Guanding had made a somewhat similar claim for Zhiyi's inheritance of Buddhism's final truth/s from his master Huisi, he never staged that moment for the reader to observe. Here, though, we are asked to watch: Faru had just finished bowing, and then, pow! *this* happened. Of course we can't see tradition flying from Hongren to Faru, but we are being asked to stand witness to the historical reality of this magical moment of zapping.

To make all this seem plausible, the narrative shifts to a quick discussion of how the transmission of total truth had supposedly worked in India. Here, the author works from a brief passage from Huiyuan's preface to the *Meditation Sūtra*—a complicated text apparently written in China at the beginning of the fifth century—about a secret transmission from the Buddha to Ānanda. With this quotation as an anchor, the author of the stele develops a sparse account of a clandestine lineage that emerged after the Buddha died. Then, rather abruptly, the narrative jumps forward about a thousand years to explain how this secret transmission of tradition was continued when Bodhidharma came to China. This passage from Faru's biography isn't easy to read, but it shows the author providing Bodhidharma with a sketchy family of truth-fathers extending back to the Buddha, with these patriarchs supposedly transmitting, via mind, a nonlinguistic form of Buddhist truth that supersedes what is in the sutras:

> In India, the essence was transmitted without written words, and those who entered by this door did so only through the transmission of thought/ meaning. Therefore, Huiyuan of Mount Lu wrote in his preface to the *Meditation Sūtra*, "Ānanda, who collected the oral teachings, was instructed

[by the Buddha] that if he met someone who was not [suitable], he should conceal the [teachings] in the spiritual court [of the mind] whose secluded gate is so rarely opened that one hardly ever sees the palace." Shortly after the Buddha died, Ānanda transmitted to Madhyāntika, Madhyāntika transmitted to Śāṇavāsa. These three responded to truth, and secretly tallied [their understanding] with the past [teaching (*mingqi yuxi*)]. Their achievements were beyond words, in that which the sutras do not mention. They must have secretly modeled themselves on the original craftsman—there was not even a thread's width of difference (between them and the Buddha). And they comprehended the measures and were good at transforming inwardly and outwardly without obstruction, and yet concealed their names and trusted [their legacies] to their traces—[thereby rendering the whole project] unrecognized and unmanifest. Persons such as these cannot be categorized with names, [and yet] it is clear that there was this other ancestral source (*zong*) [of truth].

Also, there was the southern Indian, the Tripiṭaka dharma master, Bodhidharma, who inherited this essence (*zong*), and marched with it to this eastern country [of China]. A biography (*zhuan*) says, "Magically transforming in hidden and mysterious ways (*shenhua youze*), he entered into Wei (China) and transmitted [this essence] to [Hui]ke, [Hui]ke [passed it on] to [Seng]can, [Seng]can transmitted it to [Dao]xin, [Dao]xin transmitted it to [Hong]ren, [Hong]ren transmitted it to [Fa]ru. Given that transmission cannot use words, if not for [finding] the right person, how could it be transmitted?[7]

Though Bodhidharma has now been vaguely connected to the Buddha, despite a thousand-year gap between them, the events of his life are still quite unclear: we learn only that he came from southern India, and bore the title "Tripiṭaka dharma master" which means "master of the three types of canonical Buddhist literature"—two details given in Daoxuan's *Continued Biographies* and also mentioned in the preface to the *Two Entrances*. We also shouldn't miss that, in line with the preface to the *Two Entrances,* this quick sketch of Bodhidharma gives him a Daoist glow since he was "Magically transforming in hidden and mysterious ways"— a phrase certain to evoke Daoist associations for any competent reader.

7. *Shoki zenshū*, ed. Yanagida, 487–88.

Now what should we make of this lineage that runs from Bodhidharma to Huike to Sengcan to Daoxin to Hongren to Faru? This set of patriarchs is vouched for in the narrative by citing a nameless "biography," a decidedly vague claim just when readers would have wanted some evidence for this monumental claim about Bodhidharma and his role in Faru's heritage. Now, one might think that by "biography" the author intended to refer to Bodhidharma's biography in Daoxuan's *Continued Biographies,* but, as we know, this lineage isn't found there. In short, it isn't clear where this lineage of five masters—Bodhidharma, Huike, Sengcan, Daoxin, Hongren—came from. And, given that the author gave us a clear reference to Huiyuan's preface to the *Meditation Sūtra* when he wanted to shore up his claims about transmission in India, it seems doubly odd that he left his source for the lineage unnamed. Despite the lack of clarity here, these five masters would become the basis for virtually all future lineage stories within Chan and Zen, down to the present.

Having sketched this lineage that works to connect China back to India, the author returns to the details of Faru's life. Here, we learn of Hongren's death and Faru's subsequent departure from Hongren's monastery. In this part of the narrative, Faru's whereabouts are kept particularly vague; in fact, it is claimed that his arrival at Shaolin was cloaked in secrecy. Faru's clandestine life radically changes though in 686 when he supposedly hosted a massive dharma meeting for all the monks of the nation, a meeting in which he publicly performs as a buddha:

> In the year 686, monks of the four directions congregated at Shaolin Monastery and requested Faru to reveal the Chan dharma. Everyone said, "From the latter Wei up until the Tang there have been five imperial dynasties (*didai*),[8] covering nearly two hundred years; [during these years] someone has always come forth to define the virtue of the age. All of them

---

8. For clarification of this term *didai,* see James Robson's "Formation and Fabrication in the History and Historiography of Chan Buddhism," *Harvard Journal of Asiatic Studies* 71, no. 2 (Dec. 2011): 333–34. While appearing to be evenhanded, Robson's essay gives a rather distorted account of my book *Fathering Your Father: The Zen of Fabrication in Tang Buddhism* (Berkeley: University of California Press, 2009).

bestowed upon us, the descendants, the legacy of the peerless jewel. If today you would again shake the mysterious net for your fortunate listeners, then your radiance would correctly transform us." ... He politely refused three times. But after some time had passed, he agreed saying: "When we contemplate the intent of the Perfect Man [the Buddha], it is broad and vast, deep and far-reaching. Today, [I will teach] with just the Single Dharma which is capable of causing sages and commoners alike to enter into irreversible *samādhi*. Those brave and intrepid listeners should carefully receive this teaching. When making fire, one must not leave off the task in the middle."

The whole assembly bowed and paid their respects, and then obtained the original mind. The master imprinted their minds secretly with the Dharma of One Seal, and thereby the mundane world was no longer manifest, and instead it was the dharma realm.[9]

With this grand teaching moment accomplished for the benefit of the monks-of-the-nation, the narrative turns to narrate Faru's demise in equally majestic terms:

After that, he [Faru] repeatedly instructed his disciples to quickly ask about that which they doubted. Suddenly he manifested signs of illness, and the quick-witted ones knew what the signs meant. On his last night he sat upright under a tree and pronounced his final words, again clarifying the ultimate principles of the lineage (*zongji*). He made seven days seem to be an eon and awakened them to the way [a buddha], with a finger-snap, shakes the world. The dharma neither comes nor goes. Thoughts of quickness or slowness were eliminated. Then, at noon on the twenty-seventh day of the seventh month in the year of 689, he died in perfect quietude. He was fifty-two years old. He was buried on the plains of Shaoshi [the name of the wider area where Shaolin Monastery is located]. And, on the north side, toward the high peak, his close disciples erected a stupa and placed there a stone with an image of the Udayana portrait of the Buddha on it. Then they collected his biography and engraved it on [this] buddha-stele (*fobei*). They set up this [stele] in the temple courtyard, in order for us to discipline ourselves saying: "Our master had keen perception and his motion and stillness were unfathomable. He molded flat the ten thousand

9. *Shoki Zenshū*, ed. Yanagida, 488–89.

types of bondage and served as a bridge for the vast world. He ascended into the subtleties and thereby provided a staircase so that whoever applied themselves [accordingly] would certainly accomplish [the task of obtaining enlightenment]. The merit of his legacy is limitless, equal in radiance to the sun and moon."[10]

In this closing sequence, the splendor of Faru's buddha-perfection is made clear, and though there is no mention of him reproducing an heir, we are promised that those who would diligently follow his model could expect similarly grand results. Of course, inciting monks to practice in accord with Faru's path seems odd since the narrative has said nothing of Faru's practice. Likewise, Faru's own enlightenment came not from practice, but as a gift from Hongren in that sudden moment of transmission that appears to be the opposite of the staircase to truth that the stele claims Faru offered to his students.

To get further into the logic of the Faru biography, four perspectives need to be highlighted. First, we need to see that the dynamics of endorsement are again at work here since this new version of the Bodhidharma family now serves to link up perfect Indian Buddhism with Shaolin Monastery and its recent in-house buddha, Faru. Second, though Faru's enlightenment is evoked with many references to Buddhist texts, his identity is also being seasoned with plenty of Daoist allusions and references. Thus, just like the two styles of being Buddhist in the *Two Entrances*, Faru's character seems to be a meeting ground of Buddhist and Daoist qualities. For instance, in a passage that I did not include above, we learn that Faru "held on to his [spiritual] roots (*shouben*), and was completely simple (*quanpu*)." With this kind of simplicity characterizing his persona, we are then told how, "Externally, he hid his fame and talent, and internally he harmonized the mysterious forces (*xuangong*)—this is, basically, the way of keeping close to it, and such is the manner of lofty simplicity." This packet of phrases makes Faru appear not too different from the stock image of the Daoist sage

10. Ibid., 489.

who hides his virtue, manifests absolute simplicity in his demeanor, and maintains some kind of mystical union with powerful cosmic forces.

The third point is that the biography makes Faru visible and invisible as needed—a key strategy in later Chan stories. For instance, though the text claims that Faru arrived at Shaolin in secrecy, it also seems that shortly thereafter he was immediately recognized as the leader of Chinese Buddhism. Thus as soon as the monks of the nation come to Shaolin to receive his teaching, they immediately announce that they know he is one of a series of marvelous masters who have appeared over the past two hundred years. At this point, a significant contradiction appears since, earlier, the author had claimed that this perfect form of Buddhist leadership was supposedly passed along in secrecy, even though here, at this climatic moment in the text, we are told that this series of masters to which Faru supposedly belonged had *already* been widely appreciated by the public for two hundred years. Presumably this claim about the lineage's long-standing renown was put here to deflect the potential suspicion that it was newly fabricated. What this contraction implies about levels of intentionality in Chan writing won't become clear until we see later Chan texts that work up similar rhetorical strategies to hide their attempts to rewrite the past.

At any rate, this contradiction is never resolved in the Faru stele, but anxiety regarding these historical claims is presumably alleviated when the narrative depicts Faru publicly teaching just as a buddha would. With this lavish event in view, the biography has "visibly" ratified the secret history of Faru's truth-fathers that stretches back to the Buddha. Hence, within the story, when Faru's magical spiritual powers turn *outward* to transform the teaching site from the mundane world into the dharma sphere, the reader is simply seeing the effect of that magical gift *inward* when Faru received total tradition from Hongren and, more distantly, the Buddha.

The fourth issue has to do with the role of literature in the story: Faru, as a perfect Chinese buddha, is presented as one naturally above everyone else, and definitely above the imported sutras, and yet a close look at the

narrative's phrasing makes clear that the events in his life—his enlightenment and his teaching, in particular—are made up of snippets of recycled
literature, much of it from the sutras. In a sense, then, this is another
example of deploying brand equity, but now, instead of relying solely on
Bodhidharma's growing symbolic heft, our author has turned Faru's life
history into a xylophone of sorts such that each mini-passage, as it echoes
Buddhist and non-Buddhist classics, rings with the tones of previously
established value and authority. The full complexity of the situation only
comes into view when we remember that this clever recycling of choice
bits of China's favorite literature is done in a narrative that claims that real
tradition doesn't take form in words or texts, but is relayed mind to mind.
Getting a bead on this paradox is essential for all things Chan.

Mention of master Sengcan, as Huike's disciple, raises other issues
regarding the recycling of literature. As far as we know the only place
that Sengcan appears in the pre-Faru literary record is at the top of the
list of Huike's supposed students in Fachong's biography in Daoxuan's
Continued Biographies. If this is where the author of the Faru biography
got the Huike-Sengcan connection, then we have to imagine that he
read that story in Daoxuan's encyclopedia and cherry-picked the lineage elements that were useful for his own program, discarding the rest
of the story that had to do with Fachong and the other devotees of the
Laṅkāvatāra Sūtra. Thus, as the author of Faru's biography put his chosen ancestors into the frame of Fachong's lineage, he did to the Fachong
story what the Fachong story had done to Huike's story in Daoxuan's
Continued Biographies. In both cases the new author inserted his own preferred ancestors into a high-profile lineage that had already been established in the literary record and, presumably, in public memory as well.
Reading Faru's biography in this manner might seem overly suspicious,
but the next text making use of the Bodhidharma family undeniably
performs precisely this gesture so it is worth wondering if it isn't already
present here. And, not to be forgotten, this is exactly what Guanding
had done several decades earlier when he tapped into the well-known

lineage of the twenty-four Indian masters found in the *History of the Transmission of the Dharma-Treasury* in order to find impressive truth-fathers for Zhiyi.

More could be said about how the Faru biography works as a piece of literature, but for now let's leave the discussion sure of two things. First, it seems clear that Faru, as he is presented in the stele, is who he is—a Chinese buddha—only because of his lineage; nothing else about him matters. It was never said that he was well trained, a master of the sutras, good at taming tigers and demons, and so on. Instead, his identity as master-of-tradition derives from a new cultural logic: he is a buddha-figure because of his supposed "family connections" and the genealogical narrative that provides proof of those connections. With this cultural logic taking hold in late-seventh-century China, the ultimate form of the Buddhist tradition can now be found in one man—Faru—who holds it precisely *because a certain style of storytelling was steadily gaining legitimacy for itself.* Thus we have to say that these new tools for establishing legitimacy were themselves beginning to appear more legitimate.

Second, Faru's biography is brimming with pageantry. For instance, when Hongren zapped Faru, the narrative explained, with a big to-do, how great that transfer of wisdom was in terms of the new status that it produced in Faru, and yet there is no mention of the actual content of what Faru learned. A similar mismatch of grandiosity and content is found when Faru preaches his Chan dharma to the assembly in 686: we get lots of descriptions about how wondrous its *effects* were, even though the text never gives us a hint of what Faru actually said in that teaching. Considering this problem a little more closely we ought to conclude that the Chan of the late seventh century was definitely not a new style of practice or a new philosophy or a new way to organize a Buddhist monastery. Instead, it was defined by two things: (1) a growing enthusiasm for identifying certain individuals as buddhas; and, (2) a growing body of literary strategies for making those claims acceptable to the public.

DU FEI'S *RECORD OF THE TRANSMISSION OF THE DHARMA-JEWEL:* FARU GETS A BROTHER

Some twenty years after Shaolin Monastery invented Faru's biography, Bodhidharma's family history was again shifted when Du Fei (n.d.) produced his *Record of the Transmission of the Dharma-Jewel (Chuan fabao ji).*[11] This new narrative picked up Faru's genealogy but reformulated it to support the claim that a very famous monk named Shenxiu was the most recent figure in the Bodhidharma lineage. To make this claim seem believable, several key "facts" had to be changed in Shaolin's version of Faru's "family history."[12] The first was simply to say that Hongren had had another student equal to Faru—Shenxiu, of course—and that he too had received the zap of total tradition. The second alteration was to invent a death-scene for Faru during which he supposedly told his students, "From now on, you must go study under Chan master Shenxiu at Yuquan Monastery in Jingzhou,"[13] a gesture that basically turns Faru into a signpost for Shenxiu. Figuring out why Du Fei did this will take a little sleuthing, but the basic contours of his agenda aren't too hard to pick out.

Although we don't know anything about Faru, other than what the Shaolin author wanted us to know, Shenxiu seems to have been a nationally famous monk—vouched for in several sources—who was invited to court by Empress Wu in 701. She apparently plied him with gifts and accolades, and in particular gave him that awesome title "Teacher of the Nation." When he died in 706, he seems to have received a huge, imperially sponsored funeral. With this historical background in view, it appears that Du Fei's text tries to do two things for Shenxiu's legacy. First, after Empress Wu identified Shenxiu as something like the king of

11. McRae's translation of this text is in *Northern School,* 255–69; for Yanagida's edited version of the text, based on Pelliot #3559, see his *Shoki Zenshū,* 559–93.

12. In the early 1990s, T. Griffith Foulk showed me the problematic nature of Du Fei's claims; for his perspective on the matter, see his, "The Chan *Tsung* in Medieval China: School, Lineage, or What?" *Pacific World,* n.s., no. 8 (1992): 18–31, esp., 21–22.

13. McRae, *Northern School,* 265, with changes; *Shoki Zenshū,* ed. Yanagida, 568.

Chinese Buddhism, Du Fei sought to provide him with a family of truth-fathers such that it would seem as though this state recognition resulted from a religious reality that predated it. In effect, Du Fei was trying to give the impression that Shenxiu's status as the leader of Buddhism was due to his truth-father Hongren and the Bodhidharma lineage, and not Empress Wu.

Establishing a religious origin for Shenxiu's success set the stage for the second basic agenda in the text: Du Fei claimed that Shenxiu had a living heir to whom he had secretly transmitted that essence-of-tradition just before he died. In short, Du Fei took Shenxiu's identity and first hooked it to the pipeline of Faru's ancestors in order to justify Shenxiu's nationally recognized prestige as the natural result of his "family" ties. Then, looking forward, with Shenxiu as the final section of that conduit, the end of pipe was threaded with the claim about a secret transmission in order that it could then receive the next link of pipe. In the decades that followed Du Fei's writing, two leading monks—Yifu (661–736) and Puji (651–739)—were recognized as Shenxiu's heirs and both granted the imperial title "Teacher of the Nation." We have no way of knowing if these two monks were, in fact, the secret heir/s whom Du Fei had written of, but we can nonetheless see that Du Fei's efforts bore fruit in the sense that once he had installed Shenxiu in the Bodhidharma family, a later generation of claimants managed to uphold the Bodhidharma-to-Shenxiu lineage and to establish themselves in the family as well—Du Fei's creative plumbing held up, as it were.

Du Fei's text is also remarkable for the way that it theorizes the secret moment of truth-transmission between master and disciple. Making this moment appear sensible to his readers is crucial to his history of the "dharma-jewel," and thus he goes out of his way to show how this "practice" of transmission supposedly began with the Buddha and was continued on into Tang China. Though he cites various Buddhist texts to support his position, we get a broad hint about Du Fei's thinking on the topic when he compares this kind of dharma-transmission to the way Daoist adepts secretly receive personal instructions from divine figures in their practice of alchemy. He writes: "For example, even in the refinement of cinnabar [as a means of achieving immortality], one must obtain the personal instruction of an immortal in order to create [real] cinnabar. Although one may be able to ascend heaven in broad daylight [by this method], if one relies [only] on the blue words of the jade-[encrusted] books, [one's efforts] will ultimately come to naught."[14] Daoist encounters of this type are indeed found in various pre-Chan sources and thus, ironically, Du Fei is counting on the reader's familiarity with these Daoist stories (and their related practices) to legitimize his construction of this new Buddhist reality: the transmission of total truth from one master to another.

Like Faru's biography, Du Fei's *Record* is carefully written. For our purposes it will be enough to point out several innovations. For instance, Du Fei took the list of Faru's supposed Chinese predecessors and gave each a biography. Thus, though graced with an introduction and conclusion, Du Fei's text is basically organized like a freight train, with each master's biography set up as a car filled with various materials and linked to the cars before and after it. In broader terms, by organizing a text that treated each master in the Bodhidharma family at length, Du Fei deserves credit for solidifying a whole new genre of literature—the free-standing genealogy of the masters.[15] In time this kind of text would become known as a "flame history" (*denglu* or *dengshi*)—because each master is like a lamp that receives the flame from his predecessor and hands it off to his descendant (see chapter 8 for discussion of this genre and the choice to translate *dengshi* as "flame history" and not "lamp history").

Du Fei's treatment of Bodhidharma and Huike is particularly interesting. Before filling out content for Bodhidharma's "boxcar," Du Fei

14. McRae, *Northern School*, 257; *Shoki Zenshū*, ed. Yanagida, 562.

15. The *History of the Transmission of the Dharma-Treasury* is an earlier example of a freestanding genealogy. However, though that text was put together in China, in Chinese, it is only Indian masters who were included; moreover, the content of those entries was largely drawn from older Indian texts that had been previously translated into Chinese, and the text thus appears rather stilted and un-Chinese.

gives us some general points about Bodhidharma's life in the introductory part of his text. Du Fei explains:

> Among those who traveled from India and came to this land, there was Bodhidharma. Because there was at that time in China a supremely benevolent one [Huike], he transmitted [perfect tradition] to him, silently indicating the truth realm. This [transmission] was like a weak and moribund person suddenly returning to health. Or again, it was like a great torch being illuminated in a dark room. There are no words that could describe it. But, just as there were some with uniquely lofty dispositions, there were others who just played with what they had studied, and didn't seek supreme wisdom [from Bodhidharma]. Those who were completely changed in receiving [the teachings] were extremely few. It was only Huike of the Eastern Wei, who sought it with his life; the great master transmitted it to him and then left.[16]

As Du Fei's metaphors of sickness and darkness make clear, his account of Bodhidharma's transmission of truth to Huike is energized with a range of insults for other forms of the Chinese Buddhist tradition. Of course, we can't help but notice that this part of Du Fei's "history" of Bodhidharma closely matches the preface to the *Two Entrances,* where Bodhidharma's arrival is cast in exactly the same way: Bodhidharma decided to bring real Buddhism to China, having somehow come to know, in India, that Chinese Buddhism was in decline. Du Fei's familiarity with earlier accounts of Bodhidharma becomes clearer when he struggles to refute what those prior texts had said about Bodhidharma and his teachings. For instance, Du Fei writes:

> Nowadays there are some words called the "Bodhidharma Treatise" (*Damo lun*). But this [text] is merely the work of some students who, back in the day and based on their own initiative, took these words to be a true discourse and, writing them down, treasured them. Nonetheless, the text is full of errors. Transcendent enlightenment (*chaowu*), which is received in the succession [of the lineage], is obtained in mind, thus how could there

16. McRae, *Northern School,* 256, with changes; Yanagida, *Shoki Zenshū,* 561.

be any sound, not to mention language or written words, that would be exchanged between them [the masters].[17]

Here, in dismissing the "Bodhidharma Treatise"—a vague title that probably refers to the *Two Entrances*—it seems as if Du Fei is simply trying to keep any specific doctrinal content away from Bodhidharma and the lineage since he no doubt reckoned that the transcendent truth that is supposedly being transmitted can only be diminished by associating it with a specific text or teachings. Moreover, as Du Fei latched on to the cachet of the Bodhidharma brand name, it appears that he felt it necessary to undermine prior efforts to link Bodhidharma to other agendas. No wonder then that he delivers such a harsh assessment of the "Bodhidharma Treatise" which appears now as an illegitimate, error-ridden work, cobbled together by benighted students.

A similar hostility vis-à-vis previous uses of the Bodhidharma brand name come to the fore when Du Fei presents his version of Bodhidharma's relationship with Huike:

> Bodhidharma was the third son in a Brahman family in southern India. He was gifted spiritually and completely enlightened (*jishen chaowu*), and he transmitted the great dharma-jewel with enlightenment and sagely wisdom; and, [in India,] for the sake of gods and men, he widely spread Buddha knowledge and insight. [Then], for the sake of those of us in the country of China, he navigated the oceans, and came to Mount Song. At the time, he was hardly recognized. It was only Daoyu and Huike, with the potential to understand derived from previous lives, who vigorously sought it, serving the master for six years, intent on obtaining thorough enlightenment.
>
> At that time, Bodhidharma said to Huike, "Would you be able to give your life for the dharma?" Huike cut off his arm to prove his sincerity (*chengken*). Another biography says that it was cut off by bandits, but that was an erroneous account circulated for a brief time. From then on [transmission] was secretly effected with skillful means (*fangbian*). This technique for effecting [transmission] is something that only masters and their disciples secretly employ and thus there is no way to represent it in language. Then Bodhi-

17. McRae, *Northern School*, 257, with changes; *Shoki Zenshū*, ed. Yanagida, 562.

dharma suddenly caused Huike's mind to directly enter into the dharma realm.[18]

This story of Huike cutting off his arm in order to receive the final truth of Buddhism from Bodhidharma became a favorite in the Chan tradition. It even made its way into Chan art, despite the obvious challenges involved in representing auto-amputation. Given that, in the previous chapter, we saw how Huike's arm had first been cut off— apparently by the inventive historian of Fachong's lineage—we are well placed to see what is going on here. Du Fei no doubt read the story of how Huike, like Tanlin, lost his arm to bandits and thought of a better narrative use for this amputated arm. Thus, instead of using it simply as an exciting element in the scenario designed to show off Huike's stoic qualities, Du Fei thought up a new piece of drama that suited his purposes: Huike's arm would be cut off by Huike! in order to prove his sincerity to Bodhidharma. Thus, Huike's sacrifice of his arm would, in effect, be the means by which real Buddhism entered China.[19]

With this simple refiguration of the past, future students of Chan would have to practice under the grisly challenge of Huike's arm-offering. Who could possibly come up with comparable bravery and endurance? Of course, the feat was actually accomplished with the flick of a pen as Du Fei rewrote Huike's story, as it had been given by the Fachong author, who, himself, had set a fine precedent by being equally creative in removing Huike's arm in the first place. Despite the dubious origins of this story, once it took root in the literary tradition it became a staple in Chan lore—a fact that is all the more ironic since the story

18. McRae, *Northern School*, 258–9, with slight changes; *Shoki Zenshū*, ed. Yanagida, 563–64.

19. In "The Hagiography of Bodhidharma: Reconstructing the Point of Origin of Chinese Chan Buddhism," in *India in the Chinese Imagination: Myth, Religion, and Thought*, eds. John Kieschnick and Meir Shahar, 125–38 (University of Pennsylvania Press, 2014), 128–29, McRae claims, incorrectly, that Huike's arm loss wasn't turned into a self-amputation until the Shenhui texts that appeared ca. 750. However, Du Fei is clearly the author who is to be credited with this invention. Jingjue, also writing before Shenhui, repeats Du Fei's version of this event; see chapter 4 below.

is dedicated to showing the boundless sincerity of China's first Chan master.

At this dramatic moment when Huike sacrifices his arm for truth, Du Fei doesn't claim that Huike actually awakened to some particular truth. Instead, as with the story of Hongren zapping Faru, we learn only that Bodhidharma, in response to Huike's auto-amputation, "suddenly caused Huike's mind to directly enter into the dharma realm." The gift structure of this moment has a number of interesting implications. First, according to Du Fei's logic, the dharma came to China through the unique conjunction of Bodhidharma's wisdom and Huike's willingness to sacrifice himself. As these two elements meet, truth now is installed in China, with Huike's bodily offering, and his total submission, anchoring that reception. By labeling Huike's sincerity with the Confucian-tinged adjective *chengken* and asserting that he faithfully served Bodhidharma for six years, Du Fei portrays Huike as something like the only good filial son in China. Huike was the only one who knew how to treat the father in a properly Confucian manner, and consequently got the father's patrimony—the dharma-jewel. Du Fei has said nothing about Huike's Buddhist qualities that brought this about; rather, for Du Fei, it was Huike's Confucian qualities of sincerity, submission, and ardor that introduced a perfect version of Indian Buddhism into a Chinese body. The manner in which Chinese Buddhist authors relied on Confucian structures to explain the presence of the fullest form of the Buddhist tradition will be an ongoing concern in the chapters to come, but for now it is enough to see that this development occurred just when the Chan masters were being shaped into Daoist-looking sages. Thus, Chan authors appear rather wily in the way they combined images of value selected from various pools of traditional Chinese literature.

With this part of the transmission between India and China in place, Du Fei turns to the problematic role of the *Laṅkāvatāra Sūtra* in the earlier accounts of Bodhidharma family. The problem, as discussed in chapter 2, was that in the rewritten section of Huike's biography there are several lines explaining that Bodhidharma transmitted the

Laṅkāvatāra Sūtra to Huike as the Thing that made a perfect understanding of Buddhist truth possible. Thus, if Du Fei was intent on lodging the final version of tradition in Chinese masters—and not in texts—then he had before him the task of first refuting the claim that perfect tradition lived in the *Laṅkāvatāra Sūtra.* To this end, he writes:

> Bodhidharma, four of five years later [after the transmission to Huike], looked for textual confirmation [of the transmission of true Buddhism to China] and took up the *Laṅkāvatāra Sūtra* and gave it to Huike saying, "I see that in the land of China, this text alone is suitable for converting students." For students who did not yet understand [truth], he personally transmitted it many times saying, "Take this as the future cause [of enlightenment]." In another biography there is mention of wall-contemplation and the four practices, but they were just provisional [techniques] for conversion used for a time. There may be traces of this teaching in circulation and someone may have collected them, but they are not his[*Bodhidharma's*] final position.[20]

In this passage, Du Fei is again carefully working against previous accounts of Bodhidharma, acknowledging them, but also working to undermine them. Hence the first part of this passage downplays the importance of transmitting the *Laṅkāvatāra Sūtra,* since it was supposedly a secondary teaching for those who did not yet understand truth; this naturally undercuts the sutra's singular importance in Huike's and Fachong's biographies, as found in Daoxuan's *Continued Biographies.* In addition to claiming that Bodhidharma only transmitted the *Laṅkāvatāra Sūtra* to Huike as a *supplement,* useful for instructing future students, Du Fei identifies "another biography" as equally unreliable. When he notes that this other biography mentions "wall-contemplation" and the "four practices" it would seem that he is denigrating Daoxuan's account of Bodhidharma, which includes just these details.[21]

20. McRae, *Northern School,* 259, with slight changes; *Shoki Zenshū,* ed. Yanagida, 564.
21. For Daoxuan's account, see *T* (no. 2060), 50.551c.5ff.

With a sense of Du Fei's craft and subtlety in dealing with the prior uses of the Bodhidharma brand name, let's turn to the larger problem of how he inserted Shenxiu into the Bodhidharma lineage, which was, of course, his main agenda. The first thing to notice is that Shenxiu's biography is the longest in the *Record*, with Du Fei providing abundant details regarding his pre-Buddhist life, his training, his travels, and, above all, his relations with the imperial court. In all this, Du Fei appears eager to present Shenxiu as a highly cultivated savant. After a description of his precocious childhood, we find an account of his wide reading in the non-Buddhist classics, followed by a list of all the masters he studied with and all the doctrines he mastered. In sum, we get the clear sense that Shenxiu was simply the best schooled teacher in China. Despite this flattering account of his education and training, Du Fei has trouble explaining the transmission of truth from Hongren to Shenxiu, which, of course, is the key to his story.

Du Fei claims vaguely that Shenxiu studied with Hongren, "who recognized his worth at a glance" and then, "after guiding him for some years, led him into the truth realm."[22] Clearly, there is no specific transmission moment mentioned here, and their relationship is obviously not consummated with the standard death-day transmission that Du Fei rehearses for the other masters in his genealogy. In fact, Du Fei had already said in Hongren's biography that Hongren transmitted the dharma to Faru just before he died. So Shenxiu's relationship with Hongren appears set off to the side of the straightforward advancement

22. McRae, *Northern School*, 265; *Shoki Zenshū*, ed. Yanagida, 568. Bodhidharma recognizes Huike in a similar manner in Daoxuan's entry for Bodhidharma (see chap. 2, and Broughton, *Bodhidharma Anthology*, 58). Likewise, a glance from the master is taken to be a sign of approval in the *Liezi*; see *The Book of Lieh-tzŭ*, trans. A.C. Graham (New York: Columbia University Press, 1960), 81. This Daoist work, well known in the Tang, presents developed, and often funny, conservations between masters and their disciples and/or government officials. Not to be overlooked is that many of these conversations demonstrate how a Daoist view overcomes older traditions, just as Chan texts show the masters overcoming older versions of Buddhism or even older versions of Chan. Graham also thought the *Liezi* was an important influence on early Chan writers; for his brief comment, see ibid., xiii.

of the dharma from Hongren to Faru. Or, more exactly, Shenxiu has this glancing contact, literally, with master Hongren, who nonetheless goes on to give transmission to Faru, who, when he dies, directs his students to go to Shenxiu. Standing back from the details, it seems evident that Du Fei has stolen the lineage that Shaolin created for Faru, even as he turned Faru into Shenxiu's guarantor, while also excluding the possibility that Faru might have had his own descendants, all in order that Shenxiu could appear to be in possession of perfect Buddhist truth, while also uniquely holding the rights to future dharma-transmission.

With this replumbing of the Faru lineage explained and defended, Du Fei goes on to narrate Shenxiu's successes, the first of which is that Shenxiu is nationally popular, with "students not thinking ten thousand miles too far to come to take refuge at his dharma platform (*fatan*)."[23] In so saying, Du Fei attempts to persuade the reader that Shenxiu was the center of the Buddhist world, the place where even those on the distant periphery came calling in order to cross over Shenxiu's "dharma platform" and become fully Buddhist. Granting Shenxiu this implicit ownership of the gateway into authentic Buddhism is of special interest since it echoes Faru's grand teaching moment described in the stele at Shaolin, while also prefiguring the *Platform Sūtra*, which also constructs just this kind of privately owned platform that is set before the public as the place for gaining, or rather, regaining, their Buddhist legitimacy.

Ironically, in the midst of this carefully constructed narrative that works hard to show the lineage members' mastery of culture and society, Du Fei also plays up their simplicity and naturalness. Thus, throughout the seven biographies that constitute the middle section of the *Record*, he underscores the masters' simplicity with regard to desire, teachings, practices, and culture. For our purposes it is the last one—simplicity of culture—that is the most indicative of this new strategy for writing up profiles of the masters. Du Fei's construction of Hongren's simplicity is

23. McRae, *Northern School*, 265–66; *Shoki Zenshū*, ed. Yanagida, 568.

particularly interesting for the way it celebrates truth-beyond-the-literary-tradition, while also inverting the social hierarchy. Thus, Du Fei's biography of Hongren explains that he did not read sutras but rather associated with the servants. Moreover, he supposedly did manual labor all day and meditated all night. Despite Hongren's supposed commitment to a hierarchy-free form of Buddhism, we next learn that he ended up at the peak of high society and Buddhist culture.[24] Thus, Du Fei notes that, "Because of his reputation, after he received the transmission, the number of nobleman who gathered around him doubled every day.... After a little more than ten years, eight or nine of every ten ordained and lay aspirants in the country had studied with him."[25]

According to Du Fei, then, Hongren's upside-down approach to Buddhism and society produced amazingly broad effects precisely in the two realms that he supposedly renounced—traditional Buddhism and society. In fact, Du Fei is claiming that Hongren became China's de facto "Teacher of the Nation" because 80 or 90 percent of the clergy and laity supposedly studied with him. In this telling, Hongren had total truth and thus had no use for secondary markers of status and learning, and this of course fits nicely with Du Fei's account of his echo style of teaching, which was notably spontaneous and free of "general pronouncements."[26] Thus not only is Hongren depicted as one beyond class considerations, in and outside the monastic institution, he is also in fact implicitly free of Buddhism. He doesn't need Buddhist texts, Buddhist rituals, Buddhist institutions, or Buddhist hierarchies. He has

24. Images of the supposedly uncultured master can be found in slightly older sources. For instance, Daoying's biography in the *Mingbao ji* (composed by Tanglin in the mid-seventh century), presents him as a monk who ate and drank whatever he wanted, wore layman's clothes, tended cattle, and kept his hair long. Most important, "He did not concern himself with acting dignified, but when it came to obscure meanings in the sutras and the monastic regulations, there were none that he could not explain upon first hearing them." For this biography, see Donald Gjerston's *Miraculous Retribution: A Study and Translation of T'anglin's Ming pao chi* (Berkeley, CA: Center for South and Southeast Asia Studies, 1989), 164–65; *T* (no. 2082), 51.789b.15.

25. McRae, *Northern School*, 263; *Shoki Zenshū*, ed. Yanagida, 567.

26. Ibid.

got it all, wherever he is, and meditation is the only Buddhist activity that he ever engaged in. With this illustriously low profile so clearly shaping Du Fei's version of Hongren, it is hard not to read Hongren's biography as an indictment of famous, well-educated, and certainly well-connected monks—all except for Shenxiu, of course. Thus, Hongren's simplicity generates a very potent kind of innocence, particularly useful for producing an enhanced portrait of Shenxiu, since the supposed simplicity of this truth-father works to remove Hongren and his "son" (Shenxiu) from the unsavory realm of religious and/or political competition—a very helpful pedigree given the competitive agenda that appears to be motivating Du Fei.

On another level, Hongren's supposed disregard for reading puts the reader in a double bind since he is reading about the Buddhist perfection of one who doesn't read, and certainly doesn't read about past masters. Thus, in longing for Hongren and his simplicity, the reader in fact disparages his own literary abilities and his respect for Buddhist institutions. In short, Du Fei has arranged for a reader-seduction that involves a measure of self-condemnation, a trope that will become nearly ubiquitous in later Chan writing. We should see too that Du Fei has set Hongren up as an impossibly perfect figure who cannot be contained or bested by any figure—high or low in the hierarchy—and especially cannot be domesticated by the desirous reader because he is literally that reader's opposite, especially because Hongren neither reads nor peers into the life of the other, hoping thereby to gain something.

BRIEF CONCLUSIONS

In these two early genealogical texts—Faru's biography from Shaoli Monastery and Du Fei's *Record*—we see solid evidence for thinking that the increasing clout (and glamour) of the fictive Bodhidharma family was, in fact, the result of a series of authors reworking prior literary statements in sly and careful ways. In particular, the narrator of Faru's biography, while clearly combining and editing earlier accounts of the various masters, figured out how to stage his new claims so that they would appear to have been *already* known and endorsed throughout the empire. Likewise, Du Fei masterfully undermined the earlier Bodhidharma narratives regarding: (1) the centrality of transmitting the *Laṅkāvatāra Sūtra*; (2) the teaching of "wall-contemplation" and the Two Entrances; and (3) the claim that Huike lost his arm to bandits. Du Fei also gave reasons why these mistaken statements had been created and then circulated, and in this sense he built a split-screen account of the past in which his readers are to understand that *some* Chan authors understood events and teachings properly, while *some others* didn't—a narrative strategy that was replayed prominently in later texts such as the *Platform Sūtra*. The increasing sophistication in the presentation of the Bodhidharma family in these two texts is accompanied by a penchant for making some of the masters—such as Faru or Hongren—appear preternaturally simple and decidedly Daoist in their tastes, practices, and teaching styles. Thus, these masters appear completely above and beyond traditional Buddhism, even as they go on to reproduce the Buddhist tradition with marvelous and unerring perfection, once they have received dharma-transmission. Arguably, then, even these tropes of simplicity appear as evidence of a growing literary sophistication, a perspective that most modern readers seem not to have considered.

Finally, having reviewed five cases of the Bodhidharma family being applied to various projects, it seems that the choice to categorize this situation in terms of recycling "brand equity" has held up. And yet an unexpected dynamic has also come to the fore: unlike inert "zombie brands" that simply maintain some measure of their prior symbolic heft, Bodhidharma and his growing family were clearly *gaining in stature* as they were recycled through these various texts. The more they were stolen and reapplied to new projects, the more the next generation of authors thought it was wise and necessary to steal them for their own purposes. After all, one only makes use of markers of authority that others also value and respect. Put this way, we should return to the comments in the Introduction about how longing and nostalgia work in

Chan—one wants the other's connection to the origin of tradition precisely because the other has figured out how to make that connection look so perfect.

With these two early Bodhidharma genealogies in view, let's turn to the two "histories" that followed.

4

More Local Buddhas Appear

Jingjue, Huineng, and Shenhui

OVERVIEW

In the wake of Du Fei's *Record of the Transmission of the Dharma-Jewel,* the history of the Bodhidharma family was developed in several directions. On one front, at least two masters—Puji (d. 739) and Yifu (d. 736)—came to be officially recognized as Shenxiu's descendants. When exactly this happened remains unclear. It is usually assumed that they both actually were Shenxiu's disciples and in that capacity received his sanction before he died, but, as noted in the previous chapter, Du Fei's text merely says that Shenxiu gave a secret transmission just before he died, thereby leaving the matter undecided. In fact, keeping the matter vague appears to have been part of Du Fei's agenda, suggesting that identifying Shenxiu's heir/s was still a work in progress. We shouldn't forget, too, that even Shenxiu might not have been reckoned a member of the Bodhidharma family until after his death, and thus he wouldn't have been in a position to select someone to fill out the next generation. After all, the whole point of Du Fei's text was to *put* Shenxiu in the Bodhidharma family, a task that required some careful story telling and was only undertaken some years after Shenxiu died in 706.

Besides this uncertainty regarding the timing of Puji's and Yifu's official inclusion in the Bodhidharma family, a number of sources name other masters as Shenxiu's descendants.[1] Given this jumble of competing claims, the first thing to conclude is that after Du Fei wrote the very famous Shenxiu into the Bodhidharma family, other elite Buddhists also hoped to join the clan. Thus by 730 or so, the Bodhidharma brand name appears to have achieved significant national recognition. Looked at this way, the birth of Chan isn't to be found in the transmission of some particular teaching or practice that Faru brought to Shaolin from Hongren's community, but rather in two other historical realities: (1) an increasingly widespread desire—among elite Buddhist—to be included in the Bodhidharma family; and, (2) the multiplication of techniques— literary, artistic, ritualistic and architectural—that made such claims to this legacy appear plausible. As these desires and techniques gained currency among a number of authors in the early decades of the eighth century, the cyclone of Chan began to find its axis of rotation.

Alongside attempts to find a place in Bodhidharma's family by claiming direct descent from Shenxiu, we find three, more complicated, strategies to join the family. The first strategy essentially accepted the Bodhidharma-to-Shenxiu lineage, but then rewrote the final section of the story so that Shenxiu appeared to have various "dharma-brothers" who supposedly were also Hongren's descendants. With these new truth-fathers providing a convenient link back to Hongren, authors then only needed to present histories connecting themselves to these more recently added family members. For instance, Jingjue (683–750?) wrote a genealogy explaining that Hongren had ten descendants (!) and that three of them were Teachers of the Nation—Shenxiu, Lao'an (n.d.), and Xuanze (n.d.). So, with Xuanze identified as his own master, Jingjue put

---

1. For discussion of Shenxiu's supposed disciples, see Bernard Faure, *The Will to Orthodoxy: A Critical Genealogy of Northern Chan Buddhism*, trans. Phyllis Brooks (Stanford, CA: Stanford University Press, 1997), chap. 3.

himself forward as an heir to the Bodhidharma legacy.[2] In this way, Jing-jue found a way to *gently* include himself in the Bodhidharma clan with-out having to negate or disparage Shenxiu's imperially ratified status. In fact, this narrative ploy very much needed Shenxiu's splendor to stay front and center so as to buoy his nine new dharma-brothers, who were either little known or, in fact, imaginary.

The second complicated strategy for joining the Bodhidharma family also gave Hongren new descendants but did so by arguing that the "authentic" transmission of truth had gone to neither Shenxiu or Faru, but instead to a newly invented figure named Huineng (n.d.), who was, henceforth, to be counted as the singular source of real Buddhism in China. This more aggressive revision of the Bodhidharma family was first promoted by Shenhui (d. 758) in mid-eighth century, and soon initi-ated a sea change in early Chan writing since this newly invented truth-father, Huineng, would soon be taken up by many authors who saw in him an ancestor more attractive than Shenxiu, and also more malleable.

Establishing dates for Shenhui's various writing projects—and there are at least four surviving texts connected to him—presents a number of problems, but I think it best to assume that these works weren't put into circulation until the 740s, when both Yifu and Puji were already dead.[3] One of the reasons for insisting on this relatively late date is that

2. Jingjue makes these claims in the preface to his *History of the Masters and Disciples of the Laṅkāvatāra Sūtra* (*Lengqie shizi ji*). For a French translation and useful notes on the text, see Bernard Faure, *Le bouddhisme Ch'an en mal d'histoire: Genèse d'une tradition religieuse dans le Chine des T'ang* (Paris: École française d'Extrême-Orient, 1989), 87–182, and for the above claims about Jingjue's relationship to Shenxiu and Xuanze, 88–95.

3. For more discussion of the problems surrounding the dates of Shenhui's texts, see Alan Cole, *Fathering Your Father: The Zen of Fabrication in Tang Buddhism* (Berkeley: Uni-versity of California Press, 2009), chap 6, esp. 232ff. In *The Mystique of Transmission: On an Early Chan History and Its Contents* (New York: Columbia University Press, 2007), 442n156, Wendi Adamek notes that the key text by Shenhui that attacks Puji appears to have been composed around 745, even though it claims to present discussions from the early 730s. For a very helpful summary of the Shenhui manuscripts found at Dun-huang, see Philip Yampolsky, *The Platform Sūtra of the Sixth Patriarch* (New York: Columbia University Press, 1967), 24n67.

Shenhui couldn't have attacked Puji and his place in the Bodhidharma family until Puji had been officially declared Shenxiu's heir, and, as far as I can tell, this didn't happen in any important way until Puji's funerary texts—a stele and an eulogy preserved at Dunhuang—were composed shortly after his death in 739.[4] Moreover, in both these texts, Puji is none too subtly presented as having been the king of Chinese Buddhism, and thus the sole heir to the Bodhidharma lineage. The virulence of Shenhui's attacks on Puji, along with Shenhui's counterclaim that he himself was the king of Buddhism, suggests that Shenhui was writing in response to the exceptional status granted to Puji in these two memorial texts that date from the early 740s.[5] Presumably it was just this high-profile claim to exclusively own the Bodhidharma lineage that prompted Shenhui to attack Puji's legacy so aggressively, while he left other less grandiose claimants, such as Yifu or Jingxian, unnamed in his polemics.[6] Imagining a relatively late date for his attack on Puji is also supported by the way Shenhui felt it necessary, in the midst of his attack, to explicitly address the question of why he was making these accusations so late in the day.[7]

The third complex strategy for taking hold of the prestige of the expanding Bodhidharma family appears in a number memorial projects organized by several monasteries located on Mount Song—primarily Shaolin and Songyue.[8] Although it was normal for monasteries to honor their "special dead" with various kinds of stupas and stelae, more involved strategies for managing the celebrity (and assumed power) of deceased

4. For discussion of Puji and the various memorials made in his honor, see Faure's *Will to Orthodoxy*, 91–100.

5. Adamek also believes that Shenhui's writing likely was a response to Puji's funerary texts; see her *Mystique of Transmission*, 170.

6. For a summary of Jingxian's life and relationship to Shenxiu, see Faure's *Will to Orthodoxy*, 207n33.

7. For these passages, see Cole, *Fathering Your Father*, 234–35.

8. For discussion of these monasteries, see Bernard Faure, "Relics and Flesh Bodies," in *Pilgrims and Sacred Sites in China*, eds. Susan Naquin and Chün-Fang Yü (Berkeley: University of California Press, 1992), 150–89, esp. 153ff.; and see also Faure, *Will to Orthodoxy*, 83ff.

masters appeared in the first half of the eighth century. Notable among these projects was the "Hall of the Seven Patriarchs"[9] which Puji had built somewhere on Mount Song. While the hall was clearly dedicated to celebrating the Bodhidharma lineage, we can only speculate about which seven masters were installed—was Puji himself included? Faru? Whatever the case, it still seems safe to say that Puji and his supporters thought that setting up this ancestral hall would help collect and control the iconic power—or "brand equity"—of the recent masters who had been recognized as members of the Bodhidharma family.[10]

9. For more discussion of this building, see T. Griffith Foulk and Robert H. Sharf, "On the Ritual Use of Ch'an Portraiture in Medieval China," *Cahiers d'Extrême-Asie* 7 (1993–94): 172. Foulk and Sharf assume that the ancestral hall was built at Shaolin, but I'm not so sure. Shenhui only mentions that the hall was built at Mount Song (Hu Shih, *Hu Shi chanxue an*, ed. Yanagida Seizan [Taipei: Zhengzhong shuzhu, 1975], 283 and 288), which leaves it unclear since Mount Song is the locale of both Shaolin and Songyue monasteries. This uncertainty doubles when we note that Puji seems to have had important connections with both monasteries. Faure mentions that Puji was buried in a golden coffin at Songyue, and that stupas were built there for both Puji and Shenxiu (*Will to Orthodoxy*, 95). Though it is a later source that may or may not accurately reflect Tang historical realities, the *Song Biographies of Eminent Monks* mentions that in 752, Shenhui had a "portrait hall" (*zhentang*) built in his monastery, *Heze si*, at Luoyang (*T* 2061, 50.755b.10); if true, this would suggest, again, that Shenhui was taking his cues from Puji in his attempts to take control of the Bodhidharma legacy. See further Foulk, "The Ch'an Tsung in Medieval China: School, Lineage, or What?" *Pacific World*, n.s., no. 8 (1992): 22–24; see also Foulk and Sharf, "On the Ritual Use of Ch'an Portraiture," 174–75. The main point here is that several high-profile monasteries sought, with their various building projects, to "capture" the cachet of these famous masters who, in different ways, claimed to be in the Bodhidharma fmily.

10. Whereas the various memorials on Mount Song were designed to control the power of the past, Shaolin also took steps to control the future. This can be seen in 728 when Shaolin cut in stone a new history of itself, referred to now as "the Shaolin stele"; see Tonami Mamoru, *The Shaolin Monastery Stele on Mount Song*, trans. P. A. Herbert (Kyoto: Italian School of East Asian Studies, 1990). This includes a passage (ibid., 37) announcing that, with court approval, Shaolin was to be home to a board of ten eminent monks (*shi dade*). What this board was charged with accomplishing isn't clear, but presumably the ten monks were to function as an elite body dedicated to managing Buddhist matters at a national level. This history is also important in that even though Bodhidharma and Huike are mentioned as having resided at Shaolin, neither Shenxiu or Puji are mentioned and Faru is given a dharma heir named Huichao (ibid.), suggesting that Shaolin was, at least at this particular juncture, still interested in establishing its relationship to the Bodhidharma legacy via Faru and apart from the Shenxiu "clan."

With a general sense for these strategies, let's turn to Jingjue's text, the *History of the Masters and Disciples of the Laṅkāvatāra Sūtra* (*Lengqie shizi ji*), to explore the specific techniques he developed as he sought to establish himself as a member of the Bodhidharma family.

JINGJUE AND THE *HISTORY OF THE MASTERS*
AND DISCIPLES OF THE LAṄKĀVATĀRA SŪTRA

Jingjue's text is fascinating for several reasons.[11] We aren't sure when it was written—surely after Du Fei's text—but it is pretty clear *why* it was written.[12] Jingjue, with unabashed directness, and with an artful blend of Daoist and Buddhist phrases, explains that he was enlightened under the direction of master Xuanze, who supposedly was a Teacher of the Nation, and an heir, just like Shenxiu, to Hongren's legacy. Aside from Jingjue's claims about Xuanze—made here and, in very brief passages in two other texts of his—there is no contemporaneous evidence attesting to the existence of this master Xuanze. And, Jingjue's reliability as a historian isn't helped when, among other far-fetched assertions, he claims that one day when Xuanze was in meditation, five-colored relics popped out of each of his eyes, thereby proving his buddha-status.[13]

I doubt this Xuanze ever existed, but other scholars in the field are less skeptical. My doubts are based on a number of inconsistencies in

---

11. Nine manuscripts of this text—seven in Chinese and two in Tibetan—were found at Dunhuang, suggesting that it held significant appeal for readers in the mid-to-late Tang era.

12. For a good discussion of the problems involved with dating Jingjue's text, see Faure, *Will to Orthodoxy*, 167ff. Timothy Barrett argues that some of the text was likely composed before 716; see his "The Date of the *Leng-chia shih-tzu chi*," *Journal of the Royal Asiatic Society*, 3d ser., 1, no. 2 (1991): 255–59. Jingjue was the brother of Empress Wei, the consort of Emperor Zhongzong, who was the son of Empress Wu. Empress Wei tried to take over the empire in 710, but was blocked and then executed, along with most of her extended family.

13. For this passage, see Faure, *Bouddhisme Chan*, 90; the version in the *Taishō* starts with just this passage; *T* (no. 2837), 85.1283a.5.

Jingjue's portrayal of Xuanze in the *History*.[14] Moreover, if Xuanze had been a Teacher of the Nation *and a dharma heir of Hongren's*—as Jingjue claimed—then Du Fei would have had to discredit him in order to present Shenxiu as the sole leader of Chinese Buddhism. Du Fei didn't do this. In fact, there is nothing in Du Fei's *Record* to suggest that he had any knowledge of Xuanze, and this is decidedly odd given that Du Fei appears to have been a well informed author living in the capital. So on these grounds alone Jingjue's claim that he had a nationally recognized master named Xuanze seems most unlikely. It is also true that Jingjue doesn't provide any dates for Xuanze's life, nor a birthplace or a burial site. In fact, Jingjue doesn't even provide a proper entry for Xuanze in his history of the lineage.

As literature, Jingjue's *History* presents several new elements that are crucial for understanding how Chan writing was developing.[15] First, as we have just seen, Jingjue writes about himself. Thus, though he often refers to himself in the third person, he still is informing the reader about his own place in the lineage of truth-fathers. In this gesture we have a merging of two kinds of authority: Jingjue, as a self-proclaimed Chinese buddha, also presents himself as the *historian of the Chinese bud-dhas,* a role that other authors will soon adopt. Second, Jingjue's text attempts to give content to the teachings of the truth-fathers. Thus whereas Du Fei's *Record,* like the Faru biography, had worked to establish believable historical connections between the masters, Jingjue drops all those "facts," and focuses on the teaching that supposedly flowed from

14. For consideration of these details, see Cole, *Fathering Your Father,* chap. 5.

15. The only English translation of Jingjue's text is by J.C. Cleary in his *Zen Dawn: Early Zen Texts from Tun Huang* (Boston: Shambhala, 1991), 19–78. Though there are issues with this translation, I have used it as a base since, in the following passages, it varies little from Faure's much more scholarly French translation in *Bouddhisme Ch'an,* 87–182, and seems to follow the *Taishō* edition closely. Yanagida provided an edited version of the text, and a Japanese translation with copious notes, in his *Shoki no Zenshi, I: Ryōga shijiki; Denhōbō ki* (Tokyo: Chikuma shobō, 1971), 47–326. For a handy edited version of the preface to the text, which is partly missing in the *Taishō,* one can turn to Yanagida's *Shoki Zenshū shisho no kenkyū* (Kyoto: Hōzōkan, 1967), 625–37.

each master. Now, given the title of his work, one would expect that Jingjue's account of the masters would have them all providing commentary on the *Laṅkāvatāra Sūtra*. And yet this is not how the text works at all since Jingjue fills up the interior of each master's "boxcar" with two kinds of language: (1) accounts of the masters reciting, apropos of nothing, their favorite sutra passages, and (2) enigmatic questions and zany comments presented in somewhat vernacular-looking phrases. Thus each entry in the genealogy provides a place where the reader can watch the masters articulate tradition's truths in their "own voices," even if their "spoken" rhetoric is borrowed from various sutras and then spiced up with some bizarre, zesty language, such as "Can you enter a jar?" or "Can you enter fire?"

Apparently, Jingjue wasn't much of a dramaturge, and thus this staging of the oral performance of tradition turns out to be chaotic and underdeveloped, with the masters reciting sutra quotations without any reference to time, place, or their intended audience. In fact, even the zany comments that the masters supposedly uttered are highly repetitive, with those attributed to Guṇabhadra being the norm. (Guṇabhadra was an Indian master who translated the *Laṅkāvatāra Sūtra* into Chinese in the fifth century; Jingjue sets him in the lineage just before Bodhidharma, thereby implying that Guṇabhadra was Bodhidharma's truth-father.) Jingjue reports that Guṇabhadra supposedly posed the following questions:

> "Can you enter a jar? Can you enter a pillar? Can you enter a furnace? A mountain?[16] Can a stick preach the dharma? Does your body or mind enter?" He also said: "In a room there is a jar. Is the jar also outside the room or not? Is there water in the jar? Is the jar in the water? Are there jars in all the waters in the world? What is this water?"[17]

16. The *Taishō* edition appears corrupt here, and thus the translation is tentative.

17. *T* (no. 2837), 85.1284c.14–18, trans. based on Cleary, *Zen Dawn*, 31; Faure, *Bouddhisme Ch'an*, 112–13. These questions likely echo passages in the *Liezi*, a fourth-century Daoist work in which there are numerous stories about magicians who, aided by the Dao, can enter fire, water, and solid objects; for translations, see *The Book of Lieh-tzŭ*, trans. A.C. Graham (New York: Columbia University Press, 1960), 34, 37, 40–42, 46, 61.

As one reads parallel lines for Bodhidharma, Hongren, and Shenxiu, it is hard to avoid the impression that Jingjue rather liked these phrases and thought to attribute them to his favorite ancestors. Obviously, the question to ask is: How did Jingjue know what the masters said at all? He never once cites a source for these long-dead masters' oral teachings, nor does he try to explain how these teachings might have been passed down to him.

But what to make, really, of these quirky questions and flippant comments? Structurally, we can see that these rude-sounding colloquialisms are always set at the end of the sutra material, giving the impression that they are expected to supplement the staid and shopworn sutra quotations in some way. Actually, in some cases, the colloquial statements directly challenge the authority of the sutras. For instance, Jingjue quotes Shenxiu as having said, "The *Nirvana Sūtra* says there is a bodhisattva with a boundless body who comes from the east. Since the bodhisattva's body is boundless, why then does he come from the east? Why not from the west, the south, or the north?"[18] Clearly, this question could be read as undermining the sanctity of the *Nirvana Sūtra*, and, by implication, sutras in general. It also gives the reader the impression that Shenxiu was just the kind of towering master who could ask such insulting questions of an Indian sutra, questions that presumably would have revealed the limits of the imported literary tradition.

In other cases, the zany language evokes a sense of urgency by asking about things at hand, as though even the most mundane things could reveal the final truths of Buddhism. Thus, for instance, Bodhidharma "would just point to something and call out 'What kind of thing is it? There are all sorts of things—question them all. Interchange their names, and with them changed, question them.'"[19] Likewise, Shenxiu supposedly demanded that his disciples pay attention to present experience, asking, "You hear the sound of the bell being struck? Does the

18. Cleary, *Zen Dawn*, 76, with a minor change; Faure, *Bouddhisme Ch'an*, 178; *T* (no. 2837), 85.1290c.10.

19. Cleary, *Zen Dawn*, 37, with changes; Faure, *Bouddhisme Ch'an*, 121; *T* (no. 2837), 85.1285b.20.

sound exist when the bell is struck or before the bell is struck? What sound is this sound?"[20] In either case, the reader gets the impression that these masters sought to impart a wisdom that goes beyond the stiff formality of the sutras, and, better still, that tradition's truth is on hand in an immediate and even jarring manner. Looked at this way, this local "orality" naturally offsets the masters' reliance on the imported sutras and makes the masters appear to be sources of final wisdom, a wisdom that is to be recovered in their presence, and in the experience of the moment. Thus, at this very early moment in Chan writing, we see a kind anti-literature literature (!) emerging, one in which *in the text* the masters were set up to drive discussions about the final truths of Buddhism in the present and in a manner that would challenge the reader in a direct and engaging manner, provided he looked past the words on the page and imagined himself on site with the masters. This possibility of intimacy is underscored by quoting "speech" from the masters that regularly uses the pronoun "you" (*ru*), which presumably would call out more directly to the reader.[21]

Jingjue's creativity as a "historian of the masters" is particularly evident in the way he handles Huike's story. In Jingjue's version, Huike, besides cutting off his own arm, as Du Fei had claimed, receives transmission from Bodhidharma after standing in a snowstorm for half a night, a scene that will become another iconic element in the Chan tradition. Jingjue has Huike say, "When I first generated the mind intent on enlightenment, I cut off one arm and stood in the snow from twilight until the third watch of the night, not noticing the snow pile up past my knees—I

20. Cleary, *Zen Dawn*, 76, with changes; Faure, *Bouddhisme Ch'an*, 177; *T* (no. 2837), 85.1290c.1.

21. John McRae argued that these passages reflect some new style of practice, and thus that we should infer that these "masters were involved in the extension of spiritual cultivation to all the activities of daily life" (McRae *Seeing through Zen: Encounter, Transformation, and Genealogy in Chinese Chan Buddhism* [Berkeley: University of California Press, 2003], 86). Unfortunately, he doesn't present any evidence to support this position, and clearly Jingjue's text looks like a heavily fictionalized presentation of the masters, with little or no connection to their actual lives or teachings.

[did all this] seeking the ultimate Dao."[22] The problem here is that Jing-jue seems to have lifted this detail about standing in a snowstorm from the mini-biography of Huiman—*not Huike*—that was tacked onto the end of Huike's reworked biography in Daoxuan's *Continued Biographies*.[23] That Jingjue has Huike include this snowstorm detail in his account of his own enlightenment—now powerfully set in first-person voicing—makes it hard to believe that Jingjue's adoption of this mini-narrative was an error of transcription in which he mistakenly wrote the details from Huiman's story into Huike's life. In fact, I believe we ought to conclude that Jingjue got his inspiration to rewrite Huiman's snowstorm scene into Huike's biography by noting the liberties that Du Fei had taken in refor-mulating the story of Huike's arm-loss into that frightful self-amputa-tion, an invention that would have been glaringly obvious to Jingjue when he went back and read just this entry for Huike, which explained that his arm had been lost to bandits.

With a sense for Jingjue's zeal for rearranging previous material, let's turn to the content that Jingjue presents as the teachings of the masters. Here we again find that Chinese penchant for claiming that sentient beings and the buddhas are essentially the same and that all creatures are endowed with an internal buddha-of-sorts. Jingjue articulates this view in his own voice in the preface,[24] and he then has Guṇabhadra announce the same thing slightly later.[25] The theme reappears when Jingjue has Bodhidharma rehearse the text that is attributed him, the *Two Entrances*. Huike follows with a similar statement, and so on. This shared sameness between sentient beings and the buddhas, however, doesn't prevent Jingjue from affirming, as Du Fei also did, that the secret truth of Buddhism isn't transmitted publicly and that real Buddhism is esoteric and far from literature, words, and even the two vehicles,

22. Cleary, *Zen Dawn*, 41–42, with changes; Faure, *Bouddhisme Ch'an*, 129; *T* (no. 2837), 85.1286a.14.

23. Faure spotted this problem; see *Bouddhisme Ch'an*, 129n30.

24. Ibid., 94–95.

25. Cleary, *Zen Dawn*, 29; Faure, *Bouddhisme Ch'an* 106–7; *T* (no. 2837), 85.1284b.8.

Hīnayāna and Mahāyāna.[26] In fact, clarifying that enlightenment is *privately held* is a theme that reappears several times in the discourses that Jingjue gives to his masters. For instance, he has Guṇabhadra explain, "In our land [India] we have the true dharma, but it is secret and not openly transmitted. However, when those who have an affinity for it, and whose spiritual faculties are fully prepared, meet good and wise men on the road, it is bestowed on them. If not for such encounters with good and wise teachers, there would be no [transmission from] 'father' to 'son.'"[27] Thus, it would seem that this rhetoric that privatizes truth goes hand in hand with promises that members of the general public already possess some version of this truth, even if it is, in fact, unavailable to them. Arguably, just this arrangement is basic to Chan ideology.

Jingjue's account of the arrival of tradition's final truth is set, like Du Fei's, next to a thorough condemnation of older forms of Chinese Buddhism. Jingjue has Guṇabhadra say, "Since coming to this country, I have not even seen people who cultivate the Dao, much less anyone who has pacified his mind. I often see people who go along creating karma, and who have not yet tallied with the Dao. Some are concerned with fame and reputation; some act for the sake of profit and support. They operate with the mentality of self and other; they act with the attitude of jealousy."[28] As Jingjue inserts these criticisms of Chinese Buddhists into Guṇabhadra's discourse—lines that parallel those that Du Fei had given to Bodhidharma in the *Record*—Jingjue has implicitly established a new rule of legitimacy: all those who can't prove their place in the Bodhidharma lineage appear guilty of practicing bad Buddhism, since, without that perfect inheritance gained in the secret "father to son" transmission, they are supposedly lost in delusion and self-aggrandizement.

26. Jingjue makes these claims in the poem that opens his preface; see Faure, *Bouddhisme Ch'an*, 87–88.

27. Cleary, *Zen Dawn*, 26, with changes; Faure, *Bouddhisme Ch'an*, 103; *T* (no. 2837), 85.1284a.9.

28. Cleary, *Zen Dawn*, 27, with changes; Faure, *Bouddhisme Ch'an*, 105; *T* (no. 2837), 85.1284a.19.

Jingjue also dresses up the masters with a number of Daoist motifs, and in a manner that fits the pattern that had already been established by previous genealogists. To see this, let's take the example of master Hongren. Back in Du Fei's *Record*, Hongren's Daoist-styled buddhahood was most evident in the way he went *down* in the symbolic order only to land on top; thus, he was a profound and solid fellow (*chenhou*), who did not respond to insults from his compatriots and was content to spend the day working at menial tasks, apparently avoiding Buddhism altogether, save for his nighttime meditations. Then, in a key passage, Du Fei claimed that "Although he had never *looked* at the sutras and commentaries, whatever he *heard* [of Buddhist teachings] tallied with his mind."[29] Thus, relying on the thousand-year old metaphor of the tally, Du Fei gave us a profile of Hongren in which his perfect understanding of Buddhist truths appeared to have come to him without any reliance on the literary forms of Buddhism. In short, Hongren secured truth, and his place in the Bodhidharma family, independent of Buddhist texts and separate from the normal monastic routine, with its well-maintained hierarchies.

Picking up Du Fei's claim about Hongren's non-Buddhist buddhahood, Jingjue positions Hongren to be *buddhafied by nature*, in the depths of the mountains, far from culture, literature, and the Buddhist elite at court. Thus, Jingjue has Hongren liken himself to the heavy timber of the deep forest:

> Someone asked [Hongren], "To study the Dao, why is it that you don't go to cities and town, and instead live in the mountains?" Hongren answered, "The timbers for a great hall come from the remote valleys (*yougu*), not from inhabited areas. Because they are far from humans, they have not been chopped down or damaged by their axes. One by one they grow into giant things: only then are they fit to serve as ridge beams. Thus we know how to rest the spirit in remote valleys (*qishen yougu*), to stay far away from

29. Italics added. McRae, *The Northern School and the Formation of Early Ch'an Buddhism* (Honolulu: University of Hawai'i Press, 1986), 263, read this passage somewhat differently; for the Chinese, see Yanagida, *Shoki Zenshū shisho no kenkyū*, 567.

the hubbub and dust [of the cities], to nourish our [true] nature in the mountains (*yangxing shanzhong*), and to always avoid conventional affairs. When there is nothing before the eyes, mind is, of itself, peaceful. From this the tree of the Dao blooms, and the fruits of the Chan forest come forth." The Great Master Hongren sat alone in purity. He produced no written record, but he explained the dark principle (*xuan li*) orally or transmitted it to people in silence.[30]

Here, Hongren appears as a remarkable tree-like figure grown far from the city and far from language; and, given all the Daoist phrases about nourishing the spirit in the remote valleys, he of course appears far from traditional forms of Buddhism. In fact, with only nature in view as the cause of Hongren's buddhahood, one might even be tempted to say that Jingjue has stripped Hongren's truth of any content, Buddhist or otherwise. And yet, when Hongren is made to say that it is only under these circumstances that such timber is "fit to serve as ridge beams," it is clear that Hongren's perfection in nature has some totally viable cultural functions since the best of nature is brought in, literally, to bear up culture.

Standing back from Jingjue's text, we can see that though he was a careful reader of the preceding Chan texts, he was also an inventive historian who took all sorts of liberties with the material he received. Besides boldly writing himself into the Bodhidharma family, and I believe he was the first author to do this, Jingjue is also to be credited with getting the masters—however long dead—to "speak." Moreover, as just seen just above, Jingjue has Hongren evoke comforting Daoist scenes in which we are asked to imagine that Chan masters naturally perfected themselves in the benevolent folds of remote valleys, as if to say that pristine Chinese landscape was, in fact, the real cause of Buddhist enlightenment. Jingjue was equally original in experimenting with a colloquial mode of writing the everyday "speech" of the master, one that presented these truths to the reader in an immediate and exciting

30. Cleary, *Zen Dawn*, 66–67, with minor changes; Faure, *Bouddhisme Ch'an*, 162; *T* (no. 2837), 85.1289b.14.

manner. Though clearly a literary product, this new style of discourse—
the zany and aggressive riffs of the master—would of course be essential
for what came next.

SHENHUI INVENTS HUINENG'S ALL-NATURAL ENLIGHTENMENT

Jingjue's *History* is a rich source for understanding developments in
Chan rhetoric, but the writing of Shenhui (not to be confused with
Shenxiu) is perhaps even more important. While we don't know much
about Shenhui, it appears that sometime in the middle of the eighth
century, he invited Wang Wei, a very famous poet and painter, to create a brief biography for a master named Huineng. Prior to Wang Wei's
writing, Huineng's name appeared only once in the literary record, in
Jingjue's *History,* where he is counted as one of the ten masters who supposedly received transmission from Hongren; nothing else is said about
him other than that he was from Shaozhou in the south, and that he was
just a local teacher, not a Teacher of the Nation, that is. Apparently,
then, as Wang Wei set about writing up the life of Huineng, he had
basically no sources at hand and, very likely, there were none to be had.
In fact, there is little reason to believe Huineng ever existed.

What *is* clear is that this Huineng figure was designed to provide Shenhui with a way into the Bodhidharma family. Thus near the end of the
biography, we learn that this newly invented Huineng, having received
transmission from Hongren, took Shenhui to be his unique heir—with, as
usual, no date or place given to secure the historical context of their time
together. So once again an author has worked up a scenario in which the
Bodhidharma brand name was brought in to endorse a new Chinese Buddhist item—this time the item was, of course, Shenhui.

The biography that Wang Wei provides for Huineng is poetic and
well wrought, but the profile that it creates looks most improbable, and
for two distinct reasons. First, there is a total lack of historical details:
no dates for life-events, and not even a place of birth or death. Second,

the details that are given about Huineng's life are generated by quoting lines from the Chinese classics and Buddhist sutras. Thus, as in the case of Faru, apart from recycled snippets from China's favorite texts, there is a noticeable absence of real events in Huineng's life; in short, he appears to be a paper tiger of sorts. To reveal the density of this kind of literary Frankensteinism, I have marked the references for some of the more interesting allusions in the following translation, which, not counting the preface, represents the first third of Wang Wei's text.

The Chan master was surnamed Lu, and was from such and such [sic] region and province. Names are empty and vain, [and anyway] he was not born of an aristocratic family. The dharma has no center or periphery, and he did not dwell in China. Good habits were manifest [even] in the way he played games as a child, and his sharp intellect was displayed in his youthful mind. He was not selfish, and was a companion to the stench of farming and silk production [*Zuozhuan*]; and, simply taking whatever came along, he followed the rank way of his barbarian land [*Zhuangzi; Analects*]. When he had a couple years of age, he served the great master [Hong-]Ren of Huangmei with all his strength [*Analects*]. Then he was installed in the [work] of the well and the mortar [*History of the South*], and it was there that he gouged out his mind and attained enlightenment in the wild grass [*Zhuangzi*].

Every time the master [Hongren] ascended the seat, students filled the hall, and among them one could find the levels of the three vehicles, who listened together to the one-sound dharma. The Chan master [Huineng] was silent in receiving the teachings and didn't introduce anything [new or private] [*Analects*]. And then with careful private investigation [*Analects*], he penetrated to no-self. [At that point, thoughts of] self would have been like a thirsty deer cherishing thoughts of water [when there was none] [*Laṅkāvatāra Sūtra*], or trying to catch the tracks of birds in the sky [*Vimalakīrti*].

The perfumed rice not digested [*Vimalakīrti*], and dirty clothes still worn, everyone told him that he [Huineng] should ascend the hall and enter the [master's] room [*Analects*] to fathom the ocean and survey the heavens because it was said that he had obtained the Yellow Emperor's pearl [*Zhuangzi*], and that he merited the seal of the dharma-king [*Lotus Sūtra*]. The Great Master [Hongren] knew of his achievements [*Shiji*] and [knew] that due to his modesty, he was not trumpeting them. Heaven, how could it speak [*Analects*]?

Sageliness and benevolence, who would dare claim them [*Analects*]? You and me are not as good as he [*Analects*]. As Hongren was about to die, he secretly transmitted the patriarchal robe and bowl, and said to him [Huineng], "All creatures hate those who are uniquely worthy. And people hate those who advance themselves [*Hanshu*]. After I am dead, you should go."[31]

In this swirl of snippets taken from Buddhist and non-Buddhist sources, it is clear that Wang Wei's basic agenda is to make Huineng look like a perfect backwoods buddha. Thus, against the regal and heavily ornamented image of the Indian Buddha, and, more recently, against Shenxiu's imperially celebrated grandeur and hyper-literacy, Huineng is rural, unschooled, plebian, and directly involved with odiferous food production. The net effect is that Huineng appears as the uncanny, if somewhat stinky, rustic master who is naturally endowed with all that it takes to be a buddha, independent of the cultural and institutional forms normally relied on to generate buddhas and Buddhist authority.

Also, we should not miss that Huineng's untutored perfection is obviously being generated by one of the most educated writers of the era. This means that there is a glaring mismatch between form and content here: Huineng is presented as an all-natural, bumpkin buddha, but this image is evoked with quotations from a wide range of sophisticated books, lightly alluded to, in an elegant eulogy. Similarly, there is a tension between observer and spectacle: to get the posh literary references that develop Huineng's down-home simplicity is, ironically, to find oneself on the wrong side of the fence that divides Huineng's miraculously perfected nature from the rest of mundane human culture—Buddhism included.

Besides these tensions, the story implies that real Buddhism was never at court and certainly never in the possession of Shenxiu and his

---

31. Yanagida, *Shoki Zenshū shisho no kenkyū*, 539–57. I have relied extensively on Yanagida's identification of these references. And, many thanks to Brook Ziporyn for solving some of the more difficult translation problems in this passage. For an alternative translation, see John Jorgensen, *Inventing Hui-neng, the Sixth Patriarch: Hagiography and Biography in Early Ch'an* (Leiden: Brill, 2005), 145–51.

descendants. Likewise we learn that the real lineage had reproduced itself out of sight since Hongren *secretly* gave transmission to Huineng and then told him to run away. This secrecy theme, by the way, while found in prior lineage heists, will soon get amplified until full-scale conspiracy theories are promoted by a number of mid-to-late-eighth-century Chan authors—this is, in fact, the topic of the next chapter. For the moment, the main thing to see is that Huineng's simplicity and earthiness are at the core of Shenhui's attempt to undermine the reigning Buddhist elite. More exactly, we can say that Huineng has been designed as a triple threat: he has the perfect truth of a buddha, but he holds it with Daoist simplicity that cleanses him of any competitiveness, even as this innocent perfection is ready to be turned over to his "son" Shenhui, according to Confucian models of inheritance.

Shenhui's bid to push aside Shenxiu and his descendants in order to take over the Bodhidharma legacy appears to have met with mixed results. As we have seen, throughout the eighth century many authors continued to accept Shenxiu and his supposed descendants as the legitimate holders of the Bodhidharma lineage, and yet it is also true that Shenhui did win some recognition for himself. More importantly, from this time on other authors would try to claim Huineng as their own ancestor, suggesting thereby that Shenhui's newly invented truth-father had gained appreciable clout, even if Shenhui wasn't able to control that potential for himself. While most later Chan authors would assume that Huineng really was Hongren's true descendant—and that Shenxiu was an imposter—it isn't at all clear that this was a victory that Shenhui managed to enjoy in his lifetime. In fact, it seems that in 745, Shenhui was banished from the capital, a fact that likely had to do with the charges he was leveling against the established members of the Bodhidharma family. Later he was brought back, but he apparently never won the national recognition that he sought.[32]

32. For evidence that Shenhui won some imperial acclaim, albeit posthumously, see Foulk, "Ch'an *Tsung*," 23–24.

VISITING THE MASTER OF TRUTH

Wang Wei's biography for Huineng appears as a graceful and enchanting way to establish Shenhui's new identity as China's unique master-of-truth, but several of Shenhui's other literary ventures were a good bit more confrontational. For instance, a text whose abbreviated title is *Questions and Answers on Various Topics Confirming the Doctrine* (*Wendaza zhengyi*), provides verbatim accounts of dharma discussions that Shenhui purportedly had with various important people.[33] With this kind of reportage, it is as though we get to watch—or, rather, listen to—Shenhui smoothly answer a variety of questions regarding truth and tradition. Since these discussions are presented as transcripts of *unscripted events,* Shenhui's brilliance appears to play out as a natural and uncontrived reality.

Questions and Answers begins with a very short preface by an editor named Liucheng who explains how the correct transmission of Buddhist truth came to China via Bodhidharma. He then plainly identifies Shenhui as the most recent heir in the Bodhidharma family, noting, in particular, that Shenhui occupies the seventh generation in the lineage, and that everyone loved him just in the way that one would take refuge in a father or mother, and that when anyone asked him a question, he responded simply, like a great master. With no further ado, the text opens up into forty-eight conversations, of various lengths, in which Shenhui explains Buddhist truths to his interlocutors.

33. The three surviving manuscripts for this text vary considerably on the ordering of the conversations. Paul Demiéville has collated the different ordering of the texts; see his "Deux documents de Touen-houang sur le Dhyāna chinois," in *Essays on the History of Buddhism Presented to Professor Zenryu Tsukamoto* (Kyoto: Nagai Shuppansha, 1961), 1–27, repr. in Demiéville, *Choix d'études bouddhiques, 1929–1970* (Leiden: Brill, 1973), 320-46. I have followed Pelliot 3047 since this is the manuscript Hu Shih edited and that Gernet translated in his *Entretiens du maître de dhyāna Chen-houei du Ho-tsö (668–760)* (Paris: École française d'Extrême-Orient, 1949). For a useful collection of materials connected to Shenhui, see Yang Zengwen, ed., *Shenhui heshang chanyu lu* [Records of the Chan Talks of the Venerable Shenhui] (Beijing: Zhonghua shuju, 1996). For McRae's useful reflections on the "fictional creativity" at work in staging these conversations see his *Seeing through Zen,* 93.

Reading through these conversations, it becomes obvious that quotations from sutras provide the debate topics. In fact, a large part of what Shenhui is made to say is based on passages taken from a fairly small set of Mahāyāna sutras that were favored in China, such as the *Lotus Sūtra*, the *Nirvana Sūtra*, and the *Vimalakīrti*. Sometimes these quotations run on for five or ten sentences, and one gets the distinct impression that the text is far from representing a real conversation and, instead, is providing an essayist with a convenient (and very traditional) model for developing a set of doctrinal positions. Thus, Shenhui, as the supposed great champion of sudden enlightenment and "no-thought," shows himself to be heavily involved in one of the oldest Buddhist preoccupations: sutra commentary. And yet what is decidedly new here is that Shenhui *appears* to perform live and thus his responses seem spontaneous and unprepared—as though they flowed naturally out of his everyday life. In sum, in reading the *Questions and Answers,* one feels a certain intimacy with a living, breathing, truth-speaking master. As we will see, working up ways to deliver just that sense of intimacy with the master is one of the hallmarks of Chan literature.

SHENHUI AS DRAMA KING IN *DEFINING THE TRUE AND FALSE*

The art of publicly displaying Shenhui's mastery of tradition comes through in another work that also purports to document his unscripted performances, performances that supposedly took place sometime in the 730s. In this text, the *Treatise Defining the True and False in the Southern Lineage of Bodhidharma (Puti Damo Nanzong ding shifei lun)*, Shenhui is shown engaging in a dangerous kind of debate with a certain master Chongyuan who is identified as the leader of Buddhist China, even though he isn't mentioned in any other source.[34] Once at Chongyuan's Great Cloud

34. For a fuller account of this text, see Cole, *Fathering Your Father,* chap. 6. Jorgensen also suspects that this debate is fictional; see his *Inventing Hui-neng,* 64–65. For an English translation, see Chu Dongwei, *The Wisdom of Huineng, Chinese Buddhist*

Monastery in Huatai—northeast of Luoyang—Shenhui recounts his place in the Bodhidharma lineage, apparently to no one in particular. Chongyuan then appears onstage and upbraids him in a manner that proves he has a very different view of Shenhui. A debate then ensues as they negotiate two versions of truth, one sanctified by the narrative that claims to know that Shenhui really is in the Bodhidharma family, and the other that lacks this knowledge—Chongyuan's position.

Seeing the hall decorated as if to receive important guests, Chongyuan initiates the debate with a trick question from the *Diamond Sūtra*:

> The dharma master Chongyuan took the monk's [Shenhui's] arm and scolded him asking, "Chan master, do you call this decoration?" "Yes," replied the monk [Shenhui]. [Chongyuan said,] "As the Tathāgata said, 'Decoration is not decoration.'"[35]

In this opening salvo, the narrator, who is identified as Dugu Pei, has Chongyuan initially assume the role of the Buddha since this question about decoration is one of the Buddha's lines in the *Diamond Sūtra*. Shenhui, on the other hand, starts off with underdog status, having to defend somebody's choice to decorate the hall on the day of his arrival, while also handling Chongyuan's more philosophic question about the reality of doing so. And yet, Shenhui smoothly evades the *Diamond Sūtra* question with a quote from chapter 11 of the *Vimalakīrti*:[36]

Philosopher: The Platform Sutra and Other Translations (Bloomington, IN: iUniverse, 2015), pt. 1, sec. 2; unfortunately, this book doesn't seem to have page numbers and presents a number of questionable translation choices. For an edited text and notes, see also Yang Zengwen, ed., *Shenhui heshang chanyu lu*, 15–48.

35. This translation, and those that follow, are based on the edited text that Hu Shih published in his *Two Newly Edited Texts of the Ch'an Master Shenhui from the Pelliot Collection of Tun-huang Manuscripts at the Bibliotheque Nationale in Paris. Zhongyang yanjiuyuan lishi yuyan yanjiusuo jikan* 29, no. 2 (1958) (in Chinese); I will be citing page numbers as found in the reprinted version in *Shenhui heshang yiji*, (Taibei: Hu Shi jinian guan, 1968). The above exchange begins on ibid., p. 264. Hu Shi's edited manuscript is also available online at http://tripitaka.cbeta.org/B25n0142_001 The text begins at 0042a03. For a French translation of the opening section of the text, see Gernet, *Entretiens du maître de dhyāna Chen-houei du Ho-tsö*, 81–91.

36. Hu Shih, *Two Newly Edited Texts*, 265. Gernet, *Entretiens du maître de dhyāna Chen-houei du Ho-tsö*, 88.

"It is also said in the sutras that one shouldn't finish with the compounded, nor should one abide in the uncompounded (*wuwei*)." Chongyuan replies, "But what is the meaning of [the sentence] 'one shouldn't finish with the compounded, nor should one abide in the uncompounded'?"

With this exchange, the balance of power has clearly shifted. Whereas Shenhui ducked Chongyuan's trap and countered it with another sutra quote, Chongyuan is shown falling into the orbit of the *Vimalakīrti*. As Chongyuan asks for an explanation of the passage, the narrative has advanced three "facts." First, Chongyuan's inability to interpret a widely revered text, the *Vimalakīrti*, has just been demonstrated. Second, in getting drawn into the *Vimalakīrti's* narrative, Chongyuan is shown unable to parry Shenhui's thrust and unable, too, to move the conversation into another zone of authority where he could dominate. Thus, the exchange reveals that Chongyuan can't dance between sutras, which marks him again as someone who has yet to master tradition. Third, given that Shenhui quotes the rest of the passage to him, Chongyuan's question has allowed Shenhui to step into the role of the Buddha since the next line from Shenhui is actually taken from the Buddha's response to a bodhisattva in the *Vimalakīrti*.[37] In brief, Chongyuan started out speaking like a buddha, but now he is getting lectured by one.

The redistribution of power and authority in this short conversation is immediately underscored when the narrator adds, "The dharma master Chongyuan didn't have anything to say at that moment, and waited a long time until he said the following: 'Lust and anger are the Way (*dao*); it is not in decoration.'"[38] While the first half of this line is the rough equivalent of several passages found in chapter 3 of the *Vimalakīrti*,[39] this shocking claim doesn't trap Shenhui, who answers with the realistic comment,

---

37. For a translation of this passage, see *The Vimalakīrti Sutra*, trans. Burton Watson (New York: Columbia University Press, 1997), 126.

38. The rest of the translations in this paragraph are from Hu Shih, *Two Newly Edited Texts*, 266; Gernet, *Entretiens du maître de dhyāna Chen-houei du Ho-tsö*, 88–89.

39. *Vimalakīrti Sutra*, trans. Watson, 41–43.

"If that is the case, then common people should currently obtain the Dao." Shenhui's response again throws Chongyuan off balance, and Chongyuan has to ask, "Why do you say that common people should obtain the Dao?" Shenhui retorts, "You say that desire and anger are the Dao, and since the common people are just those who follow desire and anger, how could they not obtain the Dao?" With his commonsense rebuttal of the *Vimalakīrti* position, Shenhui makes Chongyuan's claim that desire and anger are the Dao appear silly. In all this, Chongyuan appears unable to express and defend well-known Buddhist positions. Shenhui, on the other hand, can take tradition and speak for it—as when he quoted the *Vimalakīrti* to good effect in the exchange before this one—or against it, as he does here when he refutes *Vimalakīrti's* line about desire and anger being the Dao.

Standing back from the debate—which in a moment will end up even worse for Chongyuan—it is clear that the real topic of the conversation isn't the truth or falsity of various claims regarding Buddhist topics, but the truth or falsity of the *identities* of the two combatants. Thus, it doesn't make sense to say that there are two "philosophic" positions represented here; instead, we see a kind of wrestling in which each figure attempts to rid the other man of the right to speak as a final authority. In this kind of verbal jousting, the value of a jab is solely determined by the damage it can do to the other combatant. Shenhui easily wins each round of the match and, then, leading up to the crushing finale, Chongyuan is made to claim that a line that Shenhui cited from the *Lotus Sūtra* is really the talk of the devil, Mara.[40] It is at this most crucial point in the dialogue that Shenhui turns to the audience in the hall and repeats the blasphemous thing Chongyuan has said about the *Lotus Sūtra*, after reminding them of Chongyuan's national and international reputation. The narrator, apparently counting on his reading audience to know how scandalous (and dangerous!) it is to slander the *Lotus Sūtra*, has just finalized the formal and public *unenlightenment* of Chongyuan.

40. Hu Shi, *Two Newly Edited Texts*, 266–67. Gernet, *Entretiens du maître de dhyāna Chen-houei du Ho-tsö*, 89.

Then, and just as unequivocally, the narrative installs Chongyuan's lost authority in the figure of Shenhui. This is accomplished when we suddenly learn that forty dharma masters happened to be in the hall, and that they jointly verified Shenhui's triumph. Thus, in line with that authorial strategy first seen in Faru's biography, Shenhui's private claim to be the seventh patriarch at the beginning of the narrative appears now to have been publicly verified by reliable authorities who seem to stand *outside the narrative*. Equally important, Shenhui's buddha-status wasn't proven with some special Chan content, but rather by developing a complex narrative that first *gradually* divested old authority of its legitimacy and then reinstalled it in Shenhui. In sum, what is characteristically Chan about this text isn't findable in anything that was said, but rather in the careful and artful portrayal of their dharma-combat that leads the reader to identify a new Chinese buddha.

At this point in the narration of their combat, everything seems to be finished, with all agendas accomplished. However, it seems that right here someone thought to attach a long discussion—largely dedicated to explaining the *Diamond Sūtra*—that drifts far away from the closely knit drama depicting Chongyuan's ousting. Elements of this essay, which on and off still pretend to be part of the debate between Shenhui and Chongyuan at Great Cloud Monastery, will show up in the *Platform Sūtra* (discussed in chapter 6) and seem to have been potent in other ways too, but for now it will be enough to explore four key passages.

BODHIDHARMA'S ROBE AND ONE BUDDHA PER GENERATION IN *DEFINING THE TRUE AND FALSE*

The long essay that is awkwardly attached to the dramatic section of *Defining the True and False,* though highly polemical and partisan, provides some useful facts about the way lineage warfare was conducted in the middle of the eighth century. For instance, in this section of the text, there is great concern that there only be one Chinese buddha at a time. In a way, this had been the unspoken rule even back with the genealogies for Faru and Shenxiu, since they were presented as unique, king-like—or pope-like—leaders of Chinese Buddhism. Jingjue's text, as we saw above, completely opened up that system by giving Hongren ten descendants, and allowing several Teachers of the Nation at one time: Shenxiu, Xuanze, and Lao'an. Apparently hoping to shut down just such a possibility—while also seeking to overturn the claims made in the 740s that Puji had been the king of Buddhism—Shenhui is adamant that the Bodhidharma lineage served as the track for delivering *one* Chinese buddha per generation.

Presumably in order to strengthen the imperial quality of Chinese buddhahood, Shenhui invented the robe of transmission. This robe was supposedly Bodhidharma's robe and it was to be handed down, generation by generation, to each of his Chinese descendants. As Shenhui explains the robe's function, it is clear that that he wants Chinese buddhahood to be understood as a kind of kingship, one that requires ownership of this talisman:

> Chan master [Hong]ren of the Tang, at East Mountain, took the robe and gave it to Chan master [Hui]neng. Thus, up till now there have been six generations [since Bodhidharma]. Internal transmission is through accord in the dharma, and is confirmed by the mind. External transmission is with the robe, and it defines the lineage-essence (*zongzhi*). From the beginning of the transmission [sequence], one by one, each [master] gave the Bodhidharma robe as the guarantor. This robe can now be seen at Shaozhou [at Huineng's monastery] and will not be given to anyone anymore. To speak of the transmission of any other kind of object is simply ridiculous. Also, from the beginning down to the sixth generation, each generation has had only one person. Never were there two. Even when there are millions of students, only one person is allowed to inherit. Chongyuan asked, "Why is only one person per generation allowed to inherit?" The monk [Shenhui] answered, "It is like the way a kingdom only has one king. Never is it said that there are two. It is like the way that there is only one emperor (*cakravartin*) in the four [directions]. Never is it said that there are two. It is like the way that in the world, there is only one buddha who appears. Never is it said that there are two."[41]

41. My translation is based on Hu Shih's *Two Newly Edited Texts*, 281–82.

Clearly, in Shenhui's vision of the Bodhidharma lineage what matters is establishing a defendable form of *leadership,* one that he hopes to take hold of. And by setting the robe before the reader as the item that makes visible the private and invisible transmission of truth from one master to the next, we get more evidence that early Chan writers understood the difficulties involved in publicly claiming to privately own tradition. Shenhui seems to be betting that, with the robe supposedly on hand— or at least down in Shaozhou—this new history of the Bodhidharma family will look legitimate because, after all, *there's the robe to prove it.*

Chongyuan wants clarification about the one-master-per-generation rule and first seeks to draw out the difference between receiving transmission and achieving enlightenment.

> Chongyuan asks, "Everyone took Shenxiu [not *Shenhui*] to be one who had achieved the fruit of the path and to be an inconceivable person. How come he can't be permitted to be the sixth patriarch?" Shenhui answered, "It is because Chan master [Hong]ren didn't transmit to Shenxiu. So even if later he has obtained the fruit of the path, he is still not permitted to be the sixth patriarch. Why? Because Chan master [Hong]ren didn't give him a prediction [of buddhahood], so it is not permitted.[42]

Here generic enlightenment and inherited enlightenment are notably separated. The transmission of truth from Hongren is suddenly distinguishable from "the fruit of the path," and is to be understood as the sole basis for being a patriarch. According to Shenhui, masters aren't enlightened in some basic way that has to do with mastering Buddhist truths, but rather they are enlightened through a unique transmission from the previous figure in the Bodhidharma lineage. Thus, in effect, Shenhui's notion of transmission is really a kind of coronation: it is the magical (and legal) Thing that makes the next master the king of Buddhism, and this gift is separate from any generic awakening. Shenhui then argues that taking a robe to be the mark of buddha-to-buddha transmission was established back in India. In fact, he can point to a well-known Indian

42. Ibid., 283.

story about the Buddha giving one of his disciples—Mahākāśyapa—a robe and installing him inside a mountain (!) to wait for the coming Buddha, Maitreya, who will in the distant future come to collect this garment.

Shenhui was creative in other ways with the Indian side of Bodhidharma's family. To see what he was after on this front, we have to remember that in the Faru biography, and then again in Du Fei's *Record*, there was a gap of about one thousand years between the mini-lineage of patriarchs who followed the Buddha (Ānanda, Madhyāntika, Śānāvasa, etc.) and the patriarchs whom Bodhidharma supposedly generated in China in the sixth and seventh centuries. In those early genealogies, the information about the Indian patriarchs who descended from the Buddha was, apparently, taken from Huiyuan's preface to Dharmatrāta's *Meditation Sūtra*—a text dated to the first part of the fifth century. And yet the Dharmatrāta figure—the supposed author of the *Meditation Sūtra*—also came with his own little mini-lineage of several masters, who are mentioned in Huiyuan's preface and in the *Meditation Sūtra* itself.[43] Shenhui's crucial invention was to hook these three lineages together to make one continuous conduit running from the Buddha to Dharmatrātra to Bodhidharma and then into China, down to himself.

To make this fusion of the three lineages seem plausible, Shenhui simply claimed that Bodhidharma and Dharmatrāta were one and the same person and that the lineage of the five masters descending from the Buddha (Ānanda, Madhyāntika, Śānāvasa, etc. from Huiyuan's preface) poured *directly* into that little lineage related to Dharmatrāta who now, according to Shenhui, is none other than Bodhidharma himself. He also added in a certain [Maha]kāśyapa, preceding Ānanda, as the Buddha's direct heir. Apparently sensing that this messy synthesis would be challenged, Shenhui provided the following exchange in *Defining the True and False* to buttress his claims:

43. The nature of this mini-lineage in Huiyuan's preface to the *Meditation Sūtra* is quite complicated; see Elizabeth Morrison, *The Power of Patriarchs: Qisong and Lineage in Chinese Buddhism* (Leiden: Brill, 2010), 24ff.

Chongyuan asked Shenhui: "Based on what can you know that Bodhidharma was the eighth generation in India?" The monk [Shenhui] responded, "[It can be known,] according to the preface to the *Meditation Sūtra* where it clearly explains the number of generations in India. Moreover, when Huike personally asked Bodhidharma [about this] at Shaolin Monastery on Mount Song, Bodhidharma answered that it was just as it was in [Huiyuan's] preface to the *Meditation Sūtra*.[44]

This passage clearly shows Shenhui's interest in making his rearrangement of the truth-fathers seem factual. Thus, he has Chongyuan ask about evidence for this version of the lineage, and then he has key figures in the lineage—Bodhidharma and Huike—recount Shenhui's version of the "historical facts." Thus, the masters and the historian of the masters—Shenhui, that is—are shown to be in full agreement about the history of truth and the truth of history, as they must be for all this to appear truthful.

After this section of the text that presents these clever and deceitful inventions regarding Bodhidharma's lineage in India, Shenhui turns to attack the current Buddhist leadership of eighth-century China—Puji, in particular, but Shenxiu and his other descendants, as well—whom he refers to as the "Northern School." Here Shenhui explains that China has been the victim of an elaborate conspiracy since Shenxiu never received Hongren's transmission, as Du Fei and others had claimed, and thus Shenxiu and Puji can not be counted as dharma kings. He then charges Puji with willfully fabricating lineage claims, violently attacking Huineng's remains, and installing a bogus ancestral hall on Mount Song—that "Hall of the Seven Patriarchs" mentioned at the beginning of this chapter. In detailing this supposed conspiracy, he also points to that place in Du Fei's text where it says that Hongren gave transmission to *both* Faru and Shenxiu, and argues that according to the rule of unique transmission, this story must be false. Of course, Shenhui, insofar as he had Wang Wei invent Huineng as Hongren's

44. Hu Shih, *Two Newly Edited Texts*, 295.

"real" descendant, is making these charges against Puji *precisely in the context of promoting some very similar narrative inventions himself.*

BEING A BUDDHA IN PUBLIC:
THE PLATFORM SERMON

There is one more Shenhui-related text that we need to consider, the long titled *Platform Sermon of Master [Shenhui] from Nanyang, the Sudden Teaching Which Leads to Liberation through the Chan Door of Directly Seeing the [Buddha-]Nature* (*Nanyang heshang dunjiao chanmen zhiliaoxing tanyu*).[45] This mid-eighth-century text demonstrates how Shenhui and/or his disciples were beginning to combine the new lineage claims with the performance of traditional public rituals.[46] In the ritual sequence that the *Platform Sermon* presents, the leader is first shown speaking directly to an audience and leading them through a very standard Mahāyāna ritual in which each member of the audience confesses his or her sins, takes refuge in the Buddha, dharma, and sangha, and vows to attain enlightenment, and so on. Structurally, the ritual format looks traditional enough, but we shouldn't miss that it appears enhanced by a certain urgency since the leader calls on every member in the audience to become involved in the search for Buddhist perfection *today*. Though the leader of the rites remains nameless throughout the text—presumably since anyone who took themselves to be a master could step into this role—his

---

45. See ibid., 225ff.; for an English translation, see Walter Liebenthal, "The Sermon of Shen-hui," *Asia Major,* n.s., 3, no. 2 (1953): 132–55. For an edited text and notes, see also Yang Zengwen, ed., *Shenhui heshang chanyu lu,* 3–14.

46. In addition to the *Platform Sūtra's* use of the ritual formats in Shenhui's *Platform Sermon,* one can find a nonsectarian application of this model in another Dunhuang text, the *Dacheng wusheng fangbian men;* see *T* (no. 2834), 85.1273b. This text is also called the *Five Expedient Means* (*Wu fangbian*); for a translation, see McRae, *Northern School,* 171–96. For thoughtful reflections on the combination of lineage claims and ritual practices at Dunhuang, see also Sam van Schaik, *Tibetan Zen: Discovering a Lost Tradition* (Boston: Snow Lion, 2015).

function in redistributing the totality of Buddhism is made obvious when he intones:

> Today, I take the unsurpassed dharma of the Way and share it with the friends [the audience]. If you accept these words, then the six perfections [of the Mahāyāna], and all the various buddhas [as numerous as] the sands of the Ganges, as well as the 84,000 doors of samādhi, will, *in one moment*, enter into the bodies and minds of the audience.[47]

Clearly, in this sequence the leader appears to own and control the totality of Buddhism—the six perfections, all the buddhas, the 84,000 samādhis, and so on—and promises to deliver, "today" and "in one moment," this perfect form of Buddhism to anyone on site, provided that they accept these words and the whole premise of the arrangement, especially the assumption that a local Chinese leader could make such an offer.

The relationship of the leader to the participants has another twist to it: in reading the *Platform Sermon,* and even in the lines just quoted above, one can't miss the way that it is designed to produce intense desire for Buddhist goals, perhaps not unlike the way tent revivals whipped up sentiment among evangelicals in nineteenth-century America. What is odd, however, is that the leader also explains that one shouldn't desire Buddhism—that one shouldn't want enlightenment, or nirvana, or buddhahood. The leader, in fact, begins by not too subtly identifying the members of the audience as sinners, and, worse, sinners for desiring to be out of sin. In short, the audience is castigated for desiring to be where the leader supposedly is—in the sphere of enlightenment. This passage on the sin of desiring Buddhism comes in the first third of the text and works around the explanation of two types of desire:

> Friends, listen carefully as I explain deluded mind for you. What is "deluded mind"? Everyone here today came with greed and lust for wealth, sex, men, women, and so on, and was thinking of gardens, forests, and houses. This is mundane delusion, and you must not have this mind. As for subtle desire, you all don't know about it. What is "subtle desire"? [It is]

47. Hu Shih, *Two Newly Edited Texts,* 248.

when your mind hears of *bodhi*, and that incites [the desire] to grasp *bodhi*, or when your mind hears of nirvana and that incites [the desire] to grasp nirvana. Or, again, when you hear of emptiness, that incites [the desire] to grasp on to emptiness [and similarly] for purity and samādhi. This is delusion and is also a dharma fetter and a dharma view [in the negative sense of the term]—if one has such desires, one isn't going to be liberated.[48]

This passage establishes that the leader knows the audience, and he knows them to be a greedy and desirous lot. They all came to the meeting with their minds full of desires for the coarsest of things—money, sex, and property. This accusation presumably wouldn't have offended the audience, whose generic evil had been broadly exclaimed at the beginning of that confession sequence that began: "Friends, the mouths of commoners [the audience, that is] are filled with limitless evil talk and their minds are full of limitless evil thoughts, and [thus] they cycle for a long time in samsara and don't obtain liberation."[49] Hence, from the outset the text depicts two types of people in the world: commoners destined to cycle in samsara and those purified of desire who will win liberation. However, this division in humanity is further refined by creating the categories of coarse and subtle desire, since the leader also accuses the audience of desiring Buddhism and the positive items advertised in Buddhist discourses, such as nirvana, purity, and emptiness. Thus, the leader's teachings seems to include a rather daunting prohibition: if you desire those Buddhist achievements that are being dangled in front of you, then you will, by definition, fail to acquire them. Moreover, there is nothing about the discourse suggesting that anyone is to step over the line dividing commoners from the master. Surely the leader's status isn't in question, and though the commoners are to be convinced that they have been purified in some measure, they are never allowed to graduate into the master's role. Likewise, they presumably aren't being given a copy of the text at the end of the rites so

48. Ibid., 234.
49. Ibid., 226.

that they could run these meetings themselves. In short, though total freedom and enlightenment are supposedly available—today!—the basic master-slave paradigm organizing this event is expected to continue on as before.

CONCLUSIONS

Given the evidence above it ought to be abundantly clear that early Chan writing reveals a stable and confident will to improve the past. Thus, for instance, we saw authors steadily improve Huike's identity until he appeared to gain the dharma with that dramatic arm sacrifice, after standing in the snow all night long. Likewise, Hongren just gets more and more Daoist in his insouciant and all-natural practice of Buddhism. At the same time, the lineage stretching from the Buddha to Shenhui was stitched up by making Dharmatrāta and Bodhidharma out to be one person, and so on. Seeing how these figures were developed and polished in this literary "floating world" where the past was still sort of present and available for reworking, we ought to be ready for the impressive sculpting of the figure of Huineng—the topic of the next chapter.

The take-home point is this: as various textual claims about the Bodhidharma family gave birth to more versions of themselves, Chan appears to have been, first and foremost, an expanding set of writing skills that authors relied on, generation after generation, to present masters in just such a manner so as to: (1) revitalize and romanticize the image of Buddhism in China – especially for the elite, and (2) establish new, and more Chinese-looking, models for controlling leadership positions within the Buddhist hierarchy. Key to both these goals was the promise of bringing the perfected past into the present. Taking just this perspective helps us see a common theme running between Shenhui's "live" dialogues, his "public" dharma combat with Chongyuan, and his *Platform Sermon* since all three "events" require the master to play the role of a living buddha who, grounded in the perfection of the past, promises to deliver perfect Buddhism, today! Even though in each case drawing the perfected past into the present was only achievable *in the floating world of literature,* it is still the case that the authors were working hard to make this fantasy appear as a plausible reality. Making this fusion of the perfect past with the present appear real and uninvented is, I believe, a key element in Chan Buddhism.

5

Truth, Conspiracy, and Careful Writing

A New Version of Huineng

OVERVIEW

After Shenhui invented Huineng in the mid-eighth century, three texts appeared that reworked the figure of Huineng for new purposes: the *Biography of the Great Master of Caoqi (Caoqi dashi biezhuan)*, the *Platform Sūtra of the Sixth Patriarch (Liuzu tanjing)*, and the *Record of the Dharma-Jewel through the Generations (Lidai fabao ji)*. These three texts, which I explore in this chapter and the next—are quite different in style and agenda, and yet it isn't hard to see the enthusiasm they share for taking Huineng away from Shenhui and putting him to work endorsing other projects. Presumably, it was the initial success that Shenhui had in pushing the appealing story of Huineng into the public arena that led others to adopt Huineng for their own purposes.

That these three texts include conspiracy theories isn't surprising. As we saw in chapter 4, one of Shenhui's strategies in *Defining the True and False* was to charge that the genealogy of the Bodhidharma family that had been officially accepted at court was fraudulent and maintained by unscrupulous Buddhist leaders. What is particularly impressive about these three texts is that they take the trope of conspiracy and shift it from a direct charge leveled against the competition—Shenhui's strategy—and turn the accusation into a objective-looking history in which an invisible and omniscient narrator gradually gets the reader to "see" that a conspiracy has been perpetrated. Thus, each of these three "histories" reveals not only a new version of the Bodhidharma family but also how and why someone else's (bad) history came to be accepted into the public record. Hence, these narratives count as a kind of meta-writing in which one of the key elements of the story is to show how *someone else* tried to write the Bodhidharma story—how *someone else* organized a plot, in both senses of the term, that is.

Recognizing this theme of conspiracy in this strata of Chan writing is particularly thought-provoking when we remember that two of the more prominent Indian texts in the early Mahāyāna tradition—the *Lotus Sūtra* and the *Vimalakīrti*—are also structured as conspiracy theories.[1] Both these Indian texts develop their positions regarding the final truth-of-tradition by explaining that traditional Buddhism was nothing but a fictional construct that the Buddha purposefully generated in order to prepare his followers for the later revelation of real tradition, as found in either of these texts. In effect, both Indian texts work, first, to denigrate older versions of tradition, and then, second, to authorize themselves as the truest versions of tradition—just as Chan genealogies do—and to this end, the Indian texts set up elaborate split-screen dramas in which readers learn how to distinguish good versions of tradition from bad—again, just as Chan genealogies do. Given that both the *Lotus Sūtra* and the *Vimalakīrti* were very influential in East Asian Buddhism, and were often cited in early Chan works, it is likely that the Chan authors wrote up their own conspiracy theories with these earlier Indian precedents in mind.

Tracking the theme of conspiracy also has implications for how we interpret the "rhetoric of negation" that these three texts revel in. And by "rhetoric of negation" I simply mean those "zenny" sounding statements that deny the reality of basic elements in the Buddhist tradition—

---

1. I provide this kind of analysis of these two texts in *Text as Father: Paternal Seductions in Early Mahāyāna Buddhist Literature* (Berkeley: University of California Press, 2005), chaps. 2, 3, and 6.

claiming, for instance, that there is no meditation to perform, no dharma to understand, or that good and bad don't exist, or that no-thought and non-action (*wuwei*) are the essence of tradition. Of course, we have already seen several examples of this radical-sounding rhetoric—in fact, even the *Two Entrances* speaks of tradition in unthinkable terms, at least in the First Entrance. What remains to be clarified is how this negative rhetoric was so easily paired with various conspiracy narratives, narratives that appear to weave carefully around readers' assumptions about truth and tradition. If it can be shown that this rhetoric of negation was meaningfully combined with these deftly woven plots, then Chan authors will likely appear much more "philosophically" interesting than some modern interpreters have thought.

The key point here is that as Chan authors developed elaborate conspiracy theories, they show themselves to be rather adept at handling readers' consciousness in what we would today call a "phenomenological" manner, in the sense of managing the moment-to-moment way that readers move through information, building up opinions and conclusions along the way. However, just this refined sense for the reader's *processual consciousness* is precisely the opposite of the radical negations that issue forth from the masters at various moments in the narrative, statements that are characterized by the utter disavowal of *anything processual or cumulative*. Thus, though *logically* the radical negations—which are held to be the essence of the masters' teachings—might appear destined to ruin the possibility of constructing discourse, narrative, and historical accounts of Bodhidharma's family, in fact, they don't. Instead, and this might surprise some readers, the negative language seems to be part of the plot, adding exciting moments when authentic-looking Buddhist statements come bursting forth from the background matrix to enliven and ratify otherwise fairly mundane accounts of these Chinese masters. Figuring out how to think about this increasingly well-managed balance between narrative and negation has, arguably, to be at the center of any historical discussion of Chan literature.

With some sense for what is at stake here in focusing on "the truth of conspiracy," let's turn to consider some of the details of the first of these three provocative texts.

BIOGRAPHY OF THE GREAT MASTER OF CAOQI

The *Biography of the Great Master of Caoqi* presents a history of conspiracy that isn't as developed as the one in the *Platform Sūtra*, but it is nonetheless a good place to start exploring these more involved histories of Bodhidharma's family.[2] Modern scholars believe the text was written around 780, though it appears that material was later added to it. The text only survived in manuscript-form in Japan, and though it isn't clear how widely it ever circulated in China, chunks of its narrative show up in several prominent Song sources (see chapter 8 for more details). The first half of the *Biography* explains Huineng's meteoric rise to be the leader of Chinese Buddhism and then how, after his death, his robe and remains were installed at Baolin Monastery, in the village of Caoqi, apparently in modern-day Guangdong province. The basic agenda of the narrative appears parallel to Shaolin Monastery's efforts to present Faru as a recently living buddha, with the goal in both cases being to install the master's remains on monastic grounds as a kind of resident buddha-spirit. The second half of the text, not considered here, develops other agendas, unrelated to Baolin Monastery.

The *Biography* begins by explaining how in 502 a certain Indian master named Zhiyao (n.d.) came to Caoqi, built a monastery, and predicted that in 170 years, a perfect master—a "dharma jewel," that is—would come and teach there. With this Indian prediction in place—and, obviously this Zhiyao figure resembles Bodhidharma in the way he provides an Indian endorsement for a Chinese product—the story then jumps ahead 170 years to explain how Huineng arrived at the monastery as a day lab-

2. For a useful discussion of the text and its title, see John Jorgensen, *Inventing Huineng, the Sixth Patriarch: Hagiography and Biography in Early Ch'an* (Leiden: Brill, 2005), 577–95.

orer. At first we see how ordinary Huineng is, but then we learn that he had a marvelous talent: although completely unschooled in Buddhist thought and literature, he understood Buddhist sutras naturally, much like Hongren in Du Fei's *Record*. One evening after work, a nun recited the hugely complex *Nirvana Sūtra*, which regularly discourses on buddha-nature, and Huineng immediately understands it. The next morning he explains the meaning of the text to her, and she is dumbfounded, particularly because she knows he is illiterate. As she expresses her amazement, Huineng says, "The principle of buddha-nature isn't something that can be explained in terms of the written word. So why be amazed that I currently do not know how to read?"[3]

This brief vignette establishes three things. First, Huineng is presented as one able to provide a final "reading" of tradition, a reading that isn't based on actual reading, but that nevertheless supposedly gets "behind" the sutra's language to understand directly the essential principle of buddha-nature. Second, Huineng does this final "reading" of tradition in a natural, effortless, unmotivated, and unassailable manner. Third, this final knowledge of Huineng's also allows him to understand the relationship between truth and language, and thus he can confidently declare that the truth of tradition "isn't something that can be explained in terms of the written word." When the monks at Baolin Monastery learn of Huineng's instinctive knowledge of the buddha-nature, they, much like a Greek chorus, confirm the reality of the situation, declaring: "Understanding such as this is based on an innate ability to self-awaken and is not something that [ordinary] humans can achieve. It is fitting that you should become a monk and live here at Baolin Monastery."[4]

Huineng then stays with the monks cultivating the Dao (*xiu dao*) for three years, thereby fulfilling Zhiyao's prediction. Later, he hears of Chan master Yuan living in a cave in Lechang County (located in the

3. Ibid., 679; here and in some of the other citations from Jorgensen's translation in this chapter, I have introduced small changes. For the Chinese text, see *X* (no. 1598), 86.49a.3, www.cbeta.org/result/normal/X86/1598_001.htm.

4. Jorgensen, *Inventing Hui-neng*, 680.

north of modern-day Guangdong province) and goes to study seated meditation with him. Once there, he hears another sutra recited—this time it is the *Ascetic Sūtra*—and, sighing, says, "The sutra's meaning being like this, what am I doing now sitting in vain?"[5] In this sequence, it would seem that the author wants us to see that, just as Huineng first overcame the need to read and interpret the sutras, he now is overcoming the need to practice seated meditation, which, for an all-natural buddha like Huineng, could only seem like a waste of time. The mention of asceticism in the title of this otherwise unknown sutra seems to set the stage for what follows: when his master advises him to seek out Hongren on East Mountain in Huangmei, Huineng sets out alone and barefoot. The challenges of the trip appear even more severe when we learn that along the way he had to face down "many ferocious tigers."

Once he is with Hongren, the story becomes complicated. In their first conversation, Huineng announces that he came to Hongren to become a buddha, a claim that to some degree undercuts the natural buddha wisdom he has already been shown to possess. Hongren, for his part, assumes—for some unexplained reason—that since Huineng is from southern China, he can't become a buddha. Hongren's position is, of course, contrary to a very basic tenet in Buddhism: Buddhist truth is, by definition, available to anyone, regardless of their origins. Huineng seems to know this, and he makes just this point at the conclusion of his conversation with Hongren. What this brief bit of dharma combat demonstrates is that, apparently, Huineng has little or nothing to learn from Hongren since, as with his earlier "reading" of the *Nirvana Sūtra*, he seems to naturally have a correct understanding of Buddhism. And, as before, this mini-drama with Hongren is sealed with an enthusiastic appraisal when the narrator concludes: "One should say that he [Huineng] knew his own buddha-nature and was suddenly awakened to true thusness. What a profound marvel! What a marvel!"[6]

5. Ibid., 680.
6. Ibid., 681.

In the next bit of action, Huineng is sent to the kitchen to do manual work. There, for eight months he "trod the pestle," grinding rice. The ascetic motif is emphasized when we learn that, "hating the fact that he was light, he tied a large rock to his waist to give the pestle extra downward force, thereby harming his waist and feet."[7] Hongren notices this and asks him if it hurts. Huineng, shifting levels in a way that echoes lines from the *Vimalakīrti*, responds, "I do not perceive that there is a body. Who says it hurts?"[8] The reader is prepared for Huineng's insouciance vis-à-vis his body since just before this exchange it was mentioned that Huineng remained unfazed by the teasing he received while working in the kitchen, having "forgotten his body on account of the Dao."[9] Apparently impressed with Huineng's asceticism and quick wit, Hongren has Huineng come to his room at night and they further discuss the meaning of buddha-nature. This turns into an occasion for Huineng to rehearse his version of that standard claim regarding the deep sameness of buddhas and commoners. Huineng says, "Buddha-nature is not partial, and there is no difference between you and me; in fact, all sentient beings are without difference. It is simply due to one's capacity whether or not it [buddha-nature] is manifested or obscured."[10] As Huineng teaches Hongren about the universally pervasive quality of buddha-nature, we see yet another example of that Chinese predilection for *first* declaring the thoroughgoing sameness of all members of the religious hierarchy, and *then,* in the next sentence, reestablishing the hierarchy based on whether or not one recognizes this sameness.

In this section of their conversation, Hongren clearly serves as the straight man for Huineng's enlightened discourse, but the topic soon changes, and Hongren is put in charge of revealing important information about the lineage of truth-fathers. And here a fascinating thing

7. Ibid., 681–82.
8. Ibid., 682.
9. Ibid., 681.
10. Ibid., 682.

happens. The lineage history that our author puts in Hongren's mouth attempts to count a more plausible number of masters from the Indian Buddha up to eighth-century China. Thus after mentioning the first four figures after the Buddha—Mahākāśyapa, Ānanda, Śanavāsa, and Upagupta, a series that had been cited, in somewhat different forms, from Faru's biography up to Shenhui's *Defining the True and False*— Hongren mentions in passing that there were, in sum, twenty-eight masters in India, with the last being Dharmatrāta. He then explains that this Dharmatrāta was also the first patriarch in China, the one who transmitted truth to Huike. Given this list, it is clear that this author has merged Dharmatrāta with Bodhidharma, as Shenhui had done.[11] But he has done something else as well: since Hongren is shown counting the Indian patriarchs as twenty-eight, it would seem that the author is drawing on that list of the twenty-four Indian patriarchs that first appeared in the *History of the Transmission of the Dharma-Treasury* (see chapter 2). Master Simha is mentioned a few lines later, and Simha is the last of the twenty-four masters in the *History of the Transmission of the Dharma-Treasury* so, while the names of the twenty-eight patriarchs aren't all given in the *Biography,* it would seem that that list of twenty-four was drawn on to generate this slightly expanded set of twenty-eight Indian patriarchs. Though mention of these twenty-eight Indian masters might appear to be inconsequential here, this list would soon solidify into the most enduring version of the Chan tradition's history of itself.

Having established the Indian side of the lineage, Hongren quickly provides the now standard series of Huike-Sengcan-Daoxin-Hongren for the Chinese side. With this version of the lineage of truth-fathers now fully clarified, Hongren gives Huineng dharma-transmission. At

---

11. As we have seen, Shenhui's *Defining the True and False* mentions only eight masters in India from the Buddha up to Dharmatrāta, aka Bodhidharma, but another work associated with Shenhui, a poem called "The Record Revealing the Lineage" (*Xianzong ji*), mentions twenty-eight masters in India, though no names are given; see *T* (no. 2076), 51.458a.27. For an English translation, see Robert Zeuschner, "The *Hsien Tsung Chi* (An Early Ch'an [Zen] Buddhist Text)," *Journal of Chinese Philosophy* 3 (1976): 253–68.

the same time, Hongren gives Huineng the robe of transmission, claiming that it comes from the Buddha in India—something that not even Shenhui had ventured to say. The conversation between Hongren and Huineng then rehearses a version of that passage from Shenhui's *Defining the True and False* where Shenhui explained to Chongyuan how the robe functions to identify the owner of total truth, the king of Buddhism, as it were.

With the transmission history established, and the robe handed over to Huineng, the conspiracy element in the narrative comes to the fore. Actually, there had already been several hints of conspiracy. For instance, when the other disciples noticed Huineng in Hongren's room on the night of the transmission, Hongren dispersed them, "knowing that his disciples would not understand."[12] Thus Hongren's special relationship to Huineng is cast as something that Hongren thought he had to keep apart from the more public relations he maintained with his other disciples. This gap between Hongren's public disciples and his special disciple, Huineng, becomes clearer after the transmission moment since Hongren urges Huineng to flee and explains that he is going to have a lot of problems, primarily because: "Later there will be an evil dharma (*xiefa*) contending for success. Closely attaching itself to the princes and great ministers, it will [attempt to] cover over our correct dharma (*wo zhengfa*). Go well."[13] This is a revealing line since it shows the author setting up that split-screen reading of correct and incorrect dharma, while also making clear that the incorrect (and dangerous) version is the one taken up by the court, at least at first.

In this sequence of events we can also see how Huineng is being depicted as a kind of underground master who, once entrusted with the full truth of tradition, this truth's history, and, of course, the Buddha's robe, slips out the back door unseen, even as the reader learns that he is destined to fight it out with the wicked imposters that the court had

12. Jorgensen, *Inventing Hui-neng*, 682.
13. Ibid., 684.

ratified. The violence of this coming conflict is foreshadowed when we learn that as Huineng flees from Hongren's monastery, he is chased by hordes of angry people.[14] The implications of this situation are made clearer when we learn that three days later, Hongren's students ask Hongren why he isn't teaching anymore, and he replies that the buddha-dharma has left, traveling south, and that "*Later* you will know (why) I now do not speak."[15] Here, the story confirms that the transmission of truth and tradition to Huineng was a secret handoff that baffled and angered Hongren's other disciples. Thus, the story has in fact worked up two conspiracies: the one that Hongren organizes with Huineng against the monks in the monastery; and the vaguer conspiracy that the evil monks at court have orchestrated against Hongren and his "correct dharma." Of course, the two conspiracies rely on each other since Hongren's secret actions are designed to combat the lies and violence of the supposedly bogus masters at court.

PROVE IT

Having presented, in an objective-looking manner, the underground history of the "real" ownership of Buddhist truth, the narrative switches to lauding Huineng's prowess. Here we have evidence of the growing ability of Tang authors to dramatize a master's domination of tradition *for the reader.* Thus, we learn that after five years of hiding out among hunters along the border, Huineng attends some lectures on the *Nirvana Sūtra* given by a certain dharma master Yinzong, at Longxing monastery. Later in the evening, students at the monastery, observing a flag blowing in the wind, argue over the nature of perception. After various opinions are offered, "Master Huineng, in a loud voice, stopped them, saying, 'It isn't as though the flag has some supplementary kind of motion. What is referred to as 'motion' is really the person's mind moving.'"[16]

14. As with many elements in this story, this has a parallel in the *Platform Sūtra*.
15. Jorgensen, *Inventing Hui-neng,* 684; emphasis added.
16. Ibid., 686.

On the next day, when Yinzong learns of this supposed solution to the problem of how mind and matter interact, he calls Huineng to his room. Before a philosophical discussion can ensue, Yinzong first asks to see the robe of transmission. That Yinzong makes this demand apropos of nothing gives the impression that the newly invented "facts" about the transmission of the robe *within this text* were in fact already widely known and accepted around the empire, making it perfectly natural for Yinzong to ask to see it. Underscoring this point, we watch as Yinzong also briefly recounts a detail or two about Huineng's final days with Hongren, thereby again giving the reader the sense that those details, though apparently just invented in this very narrative, were facts well established for the Buddhist community at large, and thus it should appear normal that a random monk like Yinzong would know of them.

Then the discussion veers into more heady topics as Yinzong and Huineng turn to compare interpretations of the *Nirvana Sūtra*. Here the narrative comes full circle, since Huineng is now again explaining what the *Nirvana Sūtra* really means. What is different this time is that he is lecturing an authority figure, Yinzong, who not only supposedly specialized in the *Nirvana Sūtra* but, unlike the nun, is also clearly in charge of a monastery. At this point in the story, Huineng's right to contradict this establishment figure seems appropriate, given the recently revealed history in which Huineng's mastery of tradition was formally recognized by Hongren. Leaving nothing to the imagination, the narrative adds that after their conversation, Yinzong "bowed devoutly and asked to serve as his [Huineng's] pupil."[17] The next day, standing in front of his own disciples, Yinzong says,

> "What has made me happy? That I am an ordinary person who has not had to wait to sit at the feet of a dharma-bodied bodhisattva. The *Nirvana Sūtra* that I have preached to you is just like tiles and gravel. Last night I asked [the] postulant Lu [Huineng] to come by my room to discuss its meaning— now *that* [explanation] was just like gold and jade. Do you believe me or not?

17. Ibid., 688.

This sage is the person to whom Hongren of East Mountain transmitted the dharma. If you do not believe me, ask the postulant [Huineng] to take out the dharma-transmission robe and show it to you." Once they had seen it, they all bowed to the ground and expressed deep faith.[18]

Within this sequence of supposedly historical events, Huineng is now being *publicly recognized* for having already *privately received* total tradition from Hongren, and all this public recognition inside the text is being displayed to the reader as a fait accompli. That this literary gesture matches the front section of Shenhui's *Defining the True and False,* as well as the grand teaching moment given to Faru in his biography at Shaolin Monastery, leaves little doubt that this narrative strategy was solidifying into a standard trope.

In the flurry of activity that follows, several important details of closure get worked out. For instance, we learn that Huineng finally gets ordained as a monk, and this event is staged to highlight how traditional figures supposedly endorsed him. Taking care of another piece of unfinished business, the author explains that Shenhui, as an impudent thirteen-year-old, did receive a secret transmission (and a public beating) from Huineng, but not the robe, giving the sense thereby that that transmission was incomplete and certainly of secondary importance. Including these details also works to explain how some might have mistakenly taken Shenhui to be Huineng's real successor. Of course, this gesture functions in a manner parallel to the way Du Fei explained that Bodhidharma did, in fact, promote the *Laṅkāvatāra Sūtra*, but only as a second-rate technique.

With these matters resolved, the narrative picks back up, recounting what happened as Huineng left Yinzong's monastery to head back to Baolin Monastery at Caoqi. There, before he dies, he will exchange letters with the imperial court, letters that show the emperor Gaozong (r. 649–83) confirming Huineng's status as the new Chinese buddha. In one of these letters that supposedly came from the throne, the emperor

18. Ibid., 688.

is made to say that Shenxiu (along with Lao'an) knew of Huineng and had explained to the emperor that Huineng was in fact the real inheritor of tradition. The letter supposedly read: "The two virtuous monks, Lao'an and Shenxiu, being superior, were made the chiefs of the monks. When I [the emperor] enquired [about Buddhist matters], they repeatedly recommended that in the south there is Chan master [Hui]neng, who secretly received the prediction (of buddhahood) from the grand master Hongren, and transmits Bodhidharma's robe and bowl as proof of [his possession of the] dharma (*yiwei faxin*)."[19]

This new endorsement of Huineng, brazenly put in the mouth of a famous seventh century emperor, not only undermines the Chan masters formerly recognized by the throne in the early part of the eighth century, but goes the extra mile by having those long dead masters—Shenxiu and Lao'an—publicly endorse this new history of the Bodhidharma lineage and, in passing, admit their own second-rate status.[20] And, as our author makes the older authority figures endorse his new claims, we see a fine repetition of what Du Fei did to Faru in his *Record* when he claimed that Faru said on his deathbed, "Go study with Shenxiu." In both cases, the authors assumed that new claims to authority would appear more believable if old authority figures vouched for them, thereby making those older figures commit a kind symbolic suicide.

In sum, the narrative presents Huineng's ownership of truth and tradition as a reality confirmed by four sources of authority: (1) Hongren, who stands as the most recent representative of the Bodhidharma lineage; (2) Yinzong, supposedly a well-regarded master of the sutras, and the *Nirvana Sūtra*, in particular; (3) the emperor Gaozong; and (4) the truth-fathers of the older Bodhidharma lineage—Shenxiu and

19. Ibid., 691.
20. Shenxiu wasn't recognized as a "Teacher of the Nation" until some twenty-five years after Gaozong's death, so our author has created a dialogue that is historically impossible simply in terms of timing. Lao'an, for his part, was invented even later—and likely never existed.

Lao'an—as purportedly cited by the emperor. To this list of four endorsements, we should add another in the form of Nature, since when Huineng dies, all sorts of spectacular "natural" phenomena will be observed, proving that Nature too knows who Huineng really is. Supposedly after his death, the robe is installed at Baolin Monastery in Caoqi, but then the narrative moves on to explain how various other figures laid hold of the robe and took it to the capital and other places, making it appear that the initial narrative was significantly altered with later additions.

Rather than continuing into the chaos of the second half of the text, let's look closely at the involved conversation that Huineng supposedly had with the imperial courier, Xuejian, who had come down to Caoqi to demand that Huineng come to visit the emperor at the capital. Here it is important to see how a number of wild-sounding negations—the negation of truth, Buddhism, morality, and so on—live comfortably next to the rather worldly claim that Huineng was the king of Buddhism, and recognized as such by Buddhists and the throne alike. Not only does this language of negation work perfectly well with these status claims, it also seems to come forth from a thick stack of literary precedents. Seeing that these powerful-sounding negations were recycled from earlier texts, we have to imagine that Chan authors were avidly sifting through their libraries in their ongoing efforts to script the image of the perfect owner of tradition, an owner ironically presented as free of the literary tradition and of Buddhism in general.

REALLY POSITIVE NEGATIVE RHETORIC

At the beginning of their discussion, Xuejian asks Huineng to explain the relationship between meditation and enlightenment. Huineng responds by completely denying a connection:

> "The Dao is due to the mind's enlightenment. How can it be [found] in sitting? The *Diamond Sūtra* says that 'If a person says the Buddha sits or lies down, that person does not understand the meaning of what I preach....

Ultimately there is no gaining and no realization of the Dao, so why prefer sitting in meditation?'"[21]

In this hard-hitting answer, which seems to exclude meditation from the Buddhist tradition—a rather radical claim, to be sure—we see the author dramatizing Huineng's mastery of tradition by granting him the right to define what is and isn't necessary for achieving the highest levels of Buddhist awakening. And, given Huineng's supposed distance from the literary tradition, we shouldn't overlook the irony of showing Huineng shore up his negation of meditation with a sutra quote, one supposedly taken from the *Diamond Sūtra*.[22]

That these radical negations of the Buddhist tradition work perfectly well in the context of normal concerns regarding etiquette, hierarchy, and politics, is clear in the courier's response:

> Xuejian said, "If I go [back] to court, the Holy One [the emperor] is sure to question me, so I humbly request you, Master, to instruct me in the essence of mind (*xinyao*), so that I can transmit [those teachings] to the Holy One and to the students of the Dao in the capital, so that it will be like a lamp spreading light, and all those in the dark will be illuminated and there will be light without end."[23]

Even though Xuejian has rather eloquently set up this lamp metaphor to dramatize the imminent success of Huineng's teaching at the capital, Huineng negates it all, claiming, "The Dao lacks light and dark. Light and dark have the sense of replacing each other.... The *Vimalakīrti* says, 'The Dharma is incomparable because there is nothing that can relate to it.'"[24] Here, as with the Shenhui material, supposedly live Chinese discussions are getting filled out with sutra-talk in a manner

---

21. Jorgensen, *Inventing Hui-neng*, 692–93.

22. Actually, this exact passage isn't to be found in Kumarajiva's translation of the *Diamond Sūtra*, but there are others like it.

23. Jorgensen, *Inventing Hui-neng*, 693.

24. Ibid., 693, with changes. Jorgensen notes that this passage is found in chap. 3 of the *Vimalakīrti Sūtra, T* (no. 475), 14.540a. For the English, see *The Vimalakīrti Sūtra*, trans. Burton Watson (New York: Columbia University Press, 1997), 38.

such that the master always gets to inhabit the authority-structures established in the Indian sutras. Thus as with their first exchange, Huineng's initial negation rolls forward into an occasion for restaging lines from the Buddha, which now issue forth, uttered in full confidence, from the mouth of a Chinese master. Moreover, since Xuejian's lamp analogy evokes a passage from the fourth chapter of the *Vimalakīrti*, their whole conversation is, in effect, replaying the Indian text's own style of making meaning within that text's presentation of the play of form and nothingness. Thus, if we read this "conversation" in relation to the larger literary context to which it belongs, we can see that many exciting things are getting established in this exchange, even as everything is, on the surface, getting negated. Obviously, then, negation, when understood in terms of the particular *stuff-of-language in which it lives*—with its various signifiers of status and connectivity—can have a very positive role to play in the maintenance and reproduction of tradition.

Equally important to notice is that Huineng's negation of meditation and the reality of light and darkness, along with all other kinds of opposites, is completely useful for the more basic task at hand—providing the courier with teachings that he can take back to the emperor. Within the economy of this exchange, one can be sure that Huineng wouldn't be made to say, "Hey, forget about the capital and the emperor, those are just fabricated entities like light and darkness." Thus, this negative rhetoric, although threatening to explode both Buddhism and the logic of daily life, appears not to endanger or erode the practical concerns that structure the story and, instead, functions as a kind of spiritual capital since it constitutes a gift that can be handed over to the courier to be taken up to the emperor. Besides playing this role in the narrative, this staged negation of tradition also appears designed to elicit awe in the reader, who is, presumably, left wondering how the final nature of the universe could so thoroughly contravene the commonsense logic that we otherwise live with— the logic that takes light and dark to be real and distinctly different.

The conversation between Huineng and the courier winds along through several other topics, such as defining the nature of Mahāyāna

Buddhism and buddha-nature, until we get to a choice passage that seems to negate morality in a global manner. "The Master [Huineng] told Xuejian: 'If you want to take hold of the essence of mind (*xinyao*), [it is that] all good and evil are no-thought—the essence of mind is clear and quiescent, and its responsive function is natural."[25] As soon as this radical antinomianism is announced, Xuejian gets "greatly enlightened" and says:

> Master, today for the first time I know that we originally possess buddha-nature. In the past, I took it to be very distant. Today, for the first time I know that the supreme Dao is not far off, and if one practices, here it is! Today for the first time I know that nirvana is not far off and that all that one sees is *bodhi* [enlightenment]. Today for the first time I know that buddha-nature doesn't consider good and evil—it is without thought, without reflection, without action, and without abiding.[26]

With Xuejian's enlightenment depicted as a thoroughgoing antinomianism joined with an appreciation for the intimate and immediate presence of the ultimate goals of Buddhism—total truth and liberation *are right here!*—the courier respectfully takes leave of Huineng and returns to the emperor.

Our narrator hasn't explained how it was that this conversation with Huineng was preserved, but the courier supposedly takes some version of their exchange back to the emperor and, no surprise, all this casual, free-wheeling negation of good and evil simply results in the emperor writing another polite letter to Huineng, while also sending him a new robe and five hundred bolts of silk—a rather handsome gift, to be sure. In short, the most radical kind of negative language that refutes good and bad, and thought in general, rests very comfortably within the most standard Chinese concerns over status, politesse, and politics. We should even say that in this situation, radical negative rhetoric makes status, politesse and politics possible, since the author is apparently

25. Jorgensen, *Inventing Hui-neng*, 694.
26. Ibid., 694.

counting on this rhetoric of negation to appear perfectly appropriate in Huineng's message to the emperor. Nothing less would do.

CONCLUSIONS

Before we leave this narrative, it is worth trying to characterize the ingenuity so obviously on display here. On one level the entire text is another fine example of Buddhist politics—usual in China, with the goal being to prove the presence of pure tradition in this or that locale. On another level, though, I wonder if we don't also need to factor in a certain pleasure or playfulness in our assessment of what the text represents. Imagine the chutzpah it took for our author to brazenly put himself in charge of staging scenes in which a past emperor is shown submitting so thoroughly to Huineng—in writing!—while Huineng casually announces the scariest sounding negations the Buddhist tradition had thus far tolerated. Moreover, everything turns out splendidly—all tensions resolve, gifts flow from the emperor to the master, and all encounters are conducted with perfect Confucian decorum. In short, in this dramatic space, our author has created a wonderfully utopic world that he controls perfectly as he balances the various aspects of the Buddhist tradition that he cares most about—its India-based legitimacy, its Mahāyāna rhetorics of negation, its need to be accepted by the state, its desire to receive large gifts from important patrons, and so forth—while also making sure that his characters perform in accord with Confucian norms, even as Huineng stands out with his Daoist-looking mastery of Buddhism. Likewise, in this snow globe world of perfect Buddhism, our author can narrate the perfect transmission of Buddhism *in the first person,* since Xuejian wins total enlightenment from Huineng and then describes what his new vision involves. And it all happened suddenly and with no effort! Xuejian was there, just doing his job as an imperial runner, and, wham! he got the totality of the Buddhist tradition. Looked at this way, the scenes appear as a series of satisfying skits worked up by a master puppeteer, or rather, a puppeteer of masters, in which all powers, temporal and religious, perform according to his wishes.

Framing the series of events as a sophisticated and well-wrought drama leads to three basic perspectives. First, there is the issue of context: whatever is said in any one particular passage needs to be read against what happens in the surrounding scenes in order to get a fuller sense of how the text makes its meanings. Thus, it doesn't make much sense to focus exclusively on the negations of truth and tradition without noting how they are set within a carefully crafted play that presents these spectacles of negation for the reader's delight, and in strict accord with the author's various agendas. It's only in reckoning with that whole package that we can hope to get at the "philosophic" implications of the text.

Second, there's the question of intersubjectivity: it's clear that our author designed his narrative to carefully guide readers through the various scenes of action, negation, and the constitution of final authority and value. The author, in short, appears to trust his own vision of truth enough to design experiences for others in which he elicits and manages their desires, while also floating them out over the abyss of negation and emptiness, even as it all comes together in a satisfying conclusion, one that, not incidentally, is in accord with the author's basic agenda of enhancing the splendor of Baolin Monastery. Thus, since Huineng is essentially a hand puppet, all that he says or does in the story has to be understood in light of that hoped for outcome in which the reader comes to "see" these "events" as history, and not the result of a carefully designed advertisement for Baolin Monastery.

Third, there's the problem of cultural bias in our account of this text. Here, it has to be admitted that appreciation for the above art-related issues is precisely what modern readers tend to avoid when they read Chan texts, a fact that ought to raise questions about our limitations and biases as readers and thinkers. That is, once Chan literature is understood to be intimately involved in the creation of meaning *and* desire, then we have good grounds to question the modern obsession with finding meaning and truth *apart from art, context, and seduction.*

Clearly, though medieval Chan authors didn't want to posit their Buddhist truths outside carefully designed arenas of enjoyment and nostalgia, over and over again we find modern readers determined to tear a Chan "philosophy" or truth from that rich canvas of storytelling and reverie to which it belongs. Moreover, in failing to see these texts as the works of art that they most definitely are, we lose a chance to appreciate this impressive style of thought which can combine narrative and negation to produce entertaining *and* philosophically gripping experiences for the reader.

With a sense for the art-related issues at play here in the *History of the Great Master of Caoqi,* let's turn to the *Platform Sūtra,* which replays many of these themes and details, but redirects Huineng's legacy for new purposes.

6

The *Platform Sūtra* and Other
Conspiracy Theories

For many, the *Platform Sūtra* is one of the most enjoyable Chan texts ever penned, and it certainly has left a deep impression on Chan writing and thinking. Composed sometime in the late eighth century, it picks up and works over a number of claims regarding the Bodhidharma clan that had been put forth in earlier Chan works.[1] The text opens with an unusually creative "autobiography" of Huineng, one that circles around an involved conspiracy supposedly orchestrated by master Hongren. As the details of the conspiracy come into focus, the reader learns that Hongren's chosen heir was not Shenxiu, but rather Huineng. With that startling "history" newly revealed roughly one hundred years after the events supposedly took place, the narrative turns to show Huineng giving a formal dharma teaching that, in places, appears to negate many of the building blocks of the Buddhist tradition,

---

1. The *Platform Sūtra* would, in time, be edited and rewritten in important ways; to keep things simple, I will work from a Dunhuang version of the text that Philip Yampolsky edited and translated in his *The Platform Sūtra of the Sixth Patriarch* (New York: Columbia University Press, 1967). For a range of interesting essays on the text, see *Readings of the Platform Sūtra*, eds. Morten Schlütter and Stephen F. Teiser (New York: Columbia University Press, 2012); in particular, see Brook Ziporyn's "The *Platform Sūtra* and Chinese Thought," which examines the *Platform Sūtra* in the context of non-Buddhist Chinese literature and thought.

while also emphasizing the innate presence of perfect tradition within each person in the form of the buddha-nature. This radical-sounding discourse is, nonetheless, woven into a very traditional-looking ritual program, one dedicated to giving Buddhist precepts to the public in a manner quite parallel to Shenhui's *Platform Sermon*, covered at the end of chapter 4.[2] When the ritual sequence concludes, the story jumps forward forty years to narrate Huineng's death and concludes with the admonition that the whole text ought to be taken as the essence of the Buddhist tradition, with an—otherwise unknown master Fahai—instead of Shenhui—identified as Huineng's main disciple.

Given the complexities of the *Platform Sūtra*, I will simply sketch the logic of the conspiracy that figures so prominently in the autobiographical narrative, then briefly explore the nature of the negative rhetoric that is central to the teaching section of the text, and, finally, conclude with some reflections on the various roles that poetry plays in the text. Then, with a sense for the *Platform Sūtra's* various agendas, the chapter closes out with brief reflections on another late 8th-century text that takes up the motif of conspiracy: the *Record of the Dharma-Jewel through the Generations* (*Lidai fabao ji*).

HUINENG'S CHILDHOOD AND ENTRANCE INTO THE MONASTERY

Seated in front of a large audience at Dafan Temple in Shaozhou—in modern-day Guangdong province—Huineng begins to recount the details of his life. He mentions, first, that his father had been an official

2. This connection between Chan lineages and rituals for giving the Mahāyāna precepts on a public platform is also a prominent feature of another Dunhuang text, Pelliot 3913, referred to by the abbreviated title *Tanfa yize*, which is also notable for its numerous tantric elements. For more discussion, see Henrik Sørensen, "Observations on the Characteristics of the Chinese Chan Manuscripts from Dunhuang," *Studies in Central & East Asian Religions* 2 (1989): 115–39. Christoph Anderl provides a useful summary of the text in "Zen Rhetoric: An Introduction," in *Zen Buddhist Rhetoric in China, Korea, and Japan*, ed. Anderl, (Leiden: Brill, 2012)," 5n9.

in Hebei province but, for unexplained reasons, was dismissed from his post and demoted to the rank of commoner. This scandal forced the family to move to the extreme south of China—first in Xinzhou (also in Guangdong) and then in Nanhai (near the modern-day city of Guangzhou). Huineng's nameless father dies at some unspecified time along the way, leaving Huineng alone with his mother, and in poverty. Having fallen, geographically and socially, from his prior status as the son of a Hebei official, Huineng begins to climb back upward. First, while selling firewood in the marketplace in Lingnan, he bumps into an official who takes him back to a "lodging house for officials"[3]—already, arguably, a step up—where Huineng happens to hear someone reciting the *Diamond Sūtra*. Hearing the recitation, Huineng is suddenly enlightened.[4] After this magical transformation, the official, apparently wise to all things Buddhist, advises him to go north to Hongren's monastery. Once there, Huineng's upward mobility continues as he immediately has an interview with Hongren, an interview which Huineng dominates. In short, in a couple of sentences, the narrative has lifted Huineng from the bottom of the social register to the top, though his position there has yet to be ratified. In their conversation, Hongren is shown making several obvious mistakes—mistakes that parallel those he made in the *Biography of the Great Master of Caoqi*. First, he misidentifies Huineng as a real southerner and consequently labels him a barbarian—a non-Chinese, that is—even as the reader knows that Huineng is the son of a former official from Hebei, a perfect Chinese family background, to be sure.[5] Hongren then asserts that barbarians can't be enlightened, a racist claim that flies in the face of basic Buddhist principles, and one that Huineng will soon refute. Finally, Hongren

3. *Platform Sūtra*, trans. Yampolsky, 126.

4. Since the Dunhuang text is full of copyist errors, I have here and elsewhere followed Yampolsky's suggested improvements which he included in the reprinted version of the Dunhuang text provided at the back of his book.

5. For discussion of the role that Huineng's faux barbarian status plays in the narrative, see my "Conspiracy's Truth: The Zen of Narrative Cunning in the *Platform Sūtra*," *Asia Major* 28, no. 1 (2015).

sends Huineng away, supposedly worried about what others might say—hardly what one would expect from an abbot and a recognized member of the Bodhidharma family.

Hongren's doctrinal errors and his fearful attitude appear bizarre and meaningless, until we realize that they are set here because they are useful to the development of the plot. In fact, introducing Hongren's fear here accomplishes two things; first, it clarifies the presence of a dangerous and intrusive public that stands against Hongren and Huineng; and, second, the presence of this threatening public serves as a pretext for leaving this first conversation unfinished and thereby delaying Hongren's recognition of Huineng as the next patriarch. This delay is crucial since it opens up narrative space for recounting the events that supposedly produced the bad version of history: Hongren's sham transmission to Shenxiu, the master whom previous eighth-century genealogies had identified as Hongren's heir and the leader of Chinese Buddhism. Thus, this initial interview between master Hongren and the soon-to-be-master Huineng dangles in an inconclusive and tantalizing manner until the end of the story when Hongren and Huineng finally again converse, and Hongren formally recognizes Huineng as his unique heir. The basic form of the text, then, is structured like a sandwich, with these two interviews bracketing a complex interior that is taken up with explaining how the faux version of transmission made its way into the public record. It is just this kind of careful plotting that has to be kept in view, especially with regard to the relentless rhetorics-of-negation that follow.

After the initial interview is broken off, Hongren has Huineng led away to the threshing room. Seeing this new drop in status, it seems that Huineng's life is defined by bouncing from high and low zones of symbolic and social power: he begins as the son of an official from the heartland of China, but falls to selling firewood as a southern pauper; then he suddenly heads back up north to be with Hongren where he presents himself as a solid interlocutor, scoring points against a living buddha, but that encounter results in him being sent back down the social hierarchy to perform more menial labor, winnowing rice in the monastery with the other helper types. Of course, in the next phase he will—no surprise—be whisked back upstairs to the pinnacle of power and prestige. From there he is sent back down south, on the run and undercover, and only later comes back up to take "the high seat at the lecture hall" in order to preach this sermon.[6]

THE POETRY CONTEST

Directly following the very brief account of Huineng's work in the threshing room, we learn that Hongren is hosting a poetry contest in which anyone can offer a poem to demonstrate his enlightenment and thereby gain entrance into the Bodhidharma family. Hearing this, the monastery's monks conclude that the head monk, Shenxiu, really is their leader, so there is no point in competing, since surely he is to win. Then, and really for the first time in Chan writing, we are made privy to someone's thoughts as we get to "hear" Shenxiu debate with himself over his spiritual status and his chances of winning Hongren's approval. It turns out that Shenxiu is quite unnerved by the contest. It seems that he has no idea if he is enlightened or not, and, worse, finds himself in a double bind since he believes that if he competes by offering a poem, it would seem that he is doing so out of personal ambition, and yet without offering a poem, he has no chance to win the title of sixth patriarch. Shenxiu's solution to this impasse is to secretively offer his poem, and then wait to see if Hongren accepts it before claiming it as his own. He reasons: "If the fifth patriarch [Hongren] sees the verse tomorrow and is pleased with it, then I shall come forward and say that I wrote it. If he tells me that it is not worthwhile, then I shall know that the homage I have received for these several years on this mountain has been in vain, and that I have no hope of learning the Dao."[7]

6. *Platform Sūtra*, trans. Yampolsky, 125.
7. Ibid., 129n29.

The reader, now aware of this duplicitous plan, has clear "evidence" of how different Shenxiu is from Huineng. Huineng, with his accidental enlightenment from hearing the *Diamond Sūtra*, found ultimate Buddhist wisdom effortlessly, and with no thought—in fact, we never hear a word of what Huineng is thinking. Shenxiu, on the other hand, is presented as a developed site of intersubjectivity and calculation since he is thinking about how to influence the way those above and below him in the social hierarchy view him. And, quite obviously, he is more than willing to employ subterfuge to arrange things to his liking. Equally interesting, whereas Huineng's quasi-commoner status appears as an asset—presumably marking his simplicity and innocence—Shenxiu's internal reflections show him considering that his desire to be the sixth patriarch is the very thing that makes him a commoner and thus unfit to be a buddha. On the night of these events, he says to himself: "If I am seeking the patriarchship, then it cannot be justified. Then it would be like a common man usurping the saintly position."[8] In short, Shenxiu is Huineng's opposite in terms of identity and motion: Shenxiu is at the top, where he has been receiving worship for the past couple of years (oddly, since the monks should have been worshipping Hongren), and yet any action that he might take to solidify that privilege in terms of becoming the new patriarch will reduce him to commoner status. Huineng, for his part, is at the bottom of all relevant hierarchies, is totally unaware of the competition, takes no action, and yet will soon find himself effortlessly at the top—of course, all this simplicity and non-action gives Huineng quite a Daoist-looking profile.

Resolved to follow his ruse, Shenxiu writes his poem (considered below) in the middle of the night on the wall outside the master's hall. This wall, it turns out, is something of a public "canvas" since we are told that this is the surface on which scenes from the *Laṅkāvatāra Sūtra*, and the upcoming dharma-transmission, are to be painted. Now this detail about the *Laṅkāvatāra Sūtra* is important, especially since, as we

8. Ibid.

have seen, several earlier Bodhidharma-genealogies had claimed that the totality of tradition was to be found in it. For the moment, Hongren appears poised to take actions that would be in accord with those older lineage claims, and yet once these plans are established for the public *inside the text,* they will be completely reversed for the reader, though *this reversal will never be made clear to the public inside the narrative.* In short, here we begin to see how the narrative is carefully explaining how a false history of tradition's truth was manufactured and distributed to the public, just as it also works to document the supposedly reliable history of that truth, one that was withheld from the public until this very telling.

One problem with this narrative arrangement, and it will get increasingly awkward, is that Hongren stands as the origin of both good and bad versions of tradition's truth. In a sense, this isn't such an odd thing in the Buddhist tradition since in the *Lotus Sūtra,* this double role is precisely the one invented for the Buddha. And, as if echoing the *Lotus Sūtra,* Hongren's motivations—clarified below—appear aligned with those of the Buddha of the *Lotus Sūtra,* since in both cases the deceitful promotion of a low-brow version of truth is justified as an expedient means, supposedly useful to less developed trainees. This elaborate rhyme with the *Lotus Sūtra* suggests that our author was rather aware of how prior forms of Buddhist literature worked *as literature,* and consciously adopted those previous strategies in order to arrange his own refiguration of tradition.

In the morning, when Hongren notices Shenxiu's unsigned poem on the central panel of the wall, he cancels his plan to have the paintings done. Justifying his course of action to the painter, he says: "It is said in the *Diamond Sūtra*: All forms everywhere are unreal and false."[9] Now one might rightly wonder why, after planning to have these scenes from the *Laṅkāvatāra Sūtra* painted in the context of the upcoming moment of dharma-transmission, Hongren is suddenly thinking in *Diamond*

9. Ibid., 130.

Sūtra terms about the unreality of forms. As with the details considered above, if we were to take the narrative as real history, the scene would make no sense at all. However, read as a narrative designed to reveal a conspiracy, Hongren's eleventh hour shift in allegiance provides an explanation for why there are these earlier texts that explain how Hongren identified the *Laṅkāvatāra Sūtra* (and Shenxiu) as the embodiment of tradition. The narrative is, in effect, saying: "Yes, well, Hongren did for some time promote the *Laṅkāvatāra Sūtra*, but then he rejected it in favor of the *Diamond Sūtra* (and Huineng)."

This agenda becomes clearer when the narrative has Hongren announce that he plans to leave this poem of Shenxiu's on the wall since it will—he claims—aid practitioners and keep them from falling into bad rebirths.[10] In effect, then, Hongren publicly endorses Shenxiu's poem as fulfilling *some* of tradition's normal functions, just as the Buddha of the *Lotus Sūtra* is made to ratify the limited uses of old-style Buddhism. Hongren then calls together all the monks, burns incense in front of the poem, and encourages faith in this poem, even claiming that it will keep them out of bad rebirths *and* give them insight into their fundamental natures. The monks, apparently, are delighted and cry out, "How excellent!"[11]

Continuing this charade, Hongren has Shenxiu come to his room to ask him if he is the author of the poem. Once Shenxiu arrives, Hongren first explains that whoever wrote this poem will get his dharma-transmission—a bald lie, of course. Taking Hongren at his word, Shenxiu naturally claims the poem as his own, and begs Hongren to tell him if he has any understanding or not. Here, again, Shenxiu is stuck in intersubjective no-man's-land since he is begging Hongren to define his own interior. Hongren tells him directly that he doesn't have any understanding and that he stands outside the gate of the patriarchs' residence. Hongren reiterates that what Shenxiu has is a second-rate form of tradi-

10. Ibid.
11. Ibid.

tion that is useful for aiding the deluded, but useless for obtaining "ulti-mate enlightenment."

By now it is clear that Hongren, besides tricking Shenxiu (who tried to trick him), has clearly deceived his monks by leaving before them a second-rate statement of truth with the assurance that it is an effective version of tradition, while also giving them the impression that he has chosen Shenxiu as his successor. Noting all this carefully staged decep-tion suggests, once again, that the text is far from being a simple account of past deeds—actually, it is starting to look downright Shakespearean in its capacity to interweave various points of view and their attendant desires and delusions, all for the purpose of leading the reader to one very startling conclusion: Shenxiu was a fraud and Huineng is the real sixth patriarch. This impression of literary ingenuity only thickens when we conclude, as we should, that our author has introduced all this deception into a narrative that claims to be nothing but a simple illiter-ate's truthful account of real history.

The effects of Hongren's deceptive strategies are made clearer in the story when, some eight months later, a low-level trainee passes by the threshing room reciting Shenxiu's poem, which Hongren has left on the wall. When Huineng hears the poem, he immediately knows it to be a second-rate statement of enlightenment and that the author "had yet to know his own nature and to discern the great meaning."[12] Here the narrative shows us that Huineng has the very same powers of assess-ment that the current patriarch, Hongren, had displayed earlier. And yet, in a moment Huineng will ask this passing trainee to take him to the poem so that he can see it and *worship it*. Right before that moment of duplicity—a duplicity that matches Hongren's response to the poem—the poem-reciting trainee repeats everything that has hap-pened regarding the poetry-contest because Huineng, off in the thresh-ing room as he has been the past eight or more months, apparently hasn't heard anything about it.

12. Ibid., 131, with changes.

As the trainee explains to Huineng what happened with the poetry contest, the reader gets a clear view of how the bad version of history that took Shenxiu to be the sixth patriarch has so thoroughly seeped into the collective memory of the monastery. In response to this information, Huineng tells this trainee that he would like to go to the hall and pay obeisance to Shenxiu's poem in order to win rebirth in a buddha-land—motivations that he had never announced before. In fact, in his first interview with Hongren, he said he wasn't searching for anything, just "buddha-dharma"—the essence of tradition.

Once in front of Shenxiu's poem, Huineng first pays obeisance to it, and then asks that it be read to him because he is illiterate. Of course, he has already heard the poem and judged it to be junk, but this rereading gives the author a chance to make Huineng's imminent composition appear to be an unplanned response to Shenxiu's poem. Shenxiu's poem, which had been introduced slightly earlier in the story, reads as follows:

> The body is the bodhi tree;
> The mind is like a bright mirror's stand.[13]
> At all times we must strive to polish it,
> And not let dust collect [on it].[14]

As the poem is read, Huineng gets enlightened yet again, and he supposedly understands "the great meaning."[15] After this enlightenment based on Shenxiu's poem, Huineng spontaneously composes his own poem and asks that someone write it on the wall for him, since, of course, he doesn't know how to write. This sequence of events makes it clear that although Huineng did end up presenting a poem in this public place of competition, his poem was no more than an exuberant

13. Here I have followed McRae's translation, which is more literal and seems to improve on Yampolsky's; see McRae, *Seeing through Zen: Encounter, Transformation, and Genealogy in Chinese Chan Buddhism* (Berkeley: University of California Press, 2003), 61 and 64–65.

14. *Platform Sūtra*, ed. Yampolsky, 130, with slight changes.

15. Ibid., 132.

response to Shenxiu's poem. Nonetheless, it was in the midst of all this innocent and unmotivated activity that Huineng produced the piece of literature that would, with Hongren's ratification, symbolically kill off Shenxiu. Thus, in perfect accord with Daoist theories of the power and efficacy of non-action (*wuwei*), Huineng wins the competition without making any effort or, in fact, even entering it.

In the midst of this dicey narrative ploy, our author inexplicably provides two quatrains from Huineng, as though the author, unsure which of the two might look best, decided to include both:

> Bodhi originally has no tree,
> The mirror also has no stand.
> Buddha-nature is always clean and pure;
> Where is there room for dust?

> The mind is the Bodhi tree,
> The body is the mirror stand.
> The mirror is originally clean and pure,
> Where can it be stained by dust?[16]

Placing Huineng's poem/s next to Shenxiu's obviously provides the reader with a thrilling contrast: suddenly the rug is pulled out from under the traditional-sounding practice of always seeking to purify one's mind that Shenxiu was supposedly promoting and, in place of that kind of self-purification, Huineng declares the reality of an innate enlightenment that never needs to be enhanced or purified—in fact, *can't be* enhanced or purified. In this light, the figures of Shenxiu and Huineng appear to be dramatizing that fundamental duality first announced in the *Two Entrances*, with Huineng's poem/s presenting that Daoist

16. Yampolsky points out that Hu Shih long ago argued that the "unknown author of this fictionalized autobiography of Huineng was evidently experimenting with his verse writing and was not sure which verse was better" (ibid., 132n39). Actually, as Yampolsky suggests, one could argue that there are three quatrains in view since the two sentences before the two poems can be read as a quatrain and seem thematically parallel to the two poems that follow. This third poem reads: "If you do not know the original mind, studying the dharma is of no benefit. If you know the mind and see its true nature, you then awaken to the great meaning" (ibid., 132, with slight changes).

kind of Buddhism that claims to be free of practice—as did the First Entrance—while Shenxiu's poem languishes in that anxious, workaday world of normal Buddhism, as found in the Second Entrance.

Now, while the author went out of its way to make the composition of Huineng's poems on the wall appear spontaneous and unformatted by the literary tradition, it is also the case that the first of Huineng's poem could easily be mistaken for a miniature version of the *Diamond Sūtra*. Of course, such a parallel isn't too surprising since the *Platform Sūtra's* narrative has all along been claiming that Huineng has a mystical understanding of the *Diamond Sūtra*, with all its alarming and baffling negations of the normal forms of Buddhist practice and belief. While Huineng's poem echoes the *Diamond Sūtra's* rhetoric, much has shifted in this arrangement since this thoroughgoing negation of mundane Buddhism now appears to issue forth from an illiterate Chinese man, implying that a new, decidedly Chinese, origin of tradition has been found. Better still, as Huineng's poems on the final truth of Buddhism spontaneously spill out of him, it would seem that on the level of naturalness, form and content are one: the illiterate Huineng gets at the final *content* of Buddhism without reliance on literature, just as he can express it in an equally innocent *oral form* that, again, is supposedly free of literature, even though, of course, this wisdom is presented in some pretty fancy-looking poetry. Huineng has, in short, been created as the perfect reader and the perfect writer of the Buddhist tradition, even though the manner in which he masters the Buddhist tradition suggests that he is, in fact, something of a Daoist sage who mysteriously connects to the final realities of the cosmos—the "great meaning"—while also supposedly standing free of the literary tradition.

Huineng's Daoist aura warrants a bit more attention for four reasons. First, as we saw above, the second half of each of Huineng's poems completely rejects Shenxiu's likening of Buddhist practice to the diligent wiping of dust from a mirror. Now, it turns out that chapter five of the *Zhuangzi* has a passage about mirrors, dust, and worthy men, which raises the possibility that our author drew on this Daoist discussion to structure the poetry contest.[17] The key line in the *Zhuangzi* is given by a footless man named Shen Tujia who says: "But I've heard that if a mirror is bright, no dust settles on it; if dust settles, it isn't really bright. When you live around worthy men a long time, you'll be free of faults."[18] While the passage is admittedly elliptical, Shen Tujia appears to be arguing that the self or mind is a bright, mirror-like entity that *naturally* wouldn't allow the accumulation of dust when things are as they should be, and thus, by implication, there isn't really anything to do about this problem of dust accumulation, a commitment to naturalness that is underscored by the claim that simply being around worthy men frees one of faults. Although, this passage doesn't provide an exact parallel to Huineng's poems, its metaphoric logic appears close to what we find animating the second half of Huineng's two poems, both of which insist on the naturalness of enlightenment and on the lack of need for practice.

Second, it is important to note that chapter five of the *Zhuangzi* is dedicated to celebrating uncultured sages who triumph over Confucius and other sophisticates. Of course, just this theme is precisely the one shaping Huineng's character in the *Platform Sūtra*. Read in this light, the *Platform Sūtra* has cast Huineng as one of those uncultured sages, so charming for his natural mastery of the Dao, while Shenxiu appears in the role of Confucius—socially (and imperially) recognized as a sage, but out of touch with the Dao and somewhat nervous about his moral status and place in the world. In line with the distribution of the Confucian and Daoist personae, Shenxiu is shown advocating serious and unstinting practice—as Confucius does throughout the *Analects*—while Huineng, in good Zhuangzian and Laozian form, is insisting on the impossibility of practice, or, more exactly, insisting that the only

17. Paul Demiéville pointed out this parallel in his 1973 essay "Le miroir spirituel," translated as "The Mirror of the Mind" in *Sudden and Gradual Approaches to Enlightenment in Chinese Thought*, ed. Peter Gregory (Honolulu: University of Hawai'i Press, 1987), 18.

18. *Zhuangzi*, trans. Burton Watson in *The Complete Works of Chuang Tzu* (New York: Columbia University Press, 1968), 70.

practice needed is a kind of non-action in which one dodges the dictates of normal practice. In short, here at the climax of the narrative, our author is hoping to convince the reader that Huineng really is the legitimate leader of Chinese Buddhism by staging a competition in which Daoist insouciance triumphs over Confucian anxiety, a much-loved trope that is findable in some of the oldest works in the Chinese literary tradition.

Third, we should also note that chapter five of the *Zhuangzi,* along with many of the other chapters, develops a sophisticated kind of irony in which the image of Confucius, as he would have been known to the well-informed reader, is turned upside down, such that Confucius comes to endorse Daoist positions and thereby negates or diminishes his own value. Arguably, just this zeal for reversing received tradition is also central to the *Platform Sūtra's* presentation of Huineng and his supposed triumph over Shenxiu.

Finally, if we accept that these poems are recycling a mix of Buddhist and Daoist language and logic—taken from well-known classics—then it would seem that the author of the *Platform Sūtra* was relying on the heft of the *literary tradition* to make Huineng's supposedly spontaneous poems look more profound and in line with what the Chinese took to be final wisdom, be it in Daoist or Buddhist form. Coming full circle, then, our author crafted Huineng's overcoming of Shenxiu, *and the literate tradition,* knowing that it would appear acceptable *only if it accorded with the literary tradition as understood by his anticipated audience,* a fact that has been overlooked by medieval and modern readers alike. Put that way, having the illiterate Huineng accidently win the poetry contest appears as a rather clever literary ploy designed to appeal to a suitably well-read audience who could be counted on to approve—and delight in—just this kind of Daoist coup, based on their familiarity with very old patterns in the Chinese literary tradition.[19]

19. The situation here isn't too different from the way that the basic structure of Christianity is based on recycling very traditional Jewish tropes such that the Gospels

When Hongren comes along and reads the newly composed poem/s, he "realized that Huineng had a excellent understanding of the great meaning." But, *"being afraid lest the assembly know this,* he said to them: 'This still hasn't gotten at it.'"[20] This new piece of public deception, enacted for reasons that echo Hongren's fear in that initial conversation with Huineng, is secretly reversed in the next paragraph where we learn that at midnight, Hongren called Huineng to the hall and recited the *Diamond Sūtra* for him, which resulted in Huineng getting enlightened once again. Hongren then gives Huineng dharma-transmission and Bodhidharma's robe, yet *"none of the others knew about it."*[21] A certain panic then descends and Hongren decides to whisk Huineng out of the monastery on that very night because hundreds of angry people supposedly were eager to kill him. As in the *Biography of the Great Master of Caoqi,* no reason is given for this monstrous rage and it seems best to see it as a useful narrative ploy that makes clear to the reader that something of great value is being taken from the community.

Hongren's unsavory role in the story is fascinating for several reasons, but I think it is more interesting to close out our analysis of the narrative by reflecting on how well Shenxiu's "interior" is developed in that *Hamlet*-styled passage where he wrestles with himself over how to be recognized as the sixth patriarch. The first thing to remember is that the *Platform Sūtra* was probably written around 780, and thus Shenxiu had been dead for some seventy-five years. And, this scene with Hongren would have had to occur in an even more distant past, since Hongren seems to have died around 674. There is, as far as we know, no prior textual source, or hint of a source, for this event. And, in fact,

---

explain that Jesus, as a paschal lamb of sorts, was sacrificed on Passover in a grand moment of atonement, with this decidedly Jewish event offered to readers as the reason to step over Judaism, and its sacrificial system, into new structures of truth and tradition provided by the Gospels. For discussion of this problem, see my *Fetishizing Tradition: Desire and Reinvention in Buddhist and Christian Narratives* (Albany: State University of New York Press, 2015).

20. *Platform Sūtra,* trans. Yampolsky, 132; with slight changes and emphasis added.
21. Ibid., 133.

Shenxiu was only connected with Hongren in narratives written after Shenxiu's death when various authors, such as Du Fei, had reason to attach him to Hongren and the Bodhidharma family. Thus, we have to wonder where this rich and detailed interior monologue came from. If it hasn't come to the author from the literary record, then my guess is that in Shenxiu's ruminations we see something of our author's own subjectivity. After all, our author presumably had good reason to be rather familiar with the dilemma that he has projected onto Shenxiu—how to shape public opinion by secretly putting unsigned literature before the public, all in order to win acceptance for a new claim to belong to the Bodhidharma family—for surely he was playing a similar game.

TRUTH ON THE INSIDE

Having explained how he came to be a member of the Bodhidharma family, Huineng turns to deliver a discourse that should, by now, appear quite familiar. Thus, like so many masters presented in the prior texts, Huineng insists on the radical sameness of buddhas and sentient beings. And, then, in line with the *Biography of the Great Master of Caoqi,* Huineng collapses meditation and wisdom saying:

> Good friends, enlightenment (*bodhi*) and wisdom (*prajñā*) are from the out-set possessed by men of this world (*shi ren*). It is just because the mind is deluded that men cannot attain awakening themselves. [Thus,] they must seek a good teacher to show them how to see into their own natures. Good friends, if you meet awakening, wisdom will be achieved.
>
> Good friends, my teaching of the dharma takes meditation and wisdom as its basis. Never under circumstances say mistakenly that meditation and wisdom are different; they are a unity, not two things.[22]

The theme of the non-duality of practice and the attainment of wisdom—essentially arguing that the end of the path is present at the beginning,

---

22. Ibid., 135, with slight changes.

with no way *logically* to move forward on the path—is then worked over
in several different ways, with a reference back to the *Vimalakīrti* helping
to solidify the argument. Likewise, the distinction between suddenness
and gradualness is rejected from the point of view of enlightenment,
even though suddenness is still taken as the mark of the enlightened point
of view:

> Good friends, in the dharma there is no sudden or gradual, but among peo-
> ple some are keen and others are dull. The deluded recommend the grad-
> ual method, the enlightened practice the sudden teaching. To understand
> your own original mind is to see into your original nature. Once, enlight-
> ened, there is from the outset no distinction between these two methods;
> those who are not enlightened will for long eons be caught in samsara.[23]

Then the rhetoric of negation takes over:

> Good friends, in this teaching of mine, from ancient times up to the
> present, all have set up no-thought as the main doctrine, no-form as the
> substance, and non-abiding as the basis. No-form is to be separated from
> form even when associated with form. No-thought is not to think even
> when involved in thought. Non-abiding is the original nature of man.[24]

In these passages and others like them, Huineng is shown knowing the
final nature of all humans. He is the one who knows that, ultimately,
there is a kind of perfection in "the original nature of man," which can
be referred to as "non-abiding" or "no-thought" or "no-form." Regardless of the terminology—and it all seems quite fluid and more poetic
than technical—Huineng is shown declaring that the essence of tradition is already present in each and every human subject. Thus, "enlightenment and intuitive wisdom are from the outset possessed by men of
this world." Given that the totality of tradition is supposedly lodged at
the base of all of us, working on meditation and other techniques for
self-improvement would seem decidedly misguided. The one thing to

23. Ibid., 137, with slight changes.
24. Ibid., 137–38, with slight changes.

do is to find a master who understands this reality, and the way to turn deluded commoners into the buddhas they've always been.

These rather thrilling riffs on no-thought and no-form—not to mention the implicit no-practice—might suggest, again *logically,* that every thing about the world of Buddhism was on the verge of imploding, but in fact the discussion develops easily enough and nothing seems at risk. Thus, practically speaking, it would seem that Buddhism is expected to remain the same, with or without this tantalizing rhetoric of negation draped over it. Moreover, since Huineng's teachings appear to recycle many of the themes that were established in prior Chan texts—in particular, material drawn from the Shenhui texts—we have, again, to see that a virtual literary forum is taking shape, one in which Chinese authors developed ever more interesting and provocative ways to give the impression that local figures—real or invented—had mastered the essence of the Buddhist tradition, while also promising that this essence could be regained by the public, through various forms of submission and devotion, and, as we will see, by reading.

POEMS OF TRUTH AND PRESENCE

More evidence of the *Platform Sūtra's* commitment to a literary form of Buddhism comes into view when we consider the role that poetry plays within the text's promises for gaining salvation. Of course, the turn to making poetry the perfect vehicle for truth and tradition was already evident back in the contest that Hongren arranged, but in addition to those "combat poems," two other kinds of poems figure prominently in the *Platform Sūtra.* As for the first, Huineng thrice recites long poems full of radical negations,[25] claiming that the essence of the tradition is to be found within them, and that all those who recite them will be purified and come to recognize their deep sameness with the Buddha. These

---

25. Actually, Huineng gives a fourth poem (*Platform Sūtra*, trans. Yampolsky, 180), but it isn't introduced with any specific powers.

poems, when learned and "practiced" are also said to make the reciter one with Huineng. As Huineng says in the midst of one of these poems, "I am causing the sudden teaching to be transmitted [in this poem], / And one who aspires to learn it will become one with me."[26]

This enticing promise that a poem will provide a way to be one with the master comes again in the second, much longer, poem. Just after reciting it, Huineng explains, "Good friends, if all of you recite this verse and practice in accord with it, even if you are a thousand miles away from me, you will always be in my presence."[27] In short, just as Huineng's negative rhetoric served as the basis for building a relationship of exchange with the emperor Gaozong in the *Biography of the Great Master of Caoqi,* here, too, radical negations of tradition provide the verbiage that fills out a new container for tradition—the master's poem—while also establishing a new model for making the totality of tradition available: recite this poem of negation, and the dead or distant master will be magically present, and the reciter will be one with him and, by implication, with the Buddha.

A third truth-poem of this type shows up later, and like the others delights in negative rhetoric. It opens claiming:

> Nowhere is there anything true;
> Don't try to see the True in any way.
> If you try to see the True,
> Your seeing will be in no way true.
> If you yourself would gain the True
> Separate from the false; there the mind is true.
> There is no True.
> What place is there for it to be?[28]

Here Huineng appears to reject truth and vision, and yet this poem was supposedly offered by Huineng on his deathbed when he makes clear

26. Ibid., 155, with small changes.
27. Ibid., 161.
28. Ibid., 175.

that this poem is to take his place after his passing. He introduces it saying: "I shall give you a verse, the verse of the true-false, moving-still. All of you recite it, and if you understand its meaning you will be the same as I. If you practice in reliance on it, you will not lose the essence of the teaching."[29] Clearly, in the eyes of our author, radical negations, carefully composed poetry, and a kind of mystical omni-presence of Buddhist truth fit together perfectly.

The hope that poetry could hold the essence of tradition over time comes through in the second kind of poem in the *Platform Sūtra* that Huineng recites. These brief poems—simple quatrains really—are on the topic of earth and flowers, and Huineng explains that each poem was composed at the moment of dharma-transmission. Thus there are five poems for the five Chinese masters who preceded Huineng, and the masters are metaphorized as the five "petals" that Bodhidharma opened. Bodhidharma, apparently now able to compose passable Chinese poetry *and* predict the future success of his lineage, presents the effect of his arrival in China as a kind of fruitful gardening:

> I originally came to China,
> To transmit the teaching and save deluded beings;
> One flower opens five petals,
> And the fruit ripens of itself.

Huike is then shown picking up the soil-flower motif, but adds in some negations:

> Because originally there is earth,
> From this earth, seeds can bring forth flowers.
> If from the outset there were no earth,
> From where would the flowers grow?[30]

The other masters up to Huineng are given similar quatrains, which like-wise follow the soil-flower motif. Huineng, for his part, then gives two

---

29. Ibid., 174–75, with changes.
30. Ibid., 176, with changes.

such poems, which he apparently composes in the real-time of the narrative, making clear that he is about to die and that these two poems are *his* transmission poems, even though this would imply that everyone on site, and readers too, would, in effect, be receiving dharma-transmission from him.

It might not be obvious at first, but there are three layers of fertility being worked out here. First, Bodhidharma's poem sets the theme of soil and flowers (layer #1) and thereby essentially "births" the content of following poems (layer #2), which remain focused on just this theme, even as those poems serve to reproduce the next generation of the lineage (layer #3), since the poems are given at the moment of dharma-transmission. In this sense, then, the poems appear as a perfect combination of form and content, supposedly accomplishing in the world what they promise internally. In another sense this appears as a particularly clear example of religion being about itself: the supposed *content* of the lineage of truth-fathers is nothing more than a poetic explanation of the lineage's successful reproduction, a poetry that, coming full circle, actually serves to reproduce the lineage when it is recited.

Noting this tangle of poetry, male fertility, and the supposed real-world reproduction of the lineage helps contextualize passages that claim that the *Platform Sūtra* itself secures the production of the next generation of the Bodhidharma lineage. Thus we have something like a fractal situation in which *inside* the *Platform Sūtra*, poetry plays this role of reproducing the masters, even as the text, as the container of those poems and all the surrounding material, claims that it too has similar powers, but for the (reading) public at large. Thus we read:

> If one were to talk about the essence of the lineage (*zongzhi*), it lies in the transmission of the *Platform Sūtra*, and this serves as the authority. Unless a person has received the *Platform Sūtra*, he has not received the sanction. The place, date, and the name of the recipient must be made known, and these are to be attached to it when it is transmitted. Someone who does not

have the *Platform Sūtra* and the sanction is not a disciple of the Southern School.[31]

Since the text explains how the perfect form of tradition is to be reproduced with the physical transmission of this very text, we see once more that regardless of the wild negations strung throughout the *Platform Sūtra*, the text as a whole appears fundamentally conservative and dedicated to reproducing the essence of tradition *in written language*.

Setting aside the admittedly complex *Platform Sūtra*, let's return to that point from the end of the previous chapter about the pleasures of recrafting tradition. Here, as we have seen, the author has taken several pieces of earlier Chan writing and combined them in creative ways, while also making up a set of new rules defining the legitimate ownership of the ultimate version of tradition. In particular, poetry suddenly came to the fore as the container for the essence of tradition and yet enthusiasm for rewriting the rules for inheriting tradition was equally obvious in the statements declaring that the *Platform Sūtra*, as physical text, was to be the ultimate conveyor of tradition. Refiguring tradition and its rules of reproduction surely required a good deal of confidence and audacity, but in another sense, our author must have known that he belonged to a *tradition* of those who felt authorized to reconstruct the Buddhist tradition as they saw fit. Just this underground tradition of rewriting tradition will be again conspicuously present in the next conspiracy narrative—the *Record of the Dharma-Jewel through the Generations*.

RECORD OF THE DHARMA-JEWEL THROUGH THE GENERATIONS—A GREAT CHAN DIGEST

Written sometime around 780, the *Record of the Dharma-Jewel through the Generations*, or *Lidai fabao ji* (hereafter *Lidai*), presents master Wuzhu (714–74) as the most recently recognized member of the Bodhidharma family. The narrative tactics in the *Lidai* follow closely those estab-

31. Ibid., 162, with changes; see 173–74 and 182 for similar claims.

lished in the texts considered above, and thus we again get a sense that the art of reinventing tradition was itself solidifying into a tradition, based on the repetition of certain well-established literary gestures. For instance, an important strategy in the *Lidai* is to give Huineng a dharma-brother named Zhishen (609?–702?), a claim that provided the author of the *Lidai* with a new way to link back to Hongren. With Zhishen now identified as Hongren's chief heir, and Huineng pushed off to the side, the *Lidai* presents a lineage that is built from Zhishen to Chuji (669–736) to a certain Wuxiang (684–762), who supposedly was the most recent owner of the robe of transmission before Wuzhu. These mini-narratives reach their climax when the narrative explains how Wuxiang transmitted the robe and the dharma to Wuzhu, even though they never met or spoke to one another. As we will see, the layers of intrigue at work here are impressive, even novelesque.

Before exploring the *Lidai* in greater detail, it should be noted that more than a dozen manuscripts—or at least fragments of manuscripts—of the *Lidai* were found at Dunhuang, including several translated into Tibetan.[32] This suggests that the text, besides presenting Wuzhu as China's newest buddha, served some wider purposes—after all, why else would so many people take the time to copy this long manuscript if they couldn't see it having other uses? One hypothesis would be that the text, massive as it is, functioned as a "digest" of the entire Buddhist tradition. That is, reading the story of Wuzhu and his "family" turned into a way of reading "over" all of Chinese Buddhism in a pleasant, secure, and final manner. If the text was seen to provide this service—and, arguably, the *Platform Sūtra* functions somewhat like this too—then presumably readers wouldn't be put off in learning that Wuzhu was the unique holder of the essence of tradition, especially because it was Wuzhu's final authority that was the very thing that allowed this meta-history to be told.

32. For details, see Wendi L. Adamek, *The Mystique of Transmission: On an Early Chan History and Its Contents* (New York: Columbia University Press, 2007), 6 and 408n9.

Providing this overview of tradition is presumably the reason that the author begins his lineage "history" for Wuzhu by listing all the various sutras it relies on—thirty-seven, in fact[33]—before turning to explain how Buddhism came to China in the first century. Only after explaining China's romance with pre-Chan forms of Buddhism does the narrative turn to begin building a detailed account of how, centuries later, a perfect form of tradition came to China via Bodhidharma and the clan of truth-fathers. Once the narrative has "legitimately" established Wuzhu in the Bodhidharma family, the *Lidai* turns to give "verbatim" accounts of Wuzhu's teaching and his conversations with various figures. Like the Shenhui conversations presented in chapter 4, Wuzhu has no doubts about the essence of tradition, handles all questions with ease, bounces between the sutras effortlessly, and gets all his visitors to submit to him, usually in tearful joy. In short, the *Lidai* continues in that series of Chan literary efforts *to provide the reader with an intimate vision of the master's perfect domination and reenactment of tradition.*

In the account of Wuzhu's death we see something else striking: no descendant is named or even hinted at. Instead, the final paragraphs give details that suggest that the reader is to believe that the spirit of Wuzhu lives in a portrait that was secretly made of him in his final days. Of course, as with Shaolin Monastery and its story of Faru, we can assume that Wuzhu's monastery, Baotang, sought to benefit by claiming to have recently hosted a living buddha, with his on-site portrait magically preserving his presence. And yet there is little here that emphasizes that institutional angle. Instead, in the final section of the text, we hear, however briefly, the voices of his disciples explaining their joy in having received Wuzhu's instructions.[34] Thus, though the text is squarely focused on establishing Wuzhu's perfect credentials, it also appears to suggests that readers could enjoy Wuzhu's teachings as much as his disciples appear to have.

33. For a listing of these thirty-seven texts, see ibid., 300–301, and 511ff.
34. Ibid., 404.

Reading the text this way makes even more sense when we note that at several points in the story it is explicitly claimed that seeing truth in a perfect way allows one to "see" Wuzhu. That is, the text regularly promises the virtual presence of the master in return for accepting his textualized version of truth and the "history" of that truth. Thus, much like the way that the long poems worked in the *Platform Sūtra* (see above), the privatization of truth and tradition in the Bodhidharma lineage appears as but step one within a larger program of returning truth and tradition to the (reading) public in textual form.

Getting good at making these finer distinctions regarding the give-and-take of these texts is worth the trouble since in the next chapter we will encounter texts that, though very Chan-like in content, don't seem to have any specific institutional goals in view, just as they also don't endorse any particular master's ownership of tradition. Instead, such texts seem designed as exciting literary utopias where readers can supposedly absorb or, at least, behold the final truths of Buddhism without being distracted by claims regarding someone's unique ownership of tradition. Of course, other authors continued to try to pull Chan "truth" back into institutionally controlled settings, but that too is just more proof of this struggle over defining how tradition was to be owned, enjoyed, and shared out.

Though it seems right to speak of the *Lidai*'s relative generosity as I just have, it is also the case that is has been described as one of the more disingenuous narratives among the eighth-century Bodhidharma genealogies.[35] I'm not sure that I would promote this assessment since all the texts covered above appear rather disingenuous, but I would agree that the text does engage in practically *all* the strategies that the prior texts had presented. A short list of these strategies would include[36]

35. This was McRae's assessment; see his *The Northern School and the Formation of Early Ch'an Buddhism* (Honolulu: University of Hawai'i Press, 1986), 11.

36. All the following in-text page numbers refer to Adamek's *Mystique of Transmission*.

- cleverly undermining the prior owners of Bodhidharma's legacy—Jingjue (pp. 164, 309), Shenhui (pp. 349ff.), and even Huineng (pp. 331–33), all get disenfranchised;
- inventing narratives about court figures who verify the various claims regarding Wuzhu's ownership of tradition (pp. 352–56);
- recycling older lineages for new purposes (pp. 307–10);
- borrowing heavily from Daoism; in particular, a Buddhist form of *wuwei* is emphasized; and, it is even said that Wuxiang— Wuzhu's supposed master—was so simple he survived in his mountain retreat by eating dirt (p. 337); perhaps because the text traffics in so much Daoist-sounding language that it then goes out of its way to refute those who might think that Buddhism and Daoism are the same (pp. 389–91);
- arguing that all members of the Buddhist hierarchy are fundamentally equal, but only the master really knows about that deep equality, which is why he gets to be the master (pp. 364–65);
- having Wuzhu negate normal forms of Buddhist practice in order to give the impression that he is completely in charge of defining what is and isn't the essence of the Buddhist tradition (pp. 349–51); and
- concocting complex conspiracy theories.

In keeping with the themes of this chapter, and in order to keep things brief, I will simply explore the conspiracies presented in the narrative. As it turns out, there are at least three conspiracies in the *Lidai*. The first conspiracy is easy enough to spot: likely drawing on the *Biography of the Great Master of Caoqi*, the *Lidai* rehearses the story of Huineng secretly receiving the robe and the dharma-transmission from Hongren, and then slipping away to live under cover for many years.[37] Evidence suggesting that the *Biography of the Great Master of Caoqi* is the source for this

---

37. Ibid., 329–30.

version of events comes when the author recycles that story from the *Biography* in which Huineng is at Yinzong's monastery debating the meaning of the flag flapping in the wind.

What follows directly from the flag-wind debate is a most curious story, which isn't really a conspiracy but it shows a level of narrative control that is useful for the arguments in this chapter. In this mini-narrative, we learn that Empress Wu invited Huineng to court but he refused, pleading illness. She then once more sent for him, but again with no luck; finally, she asked that he send her the robe of transmission, which he agreed to do. Then, once the robe was in the palace, she organized worship of it and invited all the other Chan masters in the empire—and the list given basically covers all those masters mentioned in prior Chan texts. They all supposedly arrived and were tested with one question: "Do [you] venerable X have desires, or not?"[38] Each master, save Zhishen, claimed that he was free of desire. Zhishen, for his part, admitted that he had desires, doing so because he had been feeling ill and wanted an excuse to leave the capital and go back to his home monastery. Somehow his answer in the positive, supported with the line "That which is born has desire. That which is not born has no desire," enlightened Empress Wu. Given this unexpected success, he petitioned the empress to allow him to leave, and she agreed, sending him off with a sutra, an image of Maitreya *and the robe of transmission.* Zhishen then supposedly gave the robe to a certain Chuji and who then secretly gives it to Wuxiang.[39] While this complicated story explaining how Wuxiang ended up with Huineng's robe—and the essence of tradition—isn't really a conspiracy, it does show the author working very hard to give a counter story to the previous accounts of Huineng and his supposed disciple Shenhui.

The real conspiracy theory comes when the narrative tries to explain how it was that Wuxiang gave the robe and dharma-transmission to Wuzhu. The action begins when Wuzhu, attending a big retreat that

---

38. Ibid., 332–33, with slight changes.
39. Ibid., 334–35.

Wuxiang hosted at Jingzhong Monastery in Chengdu, hears Wuxiang repeatedly saying to the gathered crowds, "For what reason do you not go into the mountains? What good is it to stay here?"[40] No one knows what this means, or why the master is saying this—no one except Wuzhu, that is. Not having spoken directly with Wuxiang, Wuzhu nonetheless knows that this publicly broadcast message is, in fact, a private message for him, and he leaves the congregation and heads off to the mountains as directed. Once there, the private connection with Wuxiang continues but in a more impressive manner, since it turns out that they have the power to see and hear one another at a distance of over 1,000 *li*.[41] Magically skyping over these great distances, it was supposedly as though the two men were face to face.

Once the narrative has established this secret mode of communication between the two masters, it turns to explain how this conduit was used to effect the transmission of the dharma and the robe. In this section of the story, the narrative relies on that "skype connection" to control the gradual movement of the robe of transmission from Wuxiang to Wuzhu. The details quickly become complicated but the point of revealing all the twists and turns is simply to show how these behind-the-scenes transactions played out as Wuxiang managed to secretly get the robe to Wuzhu, even though no one knew about this transfer.[42]

The author's ability to establish complex split-screen stories becomes even clearer when he shows us Wuxiang's disciples, back at Jingzhong Monastery, trying to solve a number of problems that arise after Wuxiang's death. First, it seems that they don't know about Wuxiang's transmission of the robe and dharma to Wuzhu, and that's not too surprising since, after all, it happened secretly and was organized via that magical skyping. Thus when the local governmental officials arrive to ask who Wuxiang's dharma heir is, his disciples say they have no idea. Some time later, though, these monks of Jingzhong hear that a certain Wuzhu

40. Ibid., 348, with minor changes.
41. A *li* is reckoned to be around 400 or 500 meters.
42. Ibid., 351–52.

was to be invited out of the mountains by a large group of government officials who have come to believe that Wuzhu is in possession of the robe of transmission—Wuxiang's robe, that is!

Alarmed by this news, some of Wuxiang's disciples back at Jingzhong Monastery come together to plot what the narrator calls an "evil deed"—producing a facsimile of the robe of transmission, presumably in the hopes of discrediting Wuzhu and reestablishing the preeminence of their monastery. With their preparations complete, the "treacherous clique" organizes a public feast at the monastery where this fake robe is brought out and presented to the local officials as though it was *the* robe of transmission. Weeping fake tears, one of the disciples explains to the gathered people, "This is the Robe of Verification (*xinyi*) that has been passed down."[43] However, noting doubts in the audience about this claim, the monks of Jingzhong go out of their way to slander Wuzhu and advise the officials not to accept him as the leader of Chinese Buddhism. Finally, one of the officials comes forward, claims to know the real version of events, and chastises the monks for: (1) slandering Wuzhu; (2) fabricating a facsimile of the robe of transmission; and (3) preparing this elaborate public ruse. Once the stalwart official has presented the "correct" version of history, "[The faces of] the malicious clique drained of color, they were utterly at a loss. Their evil deed was thus thwarted."[44]

Given this tightly plotted narrative, we shouldn't have any doubts about our author's skill in depicting complex events that were developing simultaneously in different places. Moreover, our author has shown himself to be a talented dramaturge since the entire "history" explaining the fate of the robe of transmission has a rich theatrical quality to it. For instance, above we were made to "see" the pale faces of the monks once their plot is uncovered. Clearly, our author was comfortable handling these carefully constructed events, while also presenting Wuxiang and Wuzhu as masters of radical negation and stunning simplicity.

43. Ibid., 356.
44. Ibid.

Likewise, the conspiracy trope has become more complex. Whereas conspiracy themes first appeared in Chan texts in a rather simple form to explain how Hongren had secretly given Huineng transmission – back in the *Biography of the Great Master from Caoqi* – in the *Lidai,* that same story is simply background for a much more elaborate conspiracy that is designed to explain how it was that Wuzhu came to be the most recent owner of tradition. Thus, as mentioned above, what is being passed down—from author to author—is that set of literary techniques useful for developing more gripping accounts of how the Bodhidharma legacy was supposedly passed down from master to master. Ironically, then, behind the track of fictional Bodhidharma lineages we can see a real lineage—a lineage of authors who created, generation after generation, just those fictional Bodhidharma lineages in reliance on the writings of their "forefathers." Coming to terms with these layers of mimesis is precisely what a critical history of Chan literature ought to offer.

One last issue to consider: What, really, are we to make of the text's vicious attack on the monks back at Jingzhong Monastery, the disciples of Wuxiang, who were so thoroughly vilified by the *Lidai*'s account of *their* attempt to invent a public story about their private possession of the robe? Like that self-incriminating monologue given to Shenxiu in the *Platform Sūtra*, it would seem that the author of the *Lidai* has foisted onto the competition—the monks of Jingzhong—precisely the crime he was committing: falsely claiming to have inherited the robe of transmission, while also slandering those who might likewise be claiming ownership of it. Of course, we saw a parallel strategy emerge in Shenhui's attacks on Puji. On this front, too, then, it would seem that the author of the *Lidai* is altogether traditional in his efforts to steal tradition.

CONCLUSION: THE KINSHIP OF CONSPIRACY AND NEGATION

Standing back from these readings, there is an important theoretical problem to confront: while I have been treating conspiracy theories and the rhetorics of negation as two very different literary constructs, in another sense both are dedicated to moving authority and the essence of tradition from one place to another. Thus, as a narrative shows a master negating truth claims advocated by some other source, this master appears to stand above that older figure-of-authority since he can only perform this kind of negation if he appears as the one in possession of the final version of Buddhist truth. Consequently, this kind of negation forces the migration of authority and value from older sources to the new source that "speaks" the negation. The above conspiracy theories, of course, work in the same way, though on the level of historical "reality"; thus, they undermine the figures of authority found in older histories, even as they move the authority associated with those older figures into the new zone created by the conspiracy theory. Thus, in a basic sense, conspiracy theories and the rhetoric of negation are brother and sister: they look and act very differently, but they come from the same family of strategies inseparable from the politics of trying to convincingly claim ownership of the final form of Buddhist truth.

Now that we have a sense of Chan authors complicated relationship with their textual precedents, let's turn to several other important "voices" from the Tang—"voices" that show all sorts of intelligence and complexity, and which further set the stage for what is to come in the Song era.

7

Chan "Dialogues" from the Tang Dynasty

As we piece together a history of early Chan literature, it is important to remember that by the end of eighth century there were several, significantly different, kinds of Chan texts in circulation. Thus, besides the various "warring genealogies" covered in the preceding chapters, one also finds Chan poems, Chan "dialogues," ritual texts detailing rites to be led by Chan masters, elegant and elaborate funeral steles, and, just slightly later, an encyclopedia of all known Chan partisans, written by Zongmi (780–841).[1] It would be interesting and worthwhile to consider examples from each of these genres, but for the purposes of this book, this chapter focuses on but one category of text, which, for the sake of convenience, I am calling the "Chan dialogue." This choice makes sense because the "Chan dialogue" would become one of the hallmarks of Chan writing in the Song era, and because the "dialogues" reveal a number of important elements in the construction of Chan thought. As my use of scare quotes suggests, these "dialogues" appear to be literary creations designed for readers, and surely are not repre-

---

1. For a translation of the preface to Zongmi's text—the only section that survives—and related material, see Jeffrey L. Broughton, *Zongmi on Chan* (New York: Columbia University Press, 2009), 101–79.

sentative of oral teachings or real conversations. And yet, as we will see, it is just this talent for writing dialogues as though they had once been actual speech that is so essential to Chan writing.

Another reason for focusing on these dialogue texts is that they show little or no interest in lineage claims. That is, though the various dialogues were, in time, attributed to Bodhidharma, or Hongren, or Sengcan, the content of the conversations and their framing spends no time developing a history of the Bodhidharma family, or establishing this or that master in the Bodhidharma family, or seeking, for that matter, to celebrate a particular monastery. In place of those essentially private concerns, these texts seem almost like "podcasts" designed to deliver the voice of the consummate master to any competent reader who would take the time to read them. A sense for these texts' public generosity only deepens when we see that in these "dialogues" the supposedly enlightened masters regularly try to convince their interlocutors—and, of course, the reader—that despite their current confusion regarding Buddhist truths, they are in fact standing on a "trapdoor" that could suddenly drop them into the refuge of nirvana. In short, these texts promise readers that they can, right now (!), awaken to the final truths of Buddhism and thereby find total freedom not just from samsara, but from Buddhism itself. That is, the promise is that one can regain a cosmic totality and be done with the whole problematic cosmology that Buddhism brought to China. Not surprising, given what we've seen in the preceding chapters, this trapdoor and its promises are often presented in Daoist-sounding language.[2]

To give a taste of these dialogue texts, this chapter first considers the *Discourse on the Essentials of Cultivating Mind* (*Xiuxin yaolun*), a text that

---

2. For useful discussion of Daoist-flavored Buddhist discourse in the Tang, see Wendi L. Adamek, *The Mystique of Transmission: On an Early Chan History and Its Contents* (New York: Columbia University Press, 2007), 249–52, and also Robert H. Sharf, *Coming to Terms with Chinese Buddhism: A Reading of the Treasure Store Treatise* (Honolulu: University of Hawai'i Press, 2005).

seems somewhat older than the other dialogue texts.[3] At some point this work was attributed to Hongren, though its final section says that it was put together by his students, and even that seems like a stretch. It is unusual among the dialogue texts in that, in its second half, it offers some advice on how to meditate. However, the place of meditation in the discussion remains ambiguous since it isn't clearly connected to the main project of awakening to innate buddhahood, an awakening that is expected to arise, apparently, from the conversation itself and not from other practices such as meditation. (More on this issue below.)

Next we will turn to the *Discourse on No-Mind* (*Wuxin lun*), which is a particularly quirky dialogue since the author explains in the introduction that he has invented both the master and his disciple.[4] Though openly inviting the reader into his world of fiction, the author nonetheless promises to present an account of the final truth of Buddhism or, rather, the "great Dao," as he calls it. Thus, we have clear admission that Chan *fiction* was accepted, at least by some authors and their readers, as a viable way to get at Buddhism's final *truth*. The author's playful creativity is confirmed when, near the end of the discussion, the narrator tells us that the disciple figure in the text suddenly had a great

---

3. Nine copies of the *Discourse on the Essentials of Cultivating Mind* were found at Dunhuang, and they differ somewhat. More noteworthy, the *Discourse* was found within scrolls that held other Chan-related materials, giving the impression that the text had been selected for several "best of" collections of Chan texts at Dunhuang. For instance, Pelliot 3559 is a scroll that holds, in addition to the *Discourse,* eleven other Chan-related texts or fragments of texts. For more details, see John R. McRae, *The Northern School and the Formation of Early Ch'an Buddhism* (Honolulu: University of Hawai'i Press, 1986), 309n36. For the following analysis, I have worked from McRae's translation (ibid., 121–32), checking it against the version in the *Taishō, T* (no. 2011), 48.377a.

4. At least three other self-proclaimed faux-dialogue texts were found at Dunhuang. For more discussion, see McRae, "The Antecedents of Encounter Dialogue in Chinese Ch'an Buddhism," in *The Kōan: Texts and Contexts in Zen Buddhism,* eds. Steven Heine and Dale S. Wright (Oxford: Oxford University Press, 2000), 66-68 and 74n44. Daoist authors also used these explicitly faux-dialogue structures; see, for example, "The Mind and Eyes Discussion" (*Xinmu lun*), trans. Livia Kohn in *Sitting in Oblivion: The Heart of Daoist Meditation* (Dunedin, FL: Three Pines Press, 2010), 207–12.

enlightenment.[5] Thus, the text is, in effect, tempting the reader, as if to say: "Pay close attention to this discussion and you, too, might get that great enlightenment." The author then has the newly enlightened disciple figure stand up, bow to the master, and deliver a poem that, in about half of its lines, looks like a rough knockoff of several passages in the *Daode jing.* Thus, in this presentation it would seem that enlightenment, in which one supposedly leaves behind language, mundane thought, and literature in general, results not only in more language, but also in a kind of poetry that medieval Chinese readers would have found distinctly Daoist in tone, rhetoric, and logic. It is just this penchant for exchanging the logical and often ponderous language of traditional Buddhism for cryptic, Daoist-flavored poetry that would continue to be a key element in the emergence of Chan literature.[6]

Looking closely at these two Tang dialogue texts, it would seem that the two kinds of Buddhism that were identified in the *Two Entrances and Four Practices* (see chapter 2) have now been brought together to form a unified discourse in which the karmic form of Buddhism—the Second Entrance—is presented as something to be dreaded, while the sudden, "trapdoor" teachings promise that karmic Buddhism can be overcome as one somehow gains enlightenment and instant access to an innate form of buddhahood. In fact, in another mid-Tang text called the *Discourse on the End of Contemplation* (*Jueguan lun*), which closely resembles the *Discourse on No-Mind,* the master is given the name "Entering by Principle" (*ruli*) and his student is called "The Karmic Door" (*yuanmen*),

5. This sudden enlightenment occurs at *T* (no. 2831), 85.1269c.19.

6. The Dao-ification of Buddhist language in the mid-Tang comes after several centuries during which Daoist authors borrowed substantially from the Buddhist tradition to produce Daoist "sutras" and monastic codes. This borrowing continued into the eighth century when Daoist authors began writing texts on meditation that appear designed to compete with Chan works; see, for example, the *Discourse on Sitting in Oblivion* (*Zuowang lun*) or the *Classic on the Lingbao [Style] of Meditation and Insight* (*Lingbao dingguan lun*). On this topic of mutual Buddhist-Daoist influence, see Sharf, *Coming to Terms with Chinese Buddhism,* and *Sitting in Oblivion,* trans. Kohn, esp. chap. 7. See also Livia Kohn, "Chuang-tzu and the Chinese Ancestry of Ch'an Buddhism," *Journal of Chinese Philosophy* 13 (1986): 411–28, published under her maiden name, Livia Knaul.

making clear that their discussion was set up as a kind of forum on the Two Entrances, one which only resolves when the confused student suddenly gains enlightenment, and describes the wondrous collapse of language and communication saying: "Just as the master spoke without speaking, I, in fact, heard without hearing. With hearing and speaking becoming one, everything is quiescent and there is nothing to say."[7] Once we see similarly staged conversions in other texts, we will have good evidence for thinking that mid-Tang authors developed these "conversations" hoping to tempt the reader with the possibility of moving from karmic Buddhism into this other, unthinkable form of Buddhism that seems to be fairly Daoist in form and content.

Now, if we are right in identifying a basic dynamic of overcoming traditional Buddhism in these dialogues, then I believe Bernard Faure was right on track in arguing that there is a kind of scapegoating at work in Chan rhetoric such that without karmic Buddhism serving as the fall guy, there would be no thrill or meaning in taking up the "sudden teachings."[8] But what, exactly, is expected to happen to the

---

7. For bibliographic details on the various manuscripts of the *Discourse on the End of Contemplation*, see Sharf, *Coming to Terms with Chinese Buddhism*, p. 296n.40; see also Sharf's useful discussion of the text, ibid., 40–47. For a handy version of the text, see the *Supplement to the Dazangjing* that is made available through CBETA, *B* (no.101), 18.693a.1; the passage translated above is found at 18.705a.11. (http://tripitaka.cbeta.org /B18no101) In his *The Ceasing of Notions: An Early Zen Text from the Dunhuang Caves with Selected Comments* (Somerville, MA: Wisdom Publications, 2012), Soko Morinaga translated this passage somewhat differently; see ibid., 93. Gishin Tokiwa also produced a translation of this text; see *A Dialogue on the Contemplation-Extinguished: A Translation based on Professor Seizan Yanagida's Modern Japanese Translation and Consultations with Professor Yoshitaka Iriya* (Kyoto: Institute for Zen Studies, 1973); for Tokiwa's rendering of this passage, see ibid., 21.

8. In *The Rhetoric of Immediacy: A Cultural Critique of Chan/Zen Buddhism* (Princeton, NJ: Princeton University Press, 1991), 49, Bernard Faure develops the position that a scapegoating mechanism is essential to the Chan tradition. He also invokes the logic of scapegoating at several places in his *The Will to Orthodoxy: A Critical Genealogy of Northern Chan Buddhism*, trans. Phyllis Brooks (Stanford, CA: Stanford University Press, 1997), see 10, 98, and 182. For more reflections on the dialectics of overcoming in the building of second-order religious traditions, see my *Fetishizing Tradition: Desire and Reinvention in Buddhist and Christian Narratives* (Albany: State University of New York Press, 2015).

reader as he works through one of these works dedicated to pitting the "sudden teachings" against more traditional forms of Buddhist thought and practice? Is the reader really expected to finish with karmic Buddhism like the mythic masters of the past whose perfection is so regularly invoked in Chan literature? Or, are the "sudden teachings" merely offered as a comforting nirvanic dreamscape, one to be nurtured and enjoyed from time to time *within* the sphere of traditional, karmic Buddhism, which, otherwise, was to remain intact?

Posing this kind of question here will likely help with a larger problem that is looming on the horizon: all the radical negations of normal Buddhism—the sudden teachings of no-thought, no-practice, no-teachings, no-sutras, no-study—that appear in various Chan statements in the Tang and the Song eras seem to say next to nothing about the regular, day-to-day practice of Chinese Buddhism. To date, we have found no evidence that Chan rhetoric translated into any major shifts in the institutional realities of monastic Buddhism in the Tang.[9] In fact, all the surviving evidence suggests that throughout the Tang, monastic and lay Buddhism continued to be practiced along very traditional lines. Likewise, though Zongmi expressed concern over Chan rhetoric that he felt was too extreme, he never mentions that anyone was acting on this rhetoric or reconstructing the Buddhist tradition in any significant manner.[10] In the Song, this gap between wild-sounding Chan rhetoric and day-to-day Buddhist practices becomes even more pronounced, since, from 1103, we start to have Chan monastic handbooks that prescribe the

9. For discussion of late Tang works in which Chan masters discuss monasticism, see Mario Poceski, "Xuefeng's Code and the Chan School's Participation in the Development of Monastic Regulations," *Asia Major,* 3d ser., 16, no. 2 (2003): 33–56. Summing up the situation, Poceski concludes that the evidence "indicates that brief monastic codes written for particular monasteries associated with the Chan School were meant to serve as supplements rather than replacements of the vinaya.... *That points to a pattern of modest adaptation of conventional monasticism rather than a radical break with canonical traditions and received monastic practices*" (34; emphasis added).

10. For an example of such criticism, see Zongmi's remarks on the Hongzhou school in Jeffrey L. Broughton's, *Zongmi on Chan* (New York: Columbia University Press, 2009), 15–20.

standard form of Chan monasticism, and which leave no doubt about its deeply traditional and thoroughly conservative nature (see chapter 9 for more details).

Consequently, we need to prepare ourselves for a deep and abiding Chan irony in which masters regularly negate and disparage the practice of karmic Buddhism, even though just this kind of normal Buddhism continued to be practiced by everyone—masters included. Trying to figure out why this mismatch between rhetoric and practice turned out to be a stable and productive element in the development of Chan is one of the basic agendas of this book.[11]

DISCOURSE ON THE ESSENTIALS OF CULTIVATING MIND

The *Discourse on the Essentials of Cultivating Mind* can feel like a bewildering text to read. The author has Hongren speak about the final truths of the universe (and the self) so directly and with such confidence that one might feel that there could be no way to analyze this text. And yet, with a bit of distance, and patience, one can see that the forms of truth (and perfection) that the text offers to the reader have some very specific characteristics and, not surprisingly, have some very visible literary precedents.

After reminding readers how important it is to copy this text correctly for later students, Hongren initiates his discussion by explaining that the "essence of cultivating the Dao" (*xiudao zhi benti*) is to realize that one's mind is "inherently pure, beyond birth and death, and free of discrimination." Equally important, one is to know that "[t]he pure mind is, by its own nature, full and complete; it is the fundamental teacher and [recognizing it] is even better than recollecting all the buddhas of

---

11. In *Coming to Terms with Chinese Buddhism* (p. 15), Sharf underscores the productive quality of this gap between religious rhetoric and actual practice: "As Jonathan Z. Smith has cogently argued *the social and cognitive allure of religious systems lies in precisely this gap between the ideal and the actual*," (emphasis added).

the ten directions."[12] Thus in this opening statement, which in fact doesn't follow from a question, we see the classic Chan assumption that all humans are endowed with innate buddhahood and, consequently, that truth and tradition are to found within each believer and not externally in the form of teachers, texts, or even in the buddhas of the ten directions.

Leaving aside, for the moment, the paradox that this statement is made just after Hongren explained the importance of maintaining this discourse in correct textual form—suggesting that an external version of tradition was assumed, in fact, to be quite important—this opening salvo sets the stage for defining the three overlapping themes that follow: (1) the minds of all sentient creatures are fundamentally pure; (2) enlightenment is already present in each creature—one just needs to uncover it; and (3) though this innate buddhahood is fully present, failure to recognize it will lead on to bad rebirths and hell. To develop these themes, the author has an unnamed questioner ask about each phrase of Hongren's opening statement, beginning with the question: "How could one know that one's mind is inherently pure?"[13] Hongren responds by citing a passage that he claims is from the *Sūtra on the Ten Stages*, which develops the following analogy: "There is an adamantine buddha-nature within the bodies of sentient beings. It is like the sun [on a cloudy day] which is essentially bright, perfect, complete, and limitlessly vast—it is just that it is [temporarily] covered over by the layered clouds of the five skandhas. [Or, again,] it is like a lamp inside a jar—its light cannot shine through."[14]

After more discussion of the aptness of these analogies, the questioner turns to ask about the opening claim that this pure mind is beyond birth and death—that it is, in effect, already "in" nirvana. In response, Hongren again looks to the Buddhist literary tradition to

12. These three passages are found in McRae, *Northern School*, 121, with changes.
13. Ibid.
14. Ibid., 121–22, with changes. According to McRae (ibid., 313n42), this analogy isn't in the *Sūtra on the Ten Stages*.

shore up his claim, quoting the *Vimalakīrti* as saying, "'Suchness is without birth; suchness is without death.' The term 'suchness' refers to the suchlike buddha-nature, the mind which is the source [of all the dharmas] and which is pure in its self-nature."[15] Hongren then further develops this point of view on suchness and the mind, adding, as well, that standard claim about the fundamental sameness between buddhas and all creatures. As the discourse advances, it is clear that the author is having Hongren weave a stray passage from the *Vimalakīrti* into these broader claims about the reality of this innate buddha-mind, claims that the *Vimalakīrti* doesn't make. In short, the author has picked out one small piece of the literary tradition to make his reconstruction of tradition look traditional.

Still working through Hongren's initial statement in a steady and exegetical manner, the questioner now turns to the phrase about this internal buddha-nature being the root teacher. Here, Hongren doesn't immediately cite a sutra passage and instead builds his case arguing that "The true mind (*zhenxin*) is just naturally (*ziran*) present [within us] and doesn't arrive from the outside; nothing in the universe is dearer to us than maintaining this mind (*zi shou yu xin*). Now, as for those who know this mind and maintain it, they will reach the other shore [of nirvana]. Conversely, those who are mistaken about it, and forsake it, will fall into the three lower realms [of samsara]."[16] Hongren then sums up the importance of this "true mind," saying, "All the buddhas of the universe—past, present, and future—take their own [true] mind to be their root teacher."[17] This claim is rounded out with a line from an unnamed commentary that says, "If one guards the [true] mind with clarity, then mistaken thoughts won't arise—just this is birthlessness [nirvana, that is]. Therefore you should know that mind is the root teacher."[18] With the language in the cited sutra quotations so neatly

15. Ibid., 122.
16. Ibid., with slight changes.
17. Ibid., with changes.
18. Ibid., 123.

matching up with Hongren's initial statements, while also nicely dove-
tailing with the student's questions, it is clear that this supposed conversation is really a highly focused essay.

Among other things, we shouldn't miss that there is an interesting tension here between literature and this innate buddha-mind that Hongren
is invoking. To wit, though Hongren is shown developing his position in
reliance on sutras and other elements in the Buddhist literary tradition,
he is building a fairly radical theory of *natural enlightenment,* an enlightenment supposedly present from the beginning of time and recoverable
with this single "practice" of guarding the true mind, in lieu of any other
kind of Buddhist activity. Ironically, then, it is precisely with *literary*
precedents that the author is working to convince the reader of this internal
reality that precedes literature, culture, and traditional consciousness,
even as he is also working to produce confidence in a practice that will
supposedly render those older forms of tradition superfluous. If one over-
looks this gentle interweaving of literary precedents with claims about
natural enlightenment, the slow and careful process of rewriting Buddhist truths and practices can, mistakenly, appear as an escape from tradition and its literature, when nothing could be further from the truth. It
is only *with* the literary tradition and *through* the literary tradition that
these natural "realities" began to take hold of the Chinese imagination.

After presenting "guarding the true mind" as the summation of the
Buddhist tradition, we find several exchanges on the sameness of buddhas and sentient beings. What is somewhat unusual here is that this
theme is developed in the context of an emphasis on the horrors of
rebirth. As the questioner pointedly asks, "If the true essence of sentient beings and the buddhas is the same, then why is it that the buddhas are not subject to the laws of birth and death, but receive incalcu-
lable pleasures and are free (*zizai*) and unhindered [in their activities],
while we sentient beings have fallen into the realm of birth and death
and are subject to various kinds of suffering?"[19] Clearly, the questioner

19. Ibid.

wants to know why the *sameness of essence* between sages and ordinary creatures doesn't translate into a *sameness of destiny*. After explaining again that buddhas recognize the true mind, never generate false thoughts, and thus are no longer subject to birth and death, Hongren clarifies, via an extended chain of logic, what awaits normal sentient beings:

> Sentient beings are all deluded as to the true nature and do not discern the mind's root. [Stricken] with a variety of mistaken views and karmic [attachments], they do not cultivate correct mindfulness, and thus thoughts of revulsion and attraction arise. Due to revulsion and attraction, the vessel of the mind becomes broken and leaks. With the vessel of the mind broken and leaking, [sentient beings] are subject to birth and death. Because of birth and death, all the [various kinds of] suffering naturally appear.[20]

Reading this, the reader likely gets the distinct impression that at each moment of his life he stands at a crossroads, with the dreadful question being: Will I be able to awaken to this true mind and get free of samsara, or will I continue to produce false thoughts and thereby condemn myself to a terrifying future of endless birth and death?

The danger of the situation isn't left to the reader's imagination. After citing a sutra supporting the above assessment of the situation, Hongren directly addresses the disciple, urging him to "Make effort to understand this! If you can maintain awareness of the true mind, then false thoughts won't arise. With the [deluded] mind that claims ownership (*wu suo xin*) destroyed, you will naturally be equal to the buddhas."[21] The urgent command to make effort reappears three more times, so it doesn't appear to be a random element in the discourse,[22] and yet the question of exertion is surely a vexed one here since, though the questioner is regularly urged to awaken to this innate buddhahood, no particular practices are given to him to help in this process.

---

20. Ibid., with changes.
21. Ibid., 124, with changes.
22. See sections N, O and P of McRae's translation in *Northern School*, 126–29.

Actually, the problem of practice comes up in the very next section where Hongren admits to the questioner that there's no way to understand how it is that one awakens to the original mind,

> At this point we enter the inconceivable portion [of this teaching] which cannot be understood by the ordinary mind. One becomes enlightened by understanding the mind; one is deluded because of losing [awareness of the true] nature. *If the conditions [necessary for you to understand this] occur, then they occur—it cannot be definitively explained.* Simply trust in the ultimate truth and maintain [awareness of] your own original mind.[23]

Here it would seem that the text is admitting that, besides faith, one has basically nothing to go on in terms of getting hold of this true mind. Nonetheless, the entire "dialogue" still represents a sustained effort to persuade the questioner and reader—with logic, analogies, and scriptural evidence—to accept this cosmology in which a perfect buddha-mind supposedly lives at the base of each creature's consciousness. Later in the discussion, in what looks like an appended section of the text, seated meditation is twice discussed, but it is not directly connected to awakening to the true mind, and thus it would seem that there is no real practice other than having faith in one's inherent buddha-nature and believing that, based on unknown and uncontrollable causes, it might one day be manifest.

What follows is a fairly long passage in which Hongren develops the position that all of the Buddha's teachings are no more than metaphoric presentations of the truth of the internal buddha—put forward for "foolish sentient beings"—and thus normal Buddhist teachings really aren't truthful teachings at all. Thus "guarding the true mind" stands alone as the single teaching/practice that contains all Buddhist truths; as Hongren puts it, "This guarding of the [true] mind is the fundamental basis of nirvana, the essential gateway for entering the path, the essence of the entire Buddhist canon, and the patriarch of all the buddhas of the past,

23. Ibid., 124, with changes.

present, and future."[24] It is here that we see how the text wants to position "guarding the true mind" as the one real Thing in the Buddhist tradition since it is the essence of Buddhist teaching, practice, accomplishment, and is even the truth-father of all the buddhas. Clearly, "guarding the mind" now appears as the perfect fetish of tradition that promises to deliver everything of value in the Buddhist tradition and in the universe, at large. We should note in passing that while other early Chan texts had located the final essence of tradition in a lineage or in a text—for instance, in the Bodhidharma lineage or in the *Laṅkāvatāra Sūtra* or the *Platform Sūtra*—here it is a practice of sorts that is said to contain the essence of all things Buddhist.

Slightly later, when the questioner asks more specifically about this claim that "guarding the true mind" is the "patriarch of all the buddhas of the three times," Hongren responds, "All the buddhas of the past, present, and future are generated from within the nature of [one's own] mind. As soon as you guard [awareness] of the true mind, you won't generate false thoughts. Then, when the [deluded] mind that claims ownership has been extinguished, you become a buddha. Therefore, maintaining [awareness] of the original true mind is the patriarch of all the buddhas of the past, present, and future."[25] While this passage is ambiguous in the Chinese, it seems that the reader is being asked to believe that he himself is the magical zone from whence buddhas come forth. If this reading is correct, then the reader is being urged to conclude that the only real form of tradition is found on the reader's own "home ground," even though, obviously, the reader's dependence on this very text, and, by extension, on the supposed perfection of master Hongren, would suggest otherwise. Hence the literary fantasy developed here is that somehow—presumably with enough faith in this new discourse—one can readily drop out of time,

24. Ibid., with changes.
25. Ibid., 126, with changes. As McRae notes, this passage is problematic; consequently, this translation is tentative. See ibid., 317n82 for more discussion; the passage is findable at *T* (no. 2011), 48.378a.14.

language, suffering, and Buddhism itself, only to find oneself in a nirvana that existed all along at the base of one's being.

Right after the above passage, the second half of the text opens up and, besides being stylistically different, shifts the discussion to focus on different topics. To keep the analysis of this portion of the text relatively short, let's simply consider the two passages where the topic of meditation comes up. In the first passage, Hongren explicitly identifies a text as the source for his comments on meditation. As he puts it, "If you are just beginning to practice seated meditation, then do so according to the *Sūtra on the Contemplation of Amitābha* (*Wuliangshou guanjing*): Sit properly with the body erect, closing the eyes and mouth. Look straight ahead, with the mind visualizing a sun at an appropriate distance away. Maintain this image continuously without stopping. Regulate your breath so that it does not sound alternately coarse and fine, as this can make one sick."[26] Similar advice for a standard form of Buddhist meditation is given slightly later, with the added comment that more information on meditation techniques can found in two other sutras, with the relevant chapters mentioned.[27] Clearly, then, when meditation is directly promoted, the techniques appear borrowed from the Buddhist tradition at large, and in particular from well-established literary sources that have nothing to do with Chan or the discourse on innate enlightenment. In short, what is presented as Hongren's teaching, while perhaps appearing innovative and distinctive in some measure for its insistence on the immediacy of the internal buddha-mind, appears altogether traditional when it comes to prescribing the actual practice of meditation. In fact, this problem will reappear throughout the Chan tradition: the meditation techniques for Chan trainees seem to have been quite traditional

---

26. Ibid., 127. Right after the line about visualizing the sun, there is a phrase in the *Taishō* that isn't in McRae's translation; it urges one to "try to maintain the true mind for one day." Presumably this line was interpolated into the quoted sutra passage at some point; actually, as McRae notes, ibid., 318n88, the whole description of this kind of meditation "is noticeably different from that contained in the sutra itself."

27. Ibid., 127.

and yet these practices are conjoined with a pumped up rhetoric about the immediacy of nirvana and the innate buddha-mind.

While it is clear that the author of this section of the text thought that these meditation techniques discussed in non-Chan sources were relevant to the attempt to recognize one's internal buddha, he doesn't explain how this union of practice and vision is to be effected. Actually, just at the end of this section, Hongren says, "Do not worry if you cannot achieve concentration and do not experience the various psychological states. Just constantly maintain clear awareness of the true mind in all your actions."[28] This comment suggests that the meditation practice that is being recommended here isn't necessarily linked to the "practice" of maintaining awareness of the true mind. And since the topic of meditation only shows up here in the second half of the text, awakening to the innate true mind seems to be something that can be spoken of and reasoned about *apart from meditation.*

Looked at another way, the *theory* part of Hongren's discourse is rather thickly developed and yet there is very little to tie this radical cosmology to a daily practice. This gap between theory and practice seems to be admitted in the second half of the text when Hongren is made to say: "Make effort! And do not be pretentious! It is difficult to get a chance to hear this essential teaching. Of those who have heard it, not more than one person in a number as great as the sands of the river Ganges is able to practice it. It would be rare for even one person in a million billion eons to practice it to perfection."[29] So, though buddha-mind is supposedly always present, Hongren concedes that we have next to no chance to realize it. Of course, there is no reason to take any one of these single statements as the text's final position since it does seem to be rather imprecise and casual in the way it handles specific truth-claims. Nonetheless, the text appears to have left the reader in quite a predicament since, for as close as buddhahood supposedly is,

28. Ibid.
29. Ibid., 128.

there is no real chance to achieve it, and thus one presumably has to go back to worrying about karma, death, and terrifying rebirths. Put that way, the text's heady rhetoric provides a temporary escape from the fundamental fears that Buddhism delivers, and yet, however comforting and exciting this brief interlude might be for the convinced reader, one still has to return to the anxieties of normal, karmic Buddhism.

Regardless of how we imagine the effects of reading Hongren's teaching, there are three visible things that we can point to in order to clarify how the text works as a piece of literature. First, the text seems uninterested in developing a *style* for Hongren or his discourse. Thus Hongren remains faceless and actionless: he simply "talks" in an uninflected manner, and does little more than provide cherry-picked scriptural quotations to buttress his teachings on "guarding the true mind." Second, and in a similar vein, we can see that his rhetoric doesn't become colloquial or poetic or whimsical. In fact, his "speech" seems altogether literary, serious, and little different from the style of the sutras. And finally, unlike other "dialogues" there is no conversion experience for the questioner. Thus, authors in this early phase of writing dialogue apparently hadn't recognized the charm of demonstrating the power of the discourse by having the unenlightened party in the discussion suddenly awaken to the text's truths. As we will see, things are rather different with the *Discourse on No-Mind*.

THE DISCOURSE ON NO-MIND (WUXIN LUN)

The *Discourse on No-Mind* is a relatively short text that, in addition to an introduction and conclusion, can be usefully broken into five sections.[30]

30. Some modern scholars have claimed that the *Discourse on No-Mind* was written by someone associated with the Oxhead School, but the evidence for this is quite thin. For a critical edition and an English translation, see Urs App, *"Mushinron—Tonko shutsudo no ichi tekisuto," Zenbunka Kenkyūjo kiyō* 21 (May 1995): 1–69, and "Treatise on No-Mind: A Chan Text from Dunhuang," *Eastern Buddhist*, n.s., 28, no. 1 (1995): 70–107. See, too, Robert H. Sharf, "Mindfulness and Mindlessness in Early Chan," *Philosophy East & West*, 64, no. 4 (Oct. 2014): 933–64; see also, id., *Coming to Terms with Chinese Buddhism*, 47-51. I learned much from App and Sharf, but the following translations are my own.

In the opening line, the author introduces his discourse with the caveat that the ultimate principle is beyond language and that the great Dao is signless. Then he announces: "Now, I will set up two people to discuss the theory of no-mind."[31] With this simple staging device acknowledged, the first section of the discussion opens up with a nameless disciple asking a nameless monk whether there is mind or not. Upon learning that there is no mind—*wu xin*—the student wants to know how it is that normal cognition operates. Responding to this question, and with a subtle shift in grammar, the monk turns the phrase "no mind" into the technical term "no-mind" which, though still based on the two characters *wu xin,* now appears somewhat substantialized and serves to designate the otherwise unnameable entity that is the basis and essence of all moments of cognition. Thus, though "no-mind" sounds like a total negation at first, it actually is the name of an active and mysterious reality, one that is the source of all that is known and experienced—subject *and* object, that is.[32] The monk figure, suspecting that his disciple is getting confused—and who wouldn't be?—says, "I will explain it to you, step by step, so as to cause you to awaken to the true principle.[33]

After this initial exchange, the second main theme emerges: the student seems worried that if everything is no-mind, and thus of a great

31. *T* (no. 2831), 85.1269a.24.

32. Since the issue of Daoist influence will become important later in the text, I should note here that the term "no-mind" (*wuxin*) appears in chaps. 12 (twice), and 22 of the *Zhuangzi.* For more discussion of the term, see Fukunaga Mitsuji, "'No-mind' in Chuang-tzu and Ch'an Buddhism," trans. L. Hurvitz, *Zimbun* 12 (1969): 9–45. *The Encyclopedia of Taoism,* ed. Fabrizio Pregadio (London: Routledge, 2004), refers to no-mind in vol. 1: 119, 536, and vol. 2, 1044, 1100, and 1298.

33. *T* (no. 2831), 85.1269b.3. Whereas the disciple regularly speaks of the monk and himself in the third person, the monk figure uses a more relaxed and direct "you" and "I"—as he does in the passage just cited. Given that this pattern holds throughout the text, it would seem that the author has taken as his "speaking" position the role of the monk, with the disciple appearing more as a stick figure. Moreover, when the monk says "you" to the disciple *in the text,* it would seem that that "you" drifts towards the reader and would seem to address him as well. In short, the text appears designed for the reader to step into the role of the disciple, even as the author controls both subject positions.

sameness, then the traditional Buddhist laws of karma and rebirth couldn't work. He asks, "The monk just said that everything is just no-mind, and thus there shouldn't be any sin or merit either, so how is it that sentient beings cycle in the six realms of transmigration, being born and dying endlessly?"[34] Answering much as Hongren does in the *Discourse on the Essentials of Cultivating Mind,* the monk makes the familiar case that "sentient beings are confused and, while in the midst of no-mind, perversely produce mind and thereby generate various kinds of karma. Perversely clinging to [all this fabrication] as existent is suffi-cient to spin the wheel of samsara with its six realms, causing endless birth and death."[35] In an effort to bolster this claim about the power of bad thinking to make bad worlds appear, the monk explains that this kind of misrecognition is just like the terror that arises when, in the dark, one takes a chair to be a ghost or mistakes a rope for a snake. He adds that if "sentient beings meet a good spiritual friend [a master, that is] who *teaches them seated meditation* and they awaken to no-mind, then all karmic obstructions will be eradicated and the cycle of birth and death will cease, just as darkness is dispersed when a shaft of sunlight enters a dark space."[36] (This is the one line in the text where meditation is mentioned, so I have highlighted it and will return to discuss it below.)

With awakening to no-mind defined as the cause of buddhahood, the third topic comes into view: the student questions the reality of Buddhism and its various teachings. The monk confirms that all the language evoking suffering, enlightenment, samsara, and nirvana is definitely no-mind, and that the buddha had to rely on all this diverse terminology for sentient beings because they were attached to mind,

34. *T* (no. 2831), 85.1269b.13.
35. *T* (no. 2831), 85.1269b.16.
36. *T* (no. 2831), 85.1269b.20. The eradication of past sins appears as a key concern in the conclusion of this *Vajrasamādhi Sūtra,* where the Buddha-in-the-text promises that relying on this sutra for entrance into a "reality vision" will result in the eradication of all past evil deeds. The supposed suddenness of this karmic cleansing is underscored when the Buddha then explains that one's evil deeds will be erased just as suddenly as when darkness in room disappears when a light is brought in (*T* no. 273, 9.374b. 18ff.).

and the world of samsara and nirvana that comes with it. In fact, though, "as soon as one awakens to no-mind, there is no more suffering, samsara or nirvana, whatsoever."[37] This radical statement leads the disciple to then ask: if enlightenment and nirvana aren't ultimately real and attainable, how was it that the buddhas of the past all attained enlightenment? The monk responds with a typical two-truths answer in which he claims that "it is only in the language of conventional truth and literary terms that we say they achieved [enlightenment]. In terms of ultimate truth, there was nothing that could actually be obtained."[38] Apparently feeling the need to support this claim with a passage from the literary tradition, the author as the monk then cite a line from the *Vimalakīrti* that reaffirms that enlightenment can't be achieved by mind or body. He follows with a passage from the *Diamond Sūtra* to the same effect, but with the twist that "all the buddhas attain [enlightenment] by means of unobtainability."[39] Summing up this unthinkability at the heart of everything, the monk says, "You need to know that as long as there is mind, then there is everything, and [conversely] when there is no-mind, everything is nonexistent."[40] In short, the monk describes an ontology in which the world and everything in it, including Buddhism, is illusory and unreal such that when one realizes no-mind, it all disappears, with this disappearance being, in fact, the truth of "real Buddhism"—even though this form of Buddhist truth isn't to be reified into something obtainable or thinkable.

The discussion then strays briefly into the question of whether insentient objects are no-mind or not. As Robert Sharf has pointed out, this topic seems to have been important to several writers at this time, and the author of the *Discourse on No-Mind* carefully argues that while everything is no-mind, there still is a fundamental difference between

37. *T* (no. 2831), 85.1269b.27.
38. *T* (no. 2831), 85.1269c.4.
39. *T* (no. 2831), 85.1269c.6.
40. *T* (no. 2831), 85.1269c.7.

sentient beings and material objects.[41] Leaving this debate, the monk declares: "this no-mind is the true mind. And true mind is just no-mind."[42] Introducing the term "true mind" to qualify no-mind helps explain how, despite all the negations, the text still allows for the *practical* attainment of enlightenment and buddhahood—the discovery of "true mind," that is. The following passage makes this even clearer.

In light of this radical-sounding discourse on no-mind, the student wants to know what he should practice. Not surprisingly the monk says, "Simply, in all matters, awaken to no-mind—just this is practicing.[43] There is no other practice. Therefore you should know that no-mind is everything. Nirvana is just no-mind." And here it is that the student, presumably because of this *discussion* of no-mind, suddenly gets greatly enlightened, understanding that there are no objects outside of mind, and that there is no mind outside of objects. This new awareness supposedly shifts his way of being in the world such that all his actions became unhindered (*zizai*), and, likewise, with the nets of doubt cut, his thinking became free of obstructions. Then, in order to demonstrate his gratitude, the disciples stands up, bows to the monk, and "engraves" [his understanding of] no-mind in this poem:

41. See further Robert H. Sharf, "Is Nirvāṇa the Same as Insentience? Chinese Struggles with an Indian Buddhist Ideal," in *India in the Chinese Imagination: Myth, Religion, and Thought*, eds. John Kieschnick and Meir Shahar (Philadelphia: University of Pennsylvania Press, 2014), 141–70. Timothy Barrett rightly suggests that the mid-Tang discussion of insentience, based on the term *wuqing* (lit., "without feeling"), reaches back to Zhuangzi's use of the term (see the *Zhuangzi*, 5:22; for Burton Waton's translation, see *The Complete Works of Chuang Tzu*, 75–76). For Barrett's discussion, see *Li Ao: Buddhist, Taoist, or Neo-Confucian?* (Oxford University Press, 1992), 97–98.

42. *T* (no. 2831), 85.1269c.16.

43. I have shifted the *Taishō* punctuation so that the first sentence ends after *wuxin* instead of in front of it; *T* (no. 2831), 85.1269c.17–18.

The state of mind has all along been quiescent (*xinshen xiangji*)[44]
It has no color and no form
[Try to] observe it, and you can't see it
Listen for it, and yet there's no sound
It seems dark and yet it is not-dark
It is bright and yet not-bright
Abandon it, and nothing will be destroyed
Obtain it, and nothing will be produced.[45]

This poem continues on for another ten lines but it is clear that the student's enlightenment has rendered him an authority on the final nature of reality, and that his articulation of these newly discovered truths takes him, not just into poetry, but into a lyrical idiom that is quite close to the *Daode jing* in style and content (see, in particular, chapters 14 and 35 of the *Daode jing*). The monk, for his part, first reaffirms that no-mind is the best of all the perfections, citing the *Vimalakīrti* and the *Dharma Drum Sūtra* to shore up his claim that with no-mind one can obliterate samsara and nirvana, even though, he adds, you can't obtain anything, not even non-attainment. Then he offers his own poem:[46]

In the past, when you were mistaken, you had mind
Now that you've awakened, shazam! no-mind.
Even though no-mind is able to shine forth and function
This shining forth and use are forever quiescent and [are of the nature of] thusness.

44. The return of "mind" here, after the above dialogue worked so hard to get the reader to understand no-mind, is of course a bit tricky—presumably this mind is a no-mind, and yet the comfortable confusion of terms and levels is no doubt indicative of the overall looseness of the text.

45. *T* (no. 2831), 85.1269c.22.

46. *T* (no. 2831), 85.1270a.10. Urs App, who is an excellent translator, reads this poem and the next as spoken by the disciple (App, "Treatise on No-Mind," 104), but this is far from clear. The monk was the one most recently speaking, and the character *nai* in the phrase that introduces the poem seems to indicate that, having just said his piece about no-mind, he *then* recites this poem. Of course, given that both figures are the author's creation, it perhaps doesn't much matter.

He adds:

> No-mind doesn't shine forth and doesn't function
> Just this not shining forth and not functioning is non-action (*wuwei*)
> This is the true dharma realm of the buddhas
> And is not the same as that of the bodhisattvas or solitary realizers.
> What is called "no-mind" is just the absence of a mind of deluded thought.

This poem would seem to mark the natural ending of the text. However there is another section that follows, one that seeks to define the very Daoist-sounding term *tai shang,* which hadn't in fact been used in the discussion thus far.[47] Hence, it seems likely that this final section was added on some time after the text had been completed.

Standing back from the dialogue, it seems that four basic points are worth making. First, there is an interesting tension between the philosophic claims about the unreality of all things—especially Buddhism and its cosmology of samsara and nirvana—and the way the dialogue develops until the disciple gets enlightened. Thus, whatever might be *said* about the final nature of reality in which ultimately there are no buddhas, no enlightenment, no nirvana, and so forth, this in no way impedes the disciple's enlightenment in the real time of the narrative. In fact, the total negation of everything—enlightenment included—appears to be the catalyst that causes the student's enlightenment. In short, all that talk of nothingness really turned into something by the end of the discussion.

Second, the text seems ambivalent in its promotion of actual practices. Thus, if it was by means of this very discussion of no-mind that the disciple opens up onto his new vision of reality, what should we make of that single line in which the monk says that sentient beings need to meet a teacher who will teach them seated mediation in order to awaken to no-mind? Surely the dialogue never suggests that the disciple in the dialogue has been doing seated meditation. And, this ambiguity only deepens when the disciple directly asks the monk what to

47. *T* (no. 2831), 85.1270a.17.

practice, only to learn that awakening to no-mind in all activities is the only practice. Hence, it would seem as though there is no practical way into this version of Buddhist truth—one either gets what no-mind means when it is explained, or one doesn't.[48] Just this assessment of the power of the language *about* enlightenment needs to be kept front and center for the dialogues to be considered in the following chapters.

Third, like so many Chan-related texts, in the *Discourse on No-Mind* a split-screen or bifocal vision of reality emerges—one that has important parallels with the visions of conspiracy explored in the previous three chapters. Here, the reader is invited into a new way of being Buddhist, one that unavoidably involves seeing and thinking in two radically different ways—as the master *and* as the benighted disciple. As both positions are established in the reading experience, it would seem that there is a third point of view that emerges and it is defined by getting used to bouncing between these two extremes. To readers familiar with the two truths of Mahāyāna Buddhism—worldly truths and emptiness—this might not sound like such an important innovation. And yet what *is* new and noteworthy here is how the reader is being so directly drawn into both visions, especially when, after slogging through all the negations, one finds oneself confronted with the student's enlightenment, articulated in that Daoist-sounding poem.[49] In short, what is taken to be the final truth of Buddhism has gotten intensely

48. Sharf also wonders what we can infer about actual mediation practices from texts such as this one; see his "Mindfulness and Mindlessness," 933, 945, 949 and 955n19. However, I am not convinced by his argument that finds parallels between early Chan and "the Buddhist mindfulness movement in the 20th century" (ibid., 933). On the other hand, Sharf wisely quotes Zongmi's ninth-century complaint that Chan sources "speak a lot about the principles of Chan but say little of Chan practice" (ibid., 934; *T* no. 2015, 48.399a.24), concluding perceptively that "Zongmi was acutely aware of the apparent contradiction between what famous Chan monks and missives say on the one hand, and what Chan monks were actually doing on the other" (ibid., 938).

49. Nor should we miss that just this kind of bifocal seeing was the very talent that enabled the author to pen this dialogue in which he had to play both sides of the discussion. In sum, a certain philosophic irony is both the cause and the effect of the text, a perspective that I think is crucial for understanding Chan in general.

present and articulated in a more familiar and "local" rhetoric, one taken, apparently, from the *Daode jing*.

The final point is simply the recognition that the disciple's enlightenment produces more language, and in two interesting ways. First, obviously, the student has traded the ordinary prose of dialogue for the poetry of his monologue; second, the earlier reliance on Buddhist terminology disappears and that Daoist-sounding diction takes over in which no-mind is reckoned in language very reminiscent of the *Daode jing*.[50] On the level of narrative, then, it would seem that the author is having the disciple (and the reader) move through a zone of conflict in which the disciple is first faced with two worlds: (1) his own world of Buddhism that he brought to the conversation, one defined by suffering, samsara, and (distant) nirvana; and (2) the much happier world of the monk, where there is only no-mind and nothing else, though this no-mind is clearly referred to as a nirvanic reality of sorts. After numerous exchanges in which the disciple tries to negotiate the gap between these two worlds, the disciple suddenly bursts into a recognition of no-mind and then begins, literally, to speak his own mind by delivering a supposedly impromptu poem to express his new-won ease of no-mind in which all is nirvana and always has been. This vision, though not breaking entirely free of Buddhist terminology and cosmology, plunges into a Daoist-styled utopia of total quiescence and non-action, one where there could be no Buddhism, no language, no samsara, no anything. Thus, in this text, attaining the final truth of Buddhism ends up sounding like attaining the Dao of the *Daode jing*, even though now this is to be accomplished by finding an accomplished Buddhist master or, at least, learning to read and interpret a text like this one. Paradoxically,

---

50. Sharf, in his *Coming to Terms with Chinese Buddhism*, 49, also argues for a connection with the *Daode jing*, but he doesn't point out that these Daoist-sounding passages only appear at this certain place in the text, a fact that raises important questions about how the author is developing a narrative in which "philosophic voicings" change in the course of the exchange. In short, we see another Chan author skillfully combining radical negation with a careful narrative program designed to shape the reader's experience in a cumulative manner.

then, although the text hopes to convince the reader that a Daoist-sounding utopia is at hand, Buddhism is still the gateway to this land.

BRIEF CONCLUSIONS

Though the two texts analyzed in this chapter might appear monochromatic and underdeveloped in comparison to the flashy, startling, and sometimes "dirty" dialogues of the Song era—to be covered in the coming chapters—it is still the case that both texts rely on three basic gestures essential to later Chan writing. First, both authors seem comfortable defining a buddha-reality that is characterized as beyond words, teachings, and the knowledge of non-buddhas. Second, while claiming direct access to that buddha-reality, they confidently presented radical-sounding advice for Buddhist "practice" which made that buddha-reality appear shockingly present; and, even though the details of this "practice" are left altogether vague, the reader is nonetheless bombarded with claims that he is a buddha already, sort of, and that he could jump out of samsara anytime he liked, if he could only stop thinking like a non-buddha. The reason the situation doesn't appear hopeless is that the texts also give us the voice of buddhahood—the voice of the master "speaking" a friendly and flawless Chinese—thereby proving that the jump into nirvana can and has been made, at least in literature. And surely the reader naturally feels all the more provoked and inspired when the disciple in the *Discourse on No-Mind* gets enlightened.

Third, both authors draw heavily on Daoist vocabulary. Borrowing Daoist language for Buddhist truths—if we can speak like this—could, of course, mean several things. For my part, I suspect that this borrowing reflects a sustained effort by elite Chinese authors to make Buddhism less scary: as Buddhism was made to sound more and more Daoist—at least within the horizons of these texts—it began to glow with a range of comforting associations that diminished or even eliminated fear of future rebirths. Presumably, readers would have been thrilled to learn from the *Discourse on No-Mind* that final Buddhist wisdom took one back to the fuzzy serenity of Daoist wholeness, a "place" where Buddhist rhetoric is absent and classical Daoist idioms and cadences take over. In fact, both the *Discourse on No-Mind* and the *Discourse on the Essentials of Cultivating Mind* look back in time to find complete enlightenment, making it appear as though the Daoist preference for *returning* to the Dao has completely overwritten the Indian Buddhist assumption that buddhahood will always be off in the distant future.

In sum, if it turns out that we can't identify specific practices that were essential to Chan—and so far that seems to be the case—then we ought to consider that Chan might be better described as the growing confidence, and literary ability, to dramatize the reality of enlightenment for Chinese readers. As these visions of Buddhist truth were expressed in first-person voices—Hongren's, Huineng's, Shenhui's, or that of the fully fictional "monk" of the *Discourse on No-Mind* – Chinese readers would have naturally concluded that Buddhist truths were, quite literally, theirs for the taking.[51]

This point about the authors' audacity in writing from the buddha-position needs to be conjoined with one more perspective. Chinese authors, from the earliest days of Buddhism's presence in China, fabricated sutras purporting to be translations from Sanskrit. In those texts, Chinese authors confidently presented the voice of the Indian Buddha and got that voice to authenticate various new perspectives on Buddhist truths. Thus it is worth wondering if there wasn't a link between that long history of sutra forgery and the production of these Chan dialogues since in both cases, it is a question of inventing a buddha-figure who speaks new, and decidedly Chinese, versions of the final truths of the Buddhist tradition.[52] Looked at that way, these eighth

51. Judith Berling's essay, "Bringing the Buddha Down to Earth: Notes on the Emergence of 'Yü-lu' as a Buddhist Genre," *History of Religions* 27, no. 1 (Aug. 1987): 56–88, has many problems, but her conclusion (p. 88) somewhat parallels what I am suggesting here.

52. In their "conversation style," the *Discourse on No-Mind* and the *Discourse on the Essentials of Cultivating Mind* both, in fact, resemble the famous *Vajrasamādhi Sūtra*, composed in China or Korea in the seventh century (esp. chap. 5).

century Chan "conversations" between master and disciple likely represent the continuation of the Chinese verve and talent for rewriting tradition, a talent that had made itself abundantly evident in the numerous apocryphal works penned in the centuries before the invention of Chan.

8

Chan Compendiums from the Song Dynasty

Between the final collapse of the Tang dynasty in 907 and the reunification of the empire in 960, China went through a period called the Five Dynasties and the Ten Kingdoms in which a series of mini-states rose and fell amid rampant civil war and general chaos.[1] When this turbulent time finally passed and the empire was restored, much about life in China was different. In the newly established Song dynasty, the centralized state had been greatly strengthened, civil society was vibrant and expanding, and the economy was, in many respects, the envy of the world. While we still don't know much about what happened to Buddhism in that volatile period between the Tang and the Song, it is clear that as the new dynasty solidified its hold over the vast expanse of the empire, a more sophisticated and systematized form of Chan came into being. This new style of Chan would go on to dominate the religious landscape of China for several centuries until falling into obscurity in the mid-Ming dynasty (1368–1644); then, some 150 years later, in the early seventeenth century, it was partially resuscitated. In fact, Chan would again slip into oblivion and be revived several more times under

---

1. For more details on Chan during this period, readers should consult Benjamin Brose, *Patrons and Patriarchs: Regional Rulers and Chan Monks During the Five Dynasties and Ten Kingdoms* (Honolulu: University of Hawai'i Press, 2015).

the Qing dynasty and in the modern era, highlighting its tenuous and, in many ways, supplementary nature vis-à-vis older and more established forms of Chinese Buddhism.[2] Thus, it would seem that, like a delicately knitted shawl, Chan was draped lightly over the head and shoulders of a much more robust form of Buddhism and, in that way, could be easily slipped off or put back on. Without attempting to explain the particulars of this ebb and flow in Chan's fortune, this chapter and the next two survey three classic genres of Song-era Chan literature: (1) vast compendiums, called "flame histories" (*dengshi* or *denglu*),[3] that present information about many hundreds of past Chan masters; (2) manuals for running a monastery under Chan leadership, called "rules for purity" (*qinggui*); and (3) koan collections (*gong'an*).[4]

2. For an insightful assessment of Chan's collapse and subsequent revival, see Jiang Wu's *Enlightenment in Dispute: The Reinvention of Chan Buddhism in Seventeenth-Century China* (New York: Oxford University Press, 2008). One of the many rewarding things to be found in Wu's book is his discussion of what happened in the late Ming era when the literati—and *not* the monastics—sought to revive Chan by first reading extensively in the Song materials and then trying to act out what they saw presented there, including staging all the yelling and beatings. Some of the literati even set about trying to enlighten monks and abbots, based on their superior abilities to read and interpret the Song texts which had, by that time, fallen into obscurity (ibid., 41–45 and chap. 2). As Wu explains, "Thus some literati who were confident about their own enlightenment experiences *through reading Chan texts* challenged monks on their Chan understanding. Some even assumed the position of Chan teachers and tried to guide monks to achieve enlightenment" (64, italics added.).

3. The character translated here as "flame" (*deng*) more often than not means "lamp," and many translators thus speak of "lamp histories." However, I think T. Griffith Foulk is right in arguing that these texts relate to the movement of the flame of enlightenment as it was passed down the line of patriarchs, so it isn't a case of transmitting a lamp; rather, each recipient *is* the lamp that *receives* the flame from his predecessor (Foulk, "Chan Literature," in *Brill's Encyclopedia of Buddhism: Literature and Languages*, eds. Jonathan A. Silk and Oskar von Hinüber [Leiden: Brill, 2015], 701).

4. Some readers may be disappointed that I have not dedicated a chapter to exploring the "recorded sayings" (*yulu*). I made this choice because I am not convinced that the "recorded sayings" represent a well-defined genre and this is because so many different kinds of writing could be included in a master's recorded sayings: his sermons, his more private teachings, his poems, his doctrinal essays, and so on. In this sense, *yulu* is an imprecise, cover-all term and not representative of a distinctive genre of writing. Foulk argues otherwise, though he admits that the term was used to refer to

To better appreciate what Chan authors created during the Song, we first need to take stock of a modern historiographical problem. Until about twenty-five years ago, many scholars wrote about Song Chan as though it were a decadent and venal form of Buddhism that, in comparison with the supposedly simple and energetic spirituality of Tang Chan, was hopelessly lost in rituals, pageantry, and strategies to secure patronage and imperial privileges. This view began to change when, in the 1990s, and largely due to the work of T. Griffith Foulk, it became clear that Song-era Chan was, in fact, a powerful and creative movement, albeit concentrated at the elite levels of Chinese society.[5] Moreover, it became hard to avoid the conclusion that the inspiring images of the perfect Chan of the Tang dynasty had, actually, been manufactured by Song authors.[6] In effect, the Song authors created the perfect masters of the Tang in order to be their descendants—a grand case of fathering your father, that is. Making sense of this vast and sustained puppeteering of the patriarchs of the past remains, to this day, one of the challenges of Chan studies.

Along with perfecting images of their distant and often imaginary ancestors, part of the appeal of Song Chan appears to have derived from the standardization of genealogical claims regarding the descendants of Bodhidharma. With careful editing of the surviving Tang documents and some creative writing to connect various Song masters with their putative Tang forefathers, the image of one large, fairly homogeneous

---

all the types of literature just mentioned (ibid., 712). Mario Poceski, *The Records of Mazu and the Making of Classical Chan Literature* (New York: Oxford University Press, 2015), discusses *yulu* in chaps 4 and 5; see also Albert Welter, *The Linji Lu and the Creation of Chan Orthodoxy* (New York: Oxford University Press, 2008), chap. 2.

5. For the best account of this shift in the field, see T. Griffith Foulk, "Myth, Ritual, and Monastic Practice in Sung Ch'an Buddhism," in *Religion and Society in T'ang and Sung China*, eds. Patricia Buckley Ebrey and Peter N. Gregory (Honolulu: University of Hawai'i Press, 1993), 147–208.

6. As Christoph Anderl put is, "[I]n the case of Chan, the whole formative period was retrospectively rewritten in the context of Song orthodoxy, with the effect that this entire formative period became 'deleted' (and replaced by a normative account) in historiographical works." See his "Zen Rhetoric: An Introduction," in *Zen Buddhist Rhetoric in China, Korea, and Japan,* ed. Anderl (Leiden: Brill, 2012), 36.

Bodhidharma family was produced in the early Song. Though this family still had its preferred descendants, gone were the numerous contradictory histories of the Bodhidharma clan that had circulated in the Tang. In place of that kind of lineage warfare, authors produced the massive flame histories that promised to elucidate the lives and teachings of all relevant Chan masters, complete with the genealogical information needed to follow the unbroken flow of truth from the Indian Buddha to Bodhidharma, and then down to the masters of the Song, who, with significant help from court literati, were largely in charge of setting up this immense display.

Besides reorganizing membership in the Bodhidharma family and keeping the genealogical narratives up to date, the most remarkable thing about the flame histories is that they fashioned a new *style* for the truth-fathers.[7] Gradually, the Chan masters appear more and more like the wild, free-wheeling sages that we moderns expect them to be. Here, finally, masters start yelling, cursing, and beating their interlocutors, even if in Tang sources these very same masters appear rather staid, traditional, and altogether polite. The situation becomes more perplexing when, following the recent research of Mario Poceski and Albert Welter, we see that this wildness was introduced into their "histories" in a gradual and purposeful manner. That is, as the compendiums were regularly updated and reissued, the unruly antics of the masters mysteriously increases. Catching sight of this writing and editing process, we have to ask: to what extent did this rough-and-tumble form of Chan Buddhism ever exist as anything more than a carefully cultivated literary fantasy? And, if it turns out that free-wheeling Chan didn't exist in the Tang, and if it didn't exist in the Song either, then what should we make of its presence *in literature*?

Answering these questions won't be easy, but for now we can see that, in a basic way, the Song compendiums functioned as museums of

7. For more reflections on classic Chan rhetoric, see Dale S. Wright, "The Discourse of Awakening: Rhetorical Practice in Classic Ch'an Buddhism," *Journal of the American Academy of Religion* 61, no. 1 (Spring 1993): 23–24.

sorts, museums which held idealized images of the past masters in a kind of suspended animation: one just needed to open the book and start reading, and the masters suddenly came to life, speaking and acting in mesmerizing ways. Considered more broadly, it would seem that very old Chinese assumptions about the quasi-presence of ancestors joined forces with new and evocative literary styles that gave readers an enhanced sense of being in the company of the patriarchs as they read through these highly fictionalized "histories." Thus it was that with the new literary talents of the Song, past masters could be made to live alongside ordinary Chinese Buddhism, thereby providing attractive and inspiring examples of a Buddhism that could never exist in the real world, but could, in literary form, enhance more traditional forms of Buddhism and advance various real-world agendas.

FLAME HISTORIES AS "MUSEUMS
OF THE MASTERS"

The museum-like quality of the Song compendiums is also visible in the way they thematize the history of the masters such that the entries concentrate on the Chan-styled things that a master might have said or done. Thus, except for the Indian patriarchs, the entries generally have little biographical information about the masters and don't mention other aspects of their lives that were chronicled in older sources, unless that material appeared relevant to the larger Chan story. And, conversely, for those figures who were included in the lineage but didn't have significant Chan vignettes already attached to their biographies, Song authors seem to have added zenny dialogues or poems so that these figures would appear to talk and act more or less like their brethren in the collection. Thus whether it is the Buddha, an Indian patriarch, or a Tang master, they were all resculpted so that they conformed to Song notions of the perfect master. Below I explore examples of this kind of writing, but for the moment it is crucial to see that, on the one hand, these texts worked to draw a patriarchal essence forward from the Buddha into the present via the genealogical narrative, even as they, on the other hand, threaded a Chan style of discourse back from the Song into the Tang and to India. In short, in these works, the Buddha, Bodhidharma, and other figures from the past were made to "talk" in the idiom of a Song Chan master.

To get a better sense for how jarring this reconstruction of Buddhist history could appear, one might imagine a New York museum dedicated to American poets that set current rappers within a larger family of American poets, reaching back to the likes of Walt Whitman, who, once given their place in the display case, would also be given several rhymed lines about the thrills of gangsta life. Thus regardless of whatever else Whitman might have written and published back in the nineteenth century, what we would see in the museum under his name would be a couple lines of rap that make his taste in poetry look little different from Snoop Dogg's or Tupac Shakur's. For those visitors with knowledge of earlier poetic traditions in America, this would seem bizarre and perhaps even obscene, but for those less versed in America's diverse poetic styles, it might appear rather comforting, since rap would appear to be the one real voice of America that stretched across centuries and into the present. Naturally, too, such a history would bestow on rap, and its current producers, a sense that they were modern versions of the best of the best. With this analogy in mind, one can imagine how the effort to slot Buddhism's rich and diverse past into Chan "museums" represented a powerful technique for re-branding those past figures, while also making current Chan representatives glow with the grandeur of truth and style that was now stockpiled in the collections.

Like museums all over the world, the flame histories were heavily involved in politics.[8] For instance, in the case of the famous flame history called the *Jingde chuandeng lu* (hereafter referred to as *Chuandeng lu*), a highly placed court official named Yang Yi lead a team of editors

---

8. This overview of literati influences on the Chan compendiums relies on Albert Welter's well-researched discussion of the matter in his *Monks, Rulers, and Literati: The Political Ascendancy of Chan Buddhism.* (New York: Oxford University Press, 2006); see esp. chap. 6.

in improving the material that the monk Daoyuan had submitted to the court in 1004. The final version of the text was only issued five years later in 1009, suggesting that quite a lot of work had been done on it.[9] Ironically, then, it was secular scholars at court who found themselves in charge of finalizing literary images of Buddhism's past masters. The next compendium, the *Tiansheng guangdeng lu,* was compiled in 1036 in a similar manner, with the scholar Li Zunxu—a good friend of Yang Yi's and brother-in-law to the most recent emperor—leading the editorial team. With court literati in charge of these works, it is likely the case that they favored material and themes that presented Chan in such a way as to intensify the *reading experience* since, after all, for such editors the text and its payload mattered more than any realistic representation of life in the Buddhist monasteries, a reality with which they might not have had that much contact.

The state no doubt had multiple motivations for collecting and distributing these exciting images of past Chan masters to the reading public, but we can assume that sponsoring Chan flame histories was thought to enhance the glamour and legitimacy of the new Song rulers. Thus, by linking the throne with the illustrious Chan family of truth-fathers— and the compendiums were often named after the imperial era during which they were produced—it would have naturally seemed that the Song court itself was something of a co-inheritor in this family line. After all, now all these striking Chan masters lived in the literary "ancestor halls" constructed for them by the Song rulers. Actually, the newly established Song court avidly collected literature and works from a wide range of Chinese traditions, giving the impression that any "art" from the past was seen as worth collecting since it could be held up as proof of the new regime's legitimate place in China's dynastic history.[10]

9. For a very readable translation of the first part of this flame history, see Daoyuan, *Records of the Transmission of the Lamp,* trans. Randolph S. Whitfield, vols. 1 and 2 (Norderstedt Books on Demand, 2015).

10. For discussion of this strategy, see Johannes Kurz, "On the Politics of Collecting Knowledge: Song Taizong's Compilation Projects," *T'oung Pao,* 2nd ser., 87, fasc. 4/5 (2001): 289–316.

That the state decided to endorse Chan's deeply partisan "history" of Buddhism had profound implications for the religious politics of the day. In particular, this endorsement set the stage for the emergence of a state-controlled form of monastic leadership in which most of the larger Song monasteries would be run by Chan masters who had won the approval of state officials and who could, in particular, convincingly attach themselves to the lineages found in these state-approved compendiums. Not surprisingly, this arrangement also led to a noticeable pushback from other Buddhist leaders who, finding themselves excluded from these choice appointments, decided to attack Chan's version of Buddhist history which had sidelined them and their predecessors from the "real" story of Buddhism.[11] In some cases, these excluded leaders went about inventing their own genealogical stories about how *they* and not the Chan masters had inherited Buddhism's "past." Besides proving, yet again, the metastatic quality of genealogical claims, the literary remains of these disputes confirm Buddhist authors' tight control of their textual sources, while also giving a sense of their astute dealings with the past, the present, and one another.

THE *ANCESTOR HALL COMPENDIUM*

To begin to reckon what happened to Chan literature in this era, let's turn to explore the form and content of one of the oldest flame histories, the *Ancestor Hall Compendium* (*Zutang ji* – hereafter shortened to *Compendium*).[12]

11. T. Griffith Foulk's "Sung Controversies Concerning the 'Separate Transmission' of Ch'an," in *Buddhism in the Sung,* eds. Peter N. Gregory and Daniel Getz Jr. (Honolulu: University of Hawai'i Press, 2002), gives a good overview of this conflict. In that same volume, Kōichi Shinohara explores the Tiantai response to Chan's growing hegemony at the national level; see his "From Local History to Universal History: The Construction of the Sung T'ien-t'ai Lineage"; see also Peter Gregory's well-balanced introduction to this book, "The Vitality of Buddhism in the Sung" (ibid., 1–20).

12. For an excellent account of the *Compendium* and its place in the politics of its day, see Welter, *Monks, Rulers, and Literati,* chap. 4. There are two important precedents to the *Compendium,* the *Baolin zhuan* of 801 and the *Continued Baolin zhuan* (*Xu baolin zhuan*) composed between 907 and 911 by one of Xuefeng's disciples, Weijing.

The *Compendium* isn't exactly from the Song era but rather appears to have been compiled in 952, some eight years before the Song dynasty was founded. The text as we have it—it survived in Korea and was only redis-covered in the early twentieth century—is twenty volumes long and includes entries for 246 masters. Despite its current size, there is evidence that it was originally just a single volume work that was later significantly expanded.[13] Despite these problems surrounding the history of the text's composition, we can still assume that the preface is reliable when it announces that the text was put together in a small southern Chinese kingdom, the Southern Tang, that flourished in the chaos after the fall of the Tang and had just taken over the Min, another little kingdom, in 945. The preface also makes clear that the two monks who compiled the work did so on behalf of Wendeng (d. 972), the abbot of Zhaoqing monastery in Quanzhou (Fujian province). In building a genealogy for Wendeng, these two monks placed him in a lineage that had been recently established by the famous master Xuefeng Yicun (822–908), who had been widely sup-ported by the rulers of the Min. Although the *Compendium* claims that Wendeng was Xuefeng's spiritual "grandson," the links hooking Wendeng back to Xuefeng look suspicious.[14] In fact, Albert Welter notes that the *Compendium* itself alludes to the fact that Wendeng's lineage claims were challenged at the time.[15] Nonetheless, Wendeng was very much favored by the Min rulers and it was presumably this high-profile support that spurred the composition of the text, which, of course, made it appear as though Wendeng was the most recent "king of Buddhism." Thus it would seem that the text took form within that standard dynamic, well estab-lished in the Tang, whereby the emperor or a local potentate supported a

---

Both texts seem to have provided the editors of the *Compendium* with material and structure.

13. For this theory, see Christoph Anderl, *Studies in the Language of the Zu-tang ji* (Oslo: Unipub, 2004), 35. For Welter's discussion of the text's complex history, see his *Monks, Rulers, and Literati,* 64; see also Foulk's assessment of the problem in "Chan Lit-erature," 707–8.

14. See Welter, *Monks, Rulers, and Literati,* 101–13.

15. Ibid., 107.

Chan master and he, in time, was aggrandized with an impressive genealogy such that he seemed to possess the essence of the Buddhist tradition and could, in that capacity, endorse his political sponsor. Of course, this quid pro quo arrangement was grounded in the historical claim that Wendeng was the spiritual descendant of other masters—such as Xuefeng—who had also served in just this capacity.

Before trying to make sense of the *Compendium's* literary innovations, we need to briefly sketch the political context of this interim period between the Tang and Song. Two things are critical to understand here. First, with the widespread chaos in north China, many people—monks included—migrated to the south of China where there was, on and off, a semblance of political order. Given these important relocations we can assume that established patterns of patronage for Buddhist monks and their monasteries were greatly disrupted. Second, establishing new systems of patronage in the south would have happened in something of a Wild West atmosphere in which Buddhist leaders, recently thrown together, worked together to reestablish that symbiotic paradigm whereby Buddhist and state leaders mutually endorsed each other's rights to reign in their respective domains.

Under these shifting and unstable conditions, the production of any new genealogy for the Bodhidharma family presumably meant that elite masters from different regions—who brought with them their different and contradictory genealogies—had to work in concert to produce omnibus documents that benefitted all involved. The *Compendium* in fact looks like just such a document. Though it *does* privilege the lineage that runs through Xuefeng Yicun and up to Wendeng, it also includes and endorses other lineages and masters who are not directly in this lineage. Thus while the text is still intent on privatizing ownership of the final version of the Buddhist tradition—as all Chan genealogies are—it is notable for allowing that the inheritors of this fetishized form of tradition might be many.

Besides these important changes in lineage claims, the *Compendium* also represents the emergence of a new style of presenting the "orality" of the masters.[16] The complex nature of this "orality" will become clearer in the examples below, but for now it is enough to say that it is rather different from the straightforward and even stilted orality that had been generated for Chan masters in the Tang—as seen in the preceding chapters. In the *Compendium,* the snippets of "orality" given to the various figures in the lineage reflect a consistent set of stylistic choices that radicalize the masters and their teachings. To begin with, the master is often placed in a nonteaching situation, as though the dialogues were dangerously open-ended and not part of scripted moments within ritualized monastic routines. Then, as the conversations develop, there is often a clear divide between the language that the master's interlocutor speaks and the language with which the master replies. Thus while questioners regularly ask straightforward questions about the essence of Buddhism, masters respond in a manner that shifts levels, pushing the conversation into zones where standard forms of logic are forbidden and where the masters' oblique or bizarre comments seem to speak of another plane of reality.

Thus, with the *Compendium,* the masters become unpredictable, enigmatic and even somewhat scary, driving their polite, well-schooled interlocutors to accept final accounts of Buddhism that are free of Buddhist logic and the standard terms that tradition had relied on to explain itself and reality. Consequently, it would seem that these "conversations" are reprising that template first established in the *Two Entrances* in which an exciting Daoist-sounding version of Buddhism is set against more traditional forms of Buddhist thought and practice. What's changed since the Tang though is that *content has turned into style* such that it isn't just that the master speaks confidently of a Daoist-styled form of elite Buddhism in which *wuwei* and a deep and originary sameness hold sway; now he also performs that philosophic vision in a vivacious, unpredictable manner that underscores his freedom from normal Buddhism and

16. For a synopsis of this new style of dialogue in the compendiums, see Foulk, "Chan Literature," 706–7; for a more involved analysis, see Anderl, "Zen Rhetoric: An Introduction," esp. 44–53.

polite society, and looks more and more Zhuangzian in terms of style and playfulness.

To get a better sense of this style, let's consider the *Compendium's* presentation of the Indian Buddha. His biography is the seventh entry in the text—after the six cosmic buddhas—and is very long, drawing as it does on a wide variety of textual precedents from many different strata of Buddhist literature. After presenting an elaborate account of the Buddha's family lineage, the editors cite snippets from famous biographic accounts of the Buddha's life to give a rather standard-looking, non-Chan "history" of the Buddha's deeds leading up to his enlightenment. However, once the narrative reaches the point of the Buddha's enlightenment, the editors shift registers to insert some Chan-styled discourse. In fact, the little speech that the authors put in the Buddha's mouth on the night of his enlightenment is fairly close to the Tang "dialogues" covered in chapter 7, since it dwells at length on the original purity of the mind, the pointlessness of practice, and other related topics.

Having established that the Buddha's first teachings were distinctly Chan in flavor, the authors then inserted a set of zenny dialogues in which the Buddha engages various interlocutors who suddenly appear in the narrative after his enlightenment; these figures, of course, aren't present in the older, non-Chan sources. These quick exchanges also circle around topics already well established in the Tang Chan repertoire and, given that these "dialogues" are often presented in poetic four-character phrases, we get a clear sense of how these "dialogues" are deeply indebted to older literary traditions. Besides noting, again, the happy combination of wild-sounding negations and elegant poetry, we need to see that these radical teachings in no way upset the overall narrative logic of the situation. That is, the mishmash of non-Chan Buddhist histories sits reasonably well next to the Buddha's (new) Chan teachings that insist that there is nothing to learn or practice, and so on. This workable combination of form and formless is underscored, and made politically relevant, when the Buddha's enlightenment is dated with reference to a Chinese dynasty.

Looking at these details more closely, we see that the narrative of the Buddha's enlightenment starts with the Buddha talking with a blind dragon who wasn't always blind and claims to have witnessed the enlightenments of the past buddhas. Given his knowledge of the deep history of the buddha-lineage, the dragon confidently explains to the Buddha the nature of the Buddha's cosmic identity, while also securing for the reader the legitimacy of the upcoming events. Having convinced the Buddha of his destiny, the dragon leads him to the "Diamond Seat," where the Buddha will achieve enlightenment. Once there, the Buddha declares:

> If I do not attain supreme enlightenment,
> I vow that I will not rise from this seat!
> Then he attained complete enlightenment
> And was called "the Buddha."

> So the *Lalitavistara* says,
> "The prince was fully enlightened on the eighth day of the second
>   month,
> At the time when the morning star appeared."

> [The Buddha] then composed the following poem:
> Because of the star I reached enlightenment,
> But after I was enlightened, there was no star.
> Now, I no longer conform to the things [of the world]
> But I am not without feelings (*bu shi wuqing*).

> The time when he attained the Dao corresponds to the third year of
> The sixth Emperor, King Mu, of [this] country's Zhou dynasty, the
>   *gui-wei*, the eight day of the second month.[17]

With his enlightenment narrated, however vaguely, the authors have the Buddha begin his Chan-styled teaching:

> He taught the assembly saying,
> "As for monks who have renounced home,

17. Translation based on Anderl, *Studies in the Language of the Zu-tang ji*, 700-1, with changes. Anderl helpfully supplies the Chinese text alongside his translations and explains how he produced this edition of the text (xxiv).

They cut off desire and banish love,
And they realize the origins of their minds.
They reach the Buddha's fundamental principle,
And are enlightened to the teaching of *wuwei*.
Inside there is nothing to gain;
Outside there is nothing to seek.
The mind does not get attached to the Dao,
And is likewise not entangled by deed (karma).
There is no thought and no action;
No practice and no awakening.
Not to pass successively through all the [bodhisattva] ranks,
But [merely?] esteeming oneself (*zi chongjing*),
That is called the Dao."[18]

With this poem put in the Buddha's mouth, the reader presumably gets the clear sense that the real practice of Buddhism involves finding that "trapdoor" of enlightenment in which the "origin of the mind" is realized and karma is thrown off, resulting in a Daoist ease of non-action in which there is nothing to gain or seek. With his poetic teaching given, the narrative somewhat awkwardly shifts to a give-and-take exchange that has the Buddha talking with an unnamed monk. Here, again, in terms of topics and terminology we are very close to the Tang "dialogue" style:

There was a monk who asked:
"Why is purity the original nature?"
The Buddha said, "Because it is ultimately pure."
"Why is the original nature unknown?"
The Buddha said, "Because all dharmas are blunt/stupid (*zhufa dun gu*)."[19]

While having the Buddha explain that "all dharmas are blunt/stupid" might appear curious and arguably innovative, the two questions that had been put to him are on topics that aren't particularly new. Of course, we shouldn't miss that while the monk "speaks" in pretty

18. Ibid., 701–2.
19. Ibid., 702, with changes.

normal, sutra-sounding phraseology, the Buddha's two answers are neat, four-line phrases that match the poetry of his teaching above.

After this conversation closes out, we learn that a non-Buddhist has shown up and put a question to the Buddha that "did not ask with words, and didn't ask without words."[20] Given the apparent impossibility of such a question, the Buddha wisely stayed silent for a long time until the questioner "made a formal bow and praised him saying, 'Splendid! Splendid! The World Honored One has such great mercy; he has dispelled my clouds of ignorance and caused me to gain enlightenment.'" Ānanda, who apparently had been witnessing the exchange, then asked the Buddha, "Based on what realization did the non-Buddhist say that he gained entrance [to the Dao]?" In response, the Buddha avoids identifying any content that caused the enlightenment and instead metaphorizes the encounter as follows: "He is just like a fine horse in the world, at the sight of [even] the shadow of the whip, he takes off running."[21]

In Tang texts, passages dramatizing the achievement of enlightenment emphasized that a person's awakening was caused by hearing poems or teachings or sutra-recitations. Here, it is the Buddha's *silence* that accomplishes the task, even though the questioner had no prior familiarity with Buddhist thought or practice. In short, instead of receiving especially potent language, it is the mere presence of the master that seems to be enough to effect the enlightenment of the questioner.[22]

After this hastily staged question-and-answer session, the narrative jumps ahead to recount the Buddha's death where we again find non-Chan material mixed with elaborate Chan-styled poems. Despite showing the Buddha preparing for Mahākāśyapa to take over after his death, the narrative doesn't hide the fact that, according to a number of high-profile Indian narratives, Mahākāśyapa only arrived on site some time

20. Ibid., 703.
21. Ibid., 703, with minor changes.
22. This exchange reappears, little changed, as koan #32 in the *Gateless Entrance*.

after the Buddha died. This would be an ongoing problem for Chan "historians" who wanted to attach Mahākāśyapa more securely to the Buddha's final legacy, but here the authors simply show the Buddha transmitting the dharma to Ānanda, with instructions that he transmit it to Mahākāśyapa once he arrived.[23] Then, some fourteen days after the Buddha's death, Mahākāśyapa shows up and the Buddha's coffin magically opens to reveal his perfectly uncorrupted body, suggesting, presumably, that he was still present enough to verify the transmission to Mahākāśyapa.[24] Standing back from this presentation of the Buddha's life and death, we can see how comfortable the authors of the *Compendium* were in rewriting aspects of the Buddha's most important moments. Though some elements of the older histories were respected—such as Mahākāśyapa's absence from the Buddha's funeral—this did nothing to prevent the authors from inventing all sorts of dialogue and poetry to insert in their preferred version of the Buddha's teaching.

This cavalier attitude toward the Buddha is parallel to the way Huineng is presented in the *Compendium*. Thus, besides casually recycling and recombining material drawn from the *Biography of the Great Master of Caoqi* and the *Platform Sūtra* (covered in chapters 5 and 6 above), new scenarios were also included to give Huineng a more "zenny" profile. For instance, we read that one day Hongren came down to the threshing room and asked Huineng, "Has the rice ripened?" Huineng, apparently assuming this to be a double entendre, easily shifts registers and responds: "The rice has been ripe for a long time, it is only that there was no person as yet to winnow it."[25] Here the authors seem interested in tempting the reader with the sense that he can penetrate this "joke" that was supposedly exchanged between the master and his dharma heir. The

23. On the problem of Mahākāśyapa in Chan history, see Foulk, "Sung Controversies Concerning the 'Separate Transmission' of Ch'an," and Welter, "Mahākāśyapa's Smile: Silent Transmission and Kung-an (Kōan) Tradition," in *The Koan: Texts and Contexts in Zen Buddhism,* eds. Steve Heine and Dale S. Wright, 75–109 (New York: Oxford University Press, 2000).

24. Anderl, *Studies in the Language of the Zu-tang ji,* 705.

25. Ibid., 760–61.

astute reader of course gets that Hongren's question isn't really about rice at all, and instead is about Huineng's enlightenment and the imminent consummation of their relationship. This suspicion is confirmed when we learn that, upon hearing Huineng's cryptic but promising response, Hongren tells him to come to his room later that night, where he will formally identify Huineng as the sixth patriarch. In short, with the rice question set up as a rather obvious double entendre, the authors presumably expected readers to pass easily from the literal to the metaphoric. In this way, the reader not only acquires a sense of intimacy with the figures "on stage," but he also gets used to seeking something profound in otherwise pedestrian exchanges. This is crucial, of course, since the thrill of reading these text relies on the conviction that the secret of enlightenment must be lurking behind these roughly sketched vignettes.[26]

A similar double entendre organizes another scene in the Hongren-Huineng "history."[27] Here, after Huineng's formal inclusion in the Bodhidharma family, Hongren sends Huineng on his way by ferrying him across a river in a rowboat. Once in the boat, Huineng says, "Shouldn't I take the oars?" This is, given the ethic of filial piety, exactly what should happen; after all, Hongren is old and about to die. But Hongren says, "Don't be a bother." The next part of the exchange is hard to parse, but it's clear that it is Hongren who has to do the rowing because the whole episode is a metaphor for Hongren's gift of enlightenment to Huineng, the gift that, as the traditional idiom has it, allows Huineng to cross over to the other shore of nirvana. Again, the authors appear confident that readers will be sophisticated enough to get the point that the deeds of the masters are replaying the metaphors of tradition. And, presumably, recognizing these parallels—however tongue in cheek they might be—only

26. Foulk makes a similar point about the expectations that need to be in place in order to read koans in a traditional manner in "The Koan: The Form and Function of Koan Literature: A Historical Overview," in *The Koan: Texts and Contexts in Zen Buddhism*, eds. Steve Heine and Dale S. Wright (Oxford: Oxford University Press, 2000), 39–40.

27. Anderl, *Studies in the Language of the Zu-tang ji*, 761.

adds to the pleasure of the discerning reader who thereby feels himself included in the tapestry of tradition. In the next section we get yet another example of this when Hongren makes a pun on Huineng's name, telling Shenxiu that "only those who are *able* get enlightenment—"able" is *neng* in Chinese and it is one of the characters in Huineng's name."[28] Clearly, the authors are expecting readers to participate in such word-play and enjoy the various kinds of movement around language and meaning that are required to get the joke, pun, or metaphor.

The artful and engaging restatement of tradition appears in another way. The entries for the twenty-seven Indian masters and for the first six main Chinese masters—from Bodhidharma to Huineng—each conclude with a brief poem restating, in a minimalist manner, the events just narrated. Some of the entries for later masters also end with a poem. These poems are explicitly attributed to Jingxu, apparently another name for Wendeng, the master for whom the *Compendium* was compiled. Placing these poems at the end of the entries gives the impression that it is Wendeng who (1) understands what has happened in the life and teachings of each master; and (2) felt inspired (and entitled) to have the last word that summed up the content of the entry. Consequently, these poems give the impression that Wendeng has, in effect, mastered the masters or, and it comes to the same thing, that the Wendeng "brand" of truth is to be found in each of these past masters.[29]

Looked at another way, Wendeng is, as it were, now a speaking contemporary of each prior master since his poems finish out what the

28. Ibid., 763, with changes.
29. Things get more complicated when it turns out that there is a Dunhuang text by Wendeng, the *Praises for the Patriarchs and Masters, Newly Composed at Qianfo Monastery in Quanzhou* (*Quanzhou qianfo xinzhu zhu zushi song*, Stein 1635), that presents these very same poems as a simple sequence with no intervening material (*T* 2861, 85.1320c). This set of poems and the lineage that it articulates stops with master Mazu of the late eighth century, and thus doesn't directly link up to Wendeng, but it would still seem to be the case that Wendeng wrote these poems in the first part of the tenth century as part of an early effort to put himself forward as a legitimate inheritor of the essence of tradition, an agenda that would come to full fruition with the compilation of the *Compendium*.

masters were saying and doing in their respective historical eras.[30] Consequently, there is, by implication, a single voice attesting to the reality of each of these entries and it is the voice of Wendeng, now tucked into the received language of the past masters.[31] It is just such gestures of self-aggrandizement that will come to the fore in the koan literature (see chapter 10 below).

Another interesting thing about Wendeng's poems is their contents. Though some stanzas seem little different in tone and terminology from the "dialogue" texts of the Tang, other poems introduce new elements. Consider this poem that closes out Hongren's entry:

> The fifth patriarch, at the age of seven
> Profoundly reached what is prior to words.
> The stone oxen spits out mist;
> The wooden horse holds the vapor in its mouth.
> Body and mind are forever quiescent,
> And, principle and phenomena [together] hold the mystery.
> Without emotion, without seeds,
> A thousand years, ten thousand years.[32]

With this striking image of the stone oxen and wooden horse performing the balanced functions of giving forth and retaining visible vapors, it would seem that the author has stepped into a new and heady set of symbols, one that mixes the animate and the inanimate, and plays with beloved Chinese idioms regarding cosmic pneuma and various forms of immortality. Here, literal statements about enlightenment and history have slipped away as Buddhism disappears behind an alluring veil of Chinese poetry and Daoist-sounding vocabulary. In fact, many readers

---

30. A further odd thing to note here is that while Wendeng added a poem to the entry for Huileng, the founding abbot of Zhaoqing monastery where Wendeng lived, he didn't provide one for his supposed master Baofu; for details, see Welter, *Monks, Rulers, and Literati*, 103–4.

31. To get a clearer sense for this power play one might imagine President Barack Obama composing a book summing up the lives of the past forty-three presidents, with each entry finalized by a bit of Obama poetry.

32. Anderl, *Studies in the Language of the Zu-tang ji*, 767, with slight changes.

would likely associate a poem like this with the *Zhuangzi,* where we find similarly charming confusions regarding animate and inanimate things, along with a wistfulness for a timelessness that promises to envelop everything in a gentle totality.

Although the *Compendium* established new horizons with these more extravagant, Daoist-sounding riffs, it still relies heavily on poetry that looks little different from that found in Tang sources. For instance, some of the poems given to Bodhidharma and other figures, such as Huineng, replay that stock idiom in which the development of the lineage is metaphorized as the planting of seeds and the blossoming of flowers; thus they appear much like the five poems that had been included in the *Platform Sūtra's* presentation of the masters' transmission verses.[33] In short, the *Compendium* is a useful text for noting gradual shifts in Chan writing.

To begin to get a broader sense of the new styles emerging in Song Chan literature, let's now turn to consider, briefly, the case of master Mazu, whose records present solid evidence of the Song authors' enthusiasm for reshaping the past masters.

MAZU AND GINNED-UP ANTINOMIANISM

For historians, one of the good things about Song Chan is that a lot of its literature survives. Unlike the Tang Chan texts hastily walled up in that cave at Dunhuang, the Song texts were often canonized and cut onto woodblocks, and thus much of this literature survived. What this bountiful evidence allows for is a careful assessment of the writing process whereby Chan authors steadily reinvented the past or, at least, steadily shaped it more to their liking. The task of this final part of the chapter is to briefly summarize recent research on this writing process by following Mario Poceski's argument about how master Mazu (709–88) was refashioned in the Song era. Poceski's research leaves little doubt

---

33. See chap. 6 above and *The Platform Sūtra of the Sixth Patriarch*, trans. and ed. Philip Yampolsky (New York: Columbia University Press, 1967), 176–78.

that the famous accounts of Mazu's rude and baffling comments were only gradually added into his portfolio, long after he was dead.[34]

Setting up his reading of the wilder stories about Mazu and other Chan monks, Poceski asks this key question: "Are both traditional and contemporary writers about Chan justified when they use these stories as historical records about the classical Chan tradition, or are they perhaps mistakenly basing their interpretations on apocryphal textual materials that bear no direct relevance to the tradition they are supposed to describe?"[35] After carefully considering several presentations of Mazu, Poceski concludes that Mazu's teachings and image resulted from a steady process of reinvention. He writes, "The central feature of that process was *the refashioning of Mazu and his disciples into radical iconoclasts,* a process that reflected the changing beliefs of the Chan school and the sectarian needs of certain Chan factions."[36] While this finding is in accord with Foulk's basic position regarding Song authors' invention and reconstruction of Tang Chan masters, Poceski's fine-grained reading makes the details of this "refashioning" process much clearer and therefore more thought-provoking.

Mazu appears to have been a real person who, near the end of the eighth century, had gathered around him a sizable following, along with winning substantial support from the local governments in Fujian province, where he spent most of his life.[37] At some point it was claimed

---

34. For the following discussion I will be working from Mario Poceski's impressive essay "*Mazu yulu* and the Creation of the Chan Records of Sayings," in *The Zen Canon: Understanding the Classic Texts,* eds. Steven Heine and Dale S. Wright (New York: Oxford University Press, 2004), 53–80. David Chappell first pointed out the way in which Mazu's profile had been radicalized in the Song period. See Chappell, "Hermeneutical Phases in Chinese Buddhism," in *Buddhist Hermeneutics,* ed. Donald S. Lopez Jr. (Honolulu: University of Hawai'i Press, 1992), 175–206, esp. 197–98.

35. Poceski, "*Mazu yulu,*" 63.

36. Ibid., 71–72; emphasis added.

37. For details of Mazu's life, see Mario Poceski, *Ordinary Mind as the Way: The Hongzhou School and the Growth of Chan Buddhism* (New York: Oxford University Press, 2007), 21–44. See also Jinhua Jia, *The Hongzhou School of Chan Buddhism in Eighth- through Tenth-Century China* (Albany: State University of New York Press, 2006).

that Mazu was a descendant of Huineng via the intermediary, and shadowy, figure of Huairang (677–744), though the whole account is surely fictional.[38] The most reliable sources for Mazu's biography and his teaching are found in two steles that were cut in his honor shortly after his death. Here we see a fairly normal-looking Tang master preaching on the reality of the internal buddha, citing sutras and "speaking" in a logical and uninflected manner, as other Tang-era masters seem to have done. When, roughly two centuries after his death, the authors of the *Compendium* and the other Song flame histories wrote about his life and his teachings, we find, as Poceski has painstakingly shown, that his portfolio has been spruced up and expanded. In this new presentation of Mazu, there is still a stratum of teachings that looks very much like other Chan writings from the Tang, and yet this stratum is now accompanied by other, wilder, images of Mazu that have no precedents in the Tang material.

In this new material, the image of Mazu has shifted in three ways. First, his quoted speech becomes more colloquial and his reliance on sutra language disappears. Second, his teachings become elliptical and somewhat bizarre, with a tendency to employ non sequiturs or physical gestures in response to questions about the final truth of Buddhism. Third, he is shown as rough, unpredictable, and abrasive in his speech and action. Thus we watch Mazu suddenly seizing people or kicking them, or, more often, simply yelling at them, and it is these decidedly un-Buddhist activities that supposedly enlightened his disciples.

38. Huairang is not mentioned in any of the earliest material related to Huineng. He first appears in a stele written for Mazu and only receives his own biography in 815. Of course, if one takes Huineng to be Shenhui's literary invention, it hardly needs to be proven that Huairang wasn't Huineng's disciple. For more discussion of this problem of connecting Mazu to Huineng via Huairang, see Poceski, *Ordinary Mind as the Way*, 26–29 and 39nn42–44; for a brief list of scholars who have registered doubts about Mazu's connection to Huineng via Huairang, see John C. Maraldo, "Is There Historical Consciousness in Ch'an?" *Japanese Journal of Religious Studies* 12, nos. 2–3 (1985): 168–69n3; and, finally, for more reflections on this invention, see John R. McRae, *Seeing through Zen: Encounter, Transformation, and Genealogy in Chinese Chan Buddhism* (Berkeley: University of California Press, 2003), 82.

What is crucial to see is that as Poceski close-reads the various Song presentations of Mazu, he is able to show that the reshaping of Mazu's profile is traceable on two separate fronts. On the one hand, Mazu's more logical statements, along with his sutra-based comments, were steadily pruned back until a zennier and less thinkable Mazu emerged.[39] Then, on the other hand, completely new material was invented and added in, with these new stories presenting a wild and uncanny Mazu who resembles the one who had emerged from editing the older accounts. Thus, in either case the authors appear to have knowingly reconstructed Mazu in a manner that fulfilled certain Song expectations of what a grand master should be like.

Poceski's evidence, solid as it is, still might be thought to result from an accidental process that somehow only influenced the Mazu material. This possibility quickly melts away as soon as we look at other important figures and see that a similar process seems to have been at work as they too were refashioned during the Song dynasty. For instance, Albert Welter has convincingly shown that Linji's (d. 866) aggressive and beguiling character was developed in a similarly gradual manner in the centuries after his death.[40] Thus, in what appears to be the earliest stratum of Linji's teachings, we see a sane-sounding, sutra-based master whose teachings are altogether comprehensible. Then in the

39. Albert Welter has shown the same dynamic at work in other parts of Mazu's record. See his excellent article "Contested Identities in Chan/Zen Buddhism: The "Lost" Fragments Mazu Daoyi in the *Zongjing lu*," in *Buddhism without Borders: Proceedings of the International Conference on Globalized Buddhism, Bumthang, Bhutan, May 21–23, 2012*, eds. Dasho Karma Ura and Dendup Chophel, 268–83 (Thimphu, Bhutan: Center for Bhutan Studies, 2012).

40. See Albert Welter, *The Linji Lu and the Creation of Chan Orthodoxy*, esp. chaps. 5 and 6. While Welter does an excellent job of exploring the invention of Linji and his Chan style, he misses a chance to reckon the layers of irony and invention at work here when he asserts that this image of Linji was "the product of a *collective Chan consciousness*" (ibid., 109; emphasis added). Mario Poceski has also shown that the production of Baizhang's records fits this pattern of development as well; see his "Monastic Innovator, Iconoclast, and Teacher of Doctrine: The Varied Images of Chan Master Baizhang," in *Zen Masters*, eds. Steven Heine and Dale S. Wright (New York: Oxford University Press, 2010), 3–32.

later strata, Linji, like Mazu, appears violent, profane, and increasingly bizarre in his articulation of Buddhist truths. In short, Welter is able to point to a "fictionalizing process" by which the beloved image of Linji and his wild "encounter dialogues" gradually came into being. He adds that with this fictionalizing process, the recorded dialogues "are little more than representations of Chan masters as their caricature makers would like them to appear. If the caricatures themselves reveal little about their subjects, they do tell us something interesting about those who devised them."[41]

In sum, Poceski and Welter agree that this "fictionalizing process" created a distinctive style for Chan, and thus that Song authors were, in effect, in charge of molding the masters into the forms that *they*, and presumably their readers, most enjoyed. Of course, given what we saw with the Tang writing, this is nothing new—it has simply become both more extreme and more ordinary.

CONCLUSION: THE DOUBLE WILDNESS OF SONG CHAN

With this kind of authorial creativity and audacity well established in the Song records, we get a good look at what the Chan of that era was really made of: the talent and practical courage to rewrite the teachings of the past masters in accord with an emerging aesthetic in which the articulation of Buddhist truths was supposed to be: free of cultural norms and restraints, free of literature and especially the sutras, and downright entertaining. Whether this meant giving the Buddha zenny poems and antinomian teachings, or turning Mazu or Linji into fearsome, uncouth masters who regularly manhandled their disciples, the point is that Song authors felt that they had the vision and wherewithal to puppeteer their favorite patriarchs, all in an effort to make the Chan system appear vital, exceptional, and up-to-date. Thus, there is a double

41. For these comments, see Welter, *Linji Lu and the Creation of Chan Orthodoxy*, 139.

wildness to be accounted for here: it took a wild and freewheeling "editorial board" of authors to shift, century by century, the received images of tradition in order to turn polite and reasonable-sounding masters into the rowdy and unpredictable patriarchs who would, in time, become the beloved icons of Chan and Zen.

Of course, to some extent, this is disappointing: it is admittedly not too uplifting to learn that the images of the rough and raunchy masters—the very figures who were applauded for their distance from culture, literature, and public opinion—took form in a "fictionalizing process" whereby elite authors assembled and polished these figures *in accord with contemporary literary conventions.* However, instead of getting stuck in this disappointment, one can take the next step and begin to appreciate the steady irony of those who so lovingly (and cleverly) rewrote the past to enhance the experience of tradition in the present. Catching sight of just that talent and audacity ought to challenge modern notions of what Chan was/is made of, even as it also gives important clues about other kinds of Chan writing that appeared in the Song: the rules for purity and the koan commentaries, both of which, as the next two chapters will show, also adopt an ironic stance vis-à-vis tradition.

9

Rules for Purity

Handbooks for Running Chan Monasteries

This chapter briefly explores what we can infer about daily life in Chan monasteries based on details drawn from a genre of texts called "rules for purity" (*qinggui*).[1] The oldest Chan example of this genre, *Rules for Purity for a Chan Monastery* (*Chanyuan qinggui*) was written in 1103 by a Chan abbot named Zongze (d. 1107).[2] The guidelines that he provides for staging life in the monastery are staggeringly precise and extensive, from instructions on how to use the toilet and wash up afterwards, to details regarding the governing officers and their various tasks, and even form letters to be used in writing to government officials and important donors. Reading the text can give the impression of visiting a city since what this handbook really does is lay out, from top to bottom, a vibrant and carefully choreographed

1. Translating *qingui* as "rules *for* purity" is a slight adaption of T. Griffith Foulk's "rules *of* purity," which is, itself, a good bit better that the more common "pure rules." I prefer "rules *for* purity" because when Zongze introduces his text, he makes clear that there is a cause-and-effect relationship between following the rules and becoming pure. He writes, "If those who are on the path accept these [rules] and put them into practice, they will naturally become exceptionally pure and lofty." This translation is taken from Foulk, "*Chanyuan qinggui* and Other 'Rules of Purity' in Chinese Buddhism," in *The Zen Canon: Understanding the Classic Texts,* eds. Steven Heine and Dale S. Wright (New York: Oxford University Press, 2004), 285.

2. A digitized version of the text from the *Xuzang jing X* (no. 1245), 63.522a.10, can be found at http://tripitaka.cbeta.org/ko/X63n1245_001.

living space designed to house as many as several thousand monks at a time, along with their officers, who were organized into thirty major and minor positions.[3] And, like cities, Chan monasteries put a premium on maintaining control: control of personnel and the hierarchies that they were to inhabit, control of resources, control of contact with those outside the monastery, control of the monastery's image as it was to be presented to the public, and, of course, control of the powerful dead who were (and still are) so important in Chan, and for Buddhism in general.[4]

One of the remarkable things about Zongze's text is the way it combines historical—and largely mythical—claims regarding the Bodhidharma family with precise institutional rules for selecting the abbots who were to govern Chan monasteries. Thus, at the larger Chan monasteries that would have followed Zongze's "rules for purity," ambitious monks with promising qualities were formally set within the Bodhidharma family, trained for years, and then, having been vetted by monastic and state officials, put to work running the enormous monastic estates that dotted the Chinese landscape. Thus, as John McRae put it: "The 'success' of Chan in the Song dynasty was thus not the creation of a new monastic institution, but rather the conquest by members of Chan lineages of the highest administrative positions in the vast majority of the largest establishments within that institution." [5] In short, the prestige of

3. For a list of these offices, see Foulk, "*Chanyuan qinggui* and Other 'Rules of Purity' in Chinese Buddhism," 291–92. For discussion of the daily routines in the Song monasteries, see Foulk's "Daily Life in the Assembly," in *Buddhism in Practice,* ed. Donald S. Lopez Jr. (Princeton, NJ: Princeton University Press, 1995), 455–72.

4. For a wide-ranging collection of essays on the Buddhist *vinaya* and its interactions with other legal frameworks in different times and places, see *Buddhism and Law: An Introduction,* eds. Rebecca Redwood French and Mark A. Nathan (New York: Cambridge University Press, 2014); see also Ann Heirman, "*Vinaya* from India to China," in *The Spread of Buddhism,* eds. Heirman and Stephan Peter Bumbacher (Leiden: Brill, 2007), 167–202. For an overview of Buddhist monasticism in medieval China, see Jacques Gernet, *Buddhism in Chinese Society: An Economic History from the Fifth to the Tenth Centuries* (New York: Columbia University Press, 1995).

5. John R. McRae, *Seeing through Zen: Encounter, Transformation, and Genealogy in Chinese Chan Buddhism* (Berkeley: University of California Press, 2003), 117.

the elite "sons of Bodhidharma"—that had been slowly cultivated in Chan literature—was now drawn into a newly emerging bureaucratized system that established leadership positions within a form of monastic Buddhism that was, in most other ways, deeply traditional.

Zongze's handbook has other surprises. For instance, near the end of his instructions, he elaborates a set of official procedures designed to prevent abbots from stealing the monastery's property or abusing their powers in other ways. Seeing how Zongze's text articulates these very practical concerns regarding abbots' potential for criminality, while *also* crafting highly involved rituals for celebrating their buddhahood, we have little choice but to imagine a rather important irony at work in Zongze's thinking about the Buddhist authority that he was organizing: Chan abbots were living buddhas, to be sure!, just make sure to keep them under careful supervision, especially at the end of their service when they might be especially tempted to make off with monastic valuables.[6] This ironic view wasn't Zongze's alone since becoming a Chan abbot presumably obliged one to know and accept just these rules that put the basic morality of the abbots in question. It would seem, then, that this kind of irony differs little from that involved in the creation of Chinese buddhas in the Tang genealogical texts and then again in the Song compendiums. In all three contexts, Chan authors demonstrate their ability to create and manage the image of buddhahood, while also, apparently, being quite clear about its fabricated nature.

Before exploring the details of this situation, it is worth pausing to speculate how it was that the carefully cultivated image of the indomitable and uncouth Chan master—as found in the Song "flame histories" and elsewhere—emerged roughly at the same time that these bureau-

---

6. Those shocked and outraged by the numerous scandals surrounding Zen masters in America might be heartened to learn of these various checks and balances put in place in medieval China to keep Chan masters from abusing their considerable powers. Presumably knowing more about this side of Chan's institutional history would go a long way towards establishing more realistic expectations of today's masters.

cratic "rules for purity" were drawn up. I believe that we can imagine at least four possible explanations for this historical coincidence. First, we could read the Chan literature celebrating the wild masters as a kind of entertaining supplement to the reality of Chan monastic life. Thus, the charming and somewhat wicked stories about an all-natural Buddhism that was transmitted with humor and violence, were written and circulated to enliven the lives of elite members of the monastery who were, perhaps, bored with strict monastic routines. The second option would be to see the accounts of the free and mighty masters as a carefully produced utopic past presented to all monastic trainees, a past that was to be honored and longed for, however impossible the practical achievement of that goal might have been. The third option might sound surprising but has a lot of evidence in its favor: the Chan literature celebrating the untamed masters—the "recorded sayings," in particular—wasn't really destined for the monastic communities, and instead was written and compiled for elites outside of the monastery, with an eye to attracting the attention of potential donors and the support of powerful governmental officials.[7] The fourth option accepts that the first three explanations might be accurate to some degree, but takes a wider view in which Chan is seen as a tradition that relied on a certain kind of practical understanding, nurtured among the elite within the monastery, in which just this gap between the Chan-of-literature and the nuts-and-bolts reality of monastic life was carefully produced and purveyed for those in and outside the monastery. In this fourth view, it is understood that Chan isn't simply its self-portrayal in literature and it

7. As Morten Schlütter puts it, "Although these works [the recorded sayings of the masters] were no doubt perused by monastic Chan students, *their main audience was the educated elite,* and the reception of a Chan master's recorded sayings could have a large impact on his career." For more discussion, see his *How Zen Became Zen: The Dispute over Enlightenment and the Formation of Chan Buddhism in Song-Dynasty China* (Honolulu: University of Hawai'i Press, 2008), 8ff; emphasis added. Christoph Anderl comes to the same conclusion: *"the main target-readership of the Recorded Sayings during the Song actually were the literati and officials..."* For more details, see Anderl, "Zen Rhetoric: An Introduction," in *Zen Buddhist Rhetoric in China, Korea, and Japan,* ed. Anderl (Leiden: Brill, 2012), 60n123; emphasis added.

isn't simply its monastic realities; rather, it is the ongoing ability to profitably blend the two together.

Imagining Chan to have been based on a kind of practical savoir-faire that shrewdly integrated the practical and the romantic also helps explain how it was that the intense structure and discipline of the monastery nevertheless regularly provided certain well-scripted moments for the ritual reenactment of scenes drawn from the literary version of Chan.[8] Thus, once every five days, the reigning abbot was to ascend the dharma throne and give a brief dharma talk during which the monks and/or their officers were permitted to pose questions. Within the context of this give-and-take, participants and observers might have felt that they were, in some small way, reliving the magic moments they imagined to have been the norm for their Tang predecessors. Getting Song monastics to imagine that they were reenacting heroic Tang episodes was encouraged by having one of the abbot's attendants record the conversation, implying that what had been exchanged in the present was of value for the future and, maybe more important, rhymed with the material that had supposedly been written down in the Tang under similar conditions and then collected in the flame histories of the early Song.[9] Thus, with systematic regularity some mini-version of the wild Chan master could have been performed for the inhabitants of the monastery and for those visitors who might have been on hand. Similar performances of "Chan dialogue" were also, no doubt, part of the ritual structure defining how a trainee should visit the abbot's room to ask for his instruction.[10] In sum, the Chan monastic schedule regularly allowed for small reenactments of the literary tradition that, with all its exciting and harrowing moments, had so captivated readers over the centuries.

8. For more reflections on the ritual reenactment of Chan literature, see Foulk, "Myth, Ritual, and Monastic Practice in Sung Ch'an Buddhism," in *Religion and Society in T'ang and Sung China*, eds. Patricia Buckley Ebrey and Peter N. Gregory (Honolulu: University of Hawai'i Press, 1993), esp., 177–80, and 193.

9. Foulk makes just this point; see ibid, 179–80.

10. For more details on visiting the abbot in private, see ibid., 181–82.

SONG MONASTERIES

To better appreciate this complex interplay of the Chan-of-literature and day-to-day monastic life, it is important to note that by the early Song, there was a legal distinction between public and private monasteries.[11] Private monasteries were called "private" for the very simple reason that each serving abbot was allowed to pick his successors from among his disciples, and thus the monastery and its lands became something like the private property of this "spiritual" lineage, which, in fact, was structured much like a normal Chinese family, albeit without women. Given the closed nature of this arrangement, we shouldn't be surprised to see that the state was much less involved in the "family life" of the monastery, and that the abbot's descendants found themselves bound much more closely to the abbot, the monastery, and the other members of the "family."[12]

The public monasteries were usually the larger, more noteworthy, institutions, and enjoyed state support, but also had to endure much more state intervention, especially in the appointment of the abbots. Public monasteries had three defining characteristics: (1) any properly ordained monk could reside there for as long as he liked; (2) the abbots of public monasteries were forbidden to pick their successors, and thus once an abbot retired or died, a complex "hiring" process was initiated, one that, at least in theory, called on local elites, governmental officials, and sometimes even the emperor—along with other important Buddhist

11. The following discussion of monastic arrangements is largely indebted to Foulk's "Myth, Ritual and Monastic Practice." See also Schlütter's clear and concise presentation of Song-era monasticism in his "Vinaya Monasteries, Public Abbacies, and State Control of Buddhism under the Song (960–1279)," in *Going Forth: Visions of Buddhist Vinaya; Essays Presented in Honor of Professor Stanley Weinstein,* ed. William M. Bodiford (Honolulu: University of Hawai'i Press), 2005, 136–60.

12. For a discussion of later developments in the familial aspects of the monastic system, see Ye Derong's "'Ancestral Transmission' in Chinese Buddhist Monasteries: The Example of the Shaolin Temple," in *India in the Chinese Imagination: Myth, Religion and Thought,* eds. John Kieschnick and Meir Shahar (Philadelphia: University of Pennsylvania Press, 2014), 110–24.

leaders from neighboring monasteries—to participate in the selection of the next abbot, a situation not unlike the hiring of a president at an American university;[13] and (3) public monasteries were "branded" in the sense that they might be identified as Chan, Tiantai, or Vinaya monasteries, and that this affiliation was to be respected insofar as the new abbot was to be chosen from among those monks who could prove that they belonged to the larger spiritual "family" of the preceding abbot, albeit without being his direct descendant.

The size and complexity of the larger public monasteries is hard to exaggerate. They often had as many as fifty buildings on site, while also owning large tracts of land and other kinds of property. In terms of architecture and ritual practices, they were, in part, modeled on the imperial court. As Foulk puts it, "The major Buddhist monasteries of the Song and Yuan, for example, imitated the architecture and ground plan of the imperial court; their internal bureaucratic structure was patterned after that of the state; and their social etiquette was basically that of the literati (scholar-bureaucrat) class, from which many leading prelates [abbots] came."[14] The more prosperous monasteries also often owned and operated mills for grinding grain, maintained small flotillas of boats and barges for commercial transport, and functioned as banks. In addition to these commercial concerns, the public monasteries also maintained significant libraries and elaborate reception halls decorated with various kinds of art. In short, the wealth of these institutions was often vast and varied, and they were clearly designed to generate more wealth and to husband those gains for future expansion and stability.

13. Comparing Chan to the American university system is a useful exercise that has been suggested by several scholars in the field, as Schlütter points out in his *How Zen Became Zen*, 203n63.

14. See Foulk, "Ritual in Japanese Zen Buddhism," in *Zen Ritual: Studies of Zen Buddhist Theory in Practice*, eds. Steve Heine and Dale S. Wright (New York: Oxford University Press, 2007), 40. Yifa draws the same conclusion in her "From the Chinese Vinaya Tradition to Chan Regulations," in *Going Forth: Visions of Buddhist Vinaya*, ed. William M. Bodiford (Honolulu: University of Hawai'i Press), 2005, 129–30.

Once one sees the scale of these institutions, it quickly becomes obvious that the abbots of these monasteries, serving as they did as chief executive officers with considerable amounts of power, had to be highly skilled bureaucrats of the first order. Like the president of an American university, or the mayor of a modern city, the abbot had to be able to handle a staggering range of tasks and topics. In particular, he had to have mastered the intricacies of Buddhist thought and practice—including the exciting and mystifying Chan rhetoric that had been gradually manufactured from the eighth century on—along with the sophisticated manners of the literati and the government officials with whom he regularly interacted. Put that way, it is hard to think of a more demanding job. In sum, the abbot had to have a global knowledge of the entire environment, an environment in which the radical quality of Chan rhetoric, and Buddhist thought in general, was securely nested in a highly disciplined "city" defined by the Buddhist monastic tradition and the laws dictated by the state.[15]

An abbot also had to understand that the well-being of his monastery required that it stay in the good graces of three external power centers: (1) the imperial court, if the monastery was large and famous enough to be nationally noteworthy; (2) local officials and those well-to-do families in the area whose members filled out the literati class; and (3) other leading Buddhist monasteries, particularly those who also claimed to be run by those in the Bodhidharma "family." Moreover, as the following passage from Zongze's *Rules for Purity* makes clear, the

---

15. Yifa concludes that one of the main innovations of Zongze's work is that he blends imperial law with traditional monastic law; see her "From the Chinese Vinaya Tradition to Chan Regulations," 124–25. More evidence of state control over the Buddhist system in the Song can be found in the way that abbots could buy titles such as "Great Master," with or without the purple robes included, from the state. If a longer title was sought, its cost was determined by the number of characters in the title. Actually, since one had to renew one's right to these items yearly, they were, in effect, being rented from the state. For more details, see Yifa's *The Origins of Buddhist Monastic Codes in China: An Annotated Translation and Study of the "Chanyuan qinggui"* (Honolulu: University of Hawaii Press, 2002), 80–81.

abbot was expected to provide various spiritual services for the emperor and government officials, while also strictly maintaining the monastery's moral purity. Actually, these two concerns were intimately linked, since it was the moral purity of the monastery that was believed to supply the spiritual power that could accomplish the various tasks that the government and other sponsors demanded of the monastery. As Zongze writes of the abbot's role, "His chief duty is to ensure the monastery's purity and strict adherence to the vinaya. His other duties include providing spiritual cultivation when asked by government officials, as well as praying for the emperor's longevity."[16] It was this basic need to maintain the monastery's public image as a place of exacting moral purity—and, consequently, a source of cosmic power—that explains why Zongze's handbook is called "rules for purity."

While the Chan abbot in the *Rules for Purity* was expected to move smoothly through all social hierarchies in and outside the monastery, the ordinary monks who lived in these Chan-themed monasteries had much more limited responsibilities and a rather restricted zone of activity. They lived, ate, and slept with the other trainees in a large open room—called the "sangha hall"—where they presumably had little time for privacy or independent action. These ordinary monks, though they surely knew that they were training under an abbot who identified himself with the Bodhidharma lineage, had no way to claim membership in the Bodhidharma "family"; thus they had to content themselves with worshipping the abbot and his dharma family from afar, while also trying to benefit from the various kinds of instruction that were regularly given. In short, while the history of the Bodhidharma family was crucial for determining the legitimacy of the abbots, such claims had little practical impact on the life of an ordinary monk, who was simply expected to keep all the rules, meditate several times during the day and attentively participate in the monastic rites and rituals, all in order to produce merit for the emperor, lay patrons,

16. See Yifa, *Origins,*216.

former Buddhist sages, and members of the Bodhidharma family, particularly those who had previously served at the monastery.

The life of monastic officers was somewhat different. In particular, they had separate housing away from the ordinary monks and, though often participating in group sutra recitations, spent a large part of their time working in various departments within the monastery, such as food supply, land management, and fundraising; some also served as personal assistants to the abbot. Theoretically, monks who staffed these positions were chosen by the abbot because he deemed them smart, reliable, and well aware of the laws and customs that governed both the monastery and Chinese society at large. Somewhat ironically, then, it was the elite monks in the monastery who spent much of their time in non-religious activities. Or, rather, their religious activities were often far from the meditation hall, focused as they were on making sure the monastery ran properly. The officers were, in essence, the day-to-day guardians of the health, welfare, and integrity of the monastery. Above all, they had to follow the abbot's orders strictly, since they served at his pleasure.[17]

Within the class of officer-monks, we find a category of select monks who seem to have been thought of differently. And here things become complicated. Zongze's handbook explains that the abbot was to choose several promising monks as his close disciples. The closeness expected between these chosen disciples and the abbot is underscored when we learn that when the abbot died, this small group of monks were to be identified as his "filial sons" (*xiaozi*) and given special Confucian-style

17. Relations between abbots and their officers could, apparently, be quite strained. The *Chixiu Baizhang qinggui*, published in 1335 (*T* no. 2025, 48.1109c), known as "Baizhang's Rules for Purity," mentions that when an abbot died, the monastery should take care to prevent any of his former officers from vandalizing his coffin or remains. The fear was that officers disciplined by the abbot would want to seek revenge for what they might have perceived as unfair treatment. See *The Baizhang Zen Monastic Regulations: Taishō volume 48, number 2025*, trans. Ichimura Shōhei (Berkeley, CA: Numata Center for Buddhist Translation and Research, 2006), 122; the passage cited above is found at *T* 48.1227c.13.

mourning duties that made clear to the monastery's inhabitants, and the public at large, that they were the descendants of the deceased abbot and, in that capacity, had received dharma-transmission from him.[18] These select monks, presumably after having passed some time in the meditation hall and in other monastic offices, would spend a lot of their time in the company of the abbot, serving and assisting him, and, in the context of that proximity, learn how to do his job. In effect, this small coterie of monks was selected to "shadow" the abbot for years so that they would have a very good idea of what would be expected of them should they, in the future, be selected to serve a monastery as abbot.[19]

Below, I more closely explore the process by which the abbot turned his "filial sons" into future buddha-abbots, a process that is, of course, completely the opposite of the literary accounts of masters zapping their disciples into sudden enlightenment. For now, though, it is enough to recognize that this two-tier setup in monastic personnel—ordinary monks vs. the abbots and the abbots-to-be—mirrors, to some extent, what we have seen in Chan literature, starting with the *Two Entrances*. On the one hand, there were the ordinary monks (and laity) who were to practice a standard form of Buddhism based on keeping the precepts, developing skill in meditation, and managing karmic "accounts" through sutra recitation and other merit-making activities. On the other hand, there were the members of the Bodhidharma family who, though following all the basic monastic rules, were also expected to produce, in public, an intriguing and beguiling antinomian discourse, one in which normal Buddhism was disparaged as second-rate, and in which all the normal practices of Buddhism were declared useless for achieving enlightenment, since real enlightenment supposedly only

18. See Yifa, *Origins,* 217; for more discussion, see also my "Upside Down / Right Side Up: A Revisionist History of Buddhist Funerals in China," *History of Religions* 35, no. 4 (1996): 310–11; directions for the abbot's funeral are found in the seventh chapter of Zongze's text; see X (no. 1245), 63.542c.23; http://www.cbeta.org/result/normal /X63/1245_007.htm

19. For Foulk's discussion of this arrangement, see his "Myth, Ritual and Monastic Practice," 162.

arrived magically when it was transmitted, man-to-man, by the abbots who had already been inducted into the Bodhidharma family. In short, the antinomian style of discourse that was most characteristic of Chan appears quite involved with establishing Buddhist leadership roles; thus, it turns out that active members of the Bodhidharma family were expected to regularly demonstrate their authority and status by speaking—publicly and privately—of Buddhist truths in a rough-and-tumble manner that was often inflected with Daoist themes.[20]

Regardless of how wild these discourses might have sounded on any particular occasion, such performances never got in the way of the abbots carefully managing the entire monastic operation.[21] Thus, in line with my above four choices regarding the gap between Chan literature and Chan's institutional reality, it isn't that Chan Buddhism is found at the elite level where abbots qua masters inherited and disseminated enlightenment to their chosen "filial sons"; rather, Chan was the logic and practice of *the whole arrangement* in which this divide between the supposedly enlightened and unenlightened was clearly drawn, and in which those identities were reliably replicated, generation after generation, by relying on the flexible "history" of the Bodhidharma family, its supporting literature, and the complex body of monastic rules Zongze was standardizing.

THE CURIOUS ORIGINS OF THE CHAN MONASTIC CODES

Various details in Zongze's handbook make clear that there are several bodies of institutional rules standing behind his vision of the properly run Chan monastery. The first source for Zongze's rules was simply the

20. As Foulk points out in "Ritual in Japanese Zen Buddhism," 41: "Becoming an heir in Bodhidharma's lineage of dharma transmission, which was the fast track to high monastic office within the Buddhist sangha, entailed mastering the literature of the Chan tradition and being able to reenact it in the ritual context of the 'question and answer' exchange between master and disciple."

21. For Foulk's reflections on this tension, see his "Myth, Ritual, and Monastic Practice," 177–80.

immense body of Buddhist monastic law—the *vinaya*—that had, over the centuries, been translated from Indic sources into Chinese. Along with the Indian texts, there was an equally massive body of Chinese commentary on them; these commentaries worked to explain and legitimize various Chinese innovations in the monastic code. In fact, as Yifa has shown, after Buddhism came to China in the second and third centuries CE, a rather stock form of Buddhist monasticism got established, and it was just this sinified form of Buddhist monasticism that served as the foundation for Zongze's handbook. Thus there isn't a lot that is original among the many practices and procedures that Zongze prescribes. Moreover, it seems likely that Zongze's handbook drew on slightly older Tiantai monastic handbooks that had been published in the first decades of the eleventh century.[22] These Tiantai works, too, rested on that large body of generic Buddhist monastic rules developed in China. Thus, by the early Song, there was a widely shared set of rules governing monastic practice, regardless of how the monastery was branded—Chan or Tiantai or neither.[23] Consequently, it isn't surprising to see that non-Chan monasteries could easily be converted into Chan monasteries—all that was needed was to install portraits of Chan ancestors in the portrait hall, and recruit a new abbot who claimed to be in the Bodhidharma family and could give his lectures based on Chan literature.[24]

As has already been implied, the Confucian tradition was another source for Zongze's rules.[25] Throughout his handbook, Zongze draws

22. As Foulk puts it: "[T]he fact is that the Tiantai school had its own tradition of compiling monastic rules that went at least as far back as the eleventh century. The eminent monk Zunshi (963–1032) ... was a monastic legislator whose rules predate the compilation of the *Chanyuan qinggui* (the oldest extant Chan code) by seventy years," (Foulk, "*Chanyuan qinggui* and Other 'Rules of Purity,'"305).

23. For Yifa's discussion of this shared form of monasticism in China, see her "From the Chinese Vinaya Tradition," esp. 124–25 and 134–35.

24. See Foulk, "The Ch'an *Tsung* in Medieval China: School, Lineage, or What?" *Pacific World*, n.s., no. 8 (1992): 29, and id., "Myth, Ritual, and Monastic Practice," 165–67, 175, 180, 191–92.

25. For discussion of Confucian influences in the *Chanyuan qinggui*, see Yifa, *Origins*, 74, 86–94, 98; see also her "From the Chinese Vinaya Tradition," esp. 125, 129–34.

on a range of Confucian ritual texts and ritual formats—some dating back to Han dynasty and earlier—to shape and justify various interactions in the monastery. Thus, whether he was establishing the rules for hosting a tea ceremony or organizing the protocol for an abbot's funeral or defining various forms of greeting, Zongze makes clear that a good Chan monastery ought to be run in a very Confucian manner. Clearly, then, Zongze's Chan monastery was to be a "habitat" marked by a careful blending of Buddhist and Confucian disciplines. Moreover, we shouldn't think that the Confucian material was somehow added onto the Chan system as an afterthought. Instead, the most Confucian-looking materials collect around the figure of the abbot and his chosen "sons," where the old, non-Buddhist family codes were relied on to structure the legal reproduction of the Bodhidharma family.[26] Thus, though the entire monastery was infused with a Confucian commitment to decorum and ritual pageantry, it is also clear that Confucian templates were most heavily relied on to define and reproduce leadership roles in the monastery.[27]

The third source for Zongze's rules is imperial law. Thus, Zongze's text provides details on a range of state-defined procedures and restrictions, especially those regarding ordination, travel, and the selection of abbots. In this sense, Zongze appears eager to bring secular law into his handbook, with the clear understanding that monasteries absolutely had to follow these government directives.

With his obvious reliance on this mass of literary precedents, one might expect Zongze to have been happy to clarify the roots of his work. However, when Zongze explains the origins of his text, we see instead something far from straightforward. In his preface, Zongze claims that his handbook is basically the work of someone else—Baizhang Huaihai

26. For more details on the Confucian elements in the abbot's funeral, see my "Upside Down / Right Side Up."

27. For more reflections on this fusion of filial piety with monastic discipline, see my "Homestyle Vinaya and Docile Boys in Chinese Buddhism," *positions: east asia cultures critique* 7, no. 1 (Spring 1999): 1–49.

(749–814), a Tang master who became very famous in the Song.[28] There is no Tang-era evidence that Baizhang wrote this handbook or one like it, and, given that Zongze's handbook is chock-full of very traditional forms of Buddhist monasticism, it presumably couldn't be attributed to any one author. Foulk sums up the situation this way: "The monastic regulations contained in the *Chanyuan qinggui* and later 'rules of purity' were neither the invention of Baizhang nor the exclusive property of the Chan school. They were, in fact, the common heritage of the Chinese Buddhist tradition during the Song and Yuan. Nevertheless, by promoting the figure of Baizhang, the Chan school was able to take credit for the entire tradition of indigenous monastic rulemaking."[29] In short, in what would appear to be another branding coup, Zongze's preface gives the impression that it was a Chan master—Baizhang—who had, in the Tang, invented the Buddhist monastic tradition as it was known in the Song, and that Zongze's text was no more than a repackaging of that initial invention. In time, everyone forgot Zongze, taking Baizhang to be this most remarkable and original (!) architect of monastic rules. Thus, just as Tang authors managed to convincingly put the totality of enlightenment into the Bodhidharma lineage, Zongze's *Rules for Purity* managed to give the impression that the Bodhidharma lineage was also the source of the monastic system.

From the above introductory discussion we can draw out four main points. First, Zongze's writing shows he had an encyclopedic knowledge of several kinds of Buddhist literature, along with the Confucian classics, not to mention the expanding body of Chan literature and the various imperial laws regarding Buddhism. In sum, as a standard-issue Song-era abbot, he was remarkably literate: Zongze knew his texts, and he knew what could be done with those texts, particularly in terms of using Confucian models of inheritance to structure and render "visible" the flow of Buddhist enlightenment from the Chan abbots to their

28. For Foulk's translation of the preface, see his "*Chanyuan qinggui* and Other 'Rules of Purity,'" 284–85.
29. Ibid., 307.

"filial sons." Second, Zongze, as an experienced abbot, took it upon himself to clarify the rules for other abbots; consequently, Zongze's handbook represents a form of final authority over the figures in tradition who supposedly had final authority – the abbots, that is. The nature of this meta-view back on Buddhist authority warrants careful attention and I will return to this issue below. Third, and in a related vein, Zongze's vision of Buddhism is totalistic: as abbot and author, he is asking his readers—presumably other abbots and/or senior officers—to regard Buddhist monasticism in this totalizing manner: all is to be seen, known and controlled. Thus the vision that Zongze is constructing for the abbot qua buddha is, arguably, little different from how an emperor was to see his empire (more on this issue below).[30] Lastly, insofar as Zongze wrote his *Rules for Purity* hoping that it would be adopted by monasteries throughout the empire, we have another example of a Chan writer working to systematize and unify the Chan version of Buddhism, a goal equally evident in the flame histories. Presumably, Zongze expected that as other Chan monasteries took up his handbook as the norm, monks—elite and ordinary—could circulate around the nation, expecting to find one basic—state-approved—form of Buddhism in every corner of the empire. In fact, by the end of this chapter, we will have evidence to suggest that the strength of Zongze's system, and Song Chan in general, lay in its ability to present the image of a stable, spiritually powerful (and fertile), self-policing family of Chinese buddha-abbots who could be counted on to reliably produce a compliant, pro-state form of Buddhism throughout the land.[31]

30. This parallel between the big monasteries and the state was, in fact, explicit. Yifa points out that the abbot's role was "analogous to that of the emperor," with the Chan monastery functioning as "a microcosm of the imperial court" (*Origins*, 86)

31. In thinking about Zongze's motivations for attempting to generate a unified form of Chan monasticism for the whole of China, we shouldn't overlook that just as Zongze was writing up his *Rules for Purity*, the emperor, Huizong (r. 1101–26), was initiating one of several attempts to create a nationally syndicated clergy that was to be, after a fashion, Daoist. For more discussion of Huizong's directives, see Schlütter, *How Zen Became Zen*, 50–51.

CHAN BUDDHISM: STATE-OWNED

To get a clearer sense for the content of Zongze's *Rules for Purity*, and the intricacies of Song-era Chan, let's briefly turn to explore several key aspects of the monastic system that his text covers, including ordination, travel, and ancestor worship. What we will see at every turn is that the Chinese state essentially won every battle with the Buddhist institution; consequently, monasteries and the monks were thoroughly controlled—owned even—by a powerfully invasive state-apparatus. For instance, as is well established in modern scholarship, even the act of setting out to become a Buddhist monk in China was under state control. The key dynamic to understand here is that since monks were exempt from taxation and corvée labor, each man who became a monk represented a loss for the state coffers and for state initiated labor-projects and, of course, warfare. Thus, Chinese dynasties before and after the Tang mandated that a man who wished to become a monk needed to first receive a certificate from the state before he could legally start his training, thereby giving the state effective control over the number of citizens who could join the clergy.[32]

Then, in the middle of the eighth century, the government decided to *sell* these ordination certificates to prospective clergy, and at rather steep prices. Henceforth, any man hoping to become a monk had to raise a significant amount of capital to finance his monastic career. In the Song this practice was much expanded to the point where a monk had to have three certificates to normalize his monastic identity: his tonsure certificate, his ordination certificate, and what was called the "six awarenesses," a document that contained the signatures of his "ordination preceptors."[33] When a monk took up residence at a monastery, he was expected to surrender these documents to the monastery's senior officers, who would send them on to the local government offi-

32. For a useful overview of the rules regarding various certificates, see Yifa, *Origins*, 75–78.
33. Ibid., 78.

cials for inspection. In effect, then, the state vigorously taxed and tracked every member of the clergy. It also instituted yearly and tri-annual reregistration fees. So, rather than being the longed-for moment when one renounced the world, becoming a monk in China meant entering into a complex relationship with a very suspicious and demanding state bureaucracy.

Once a monk had managed to obtain his proper certificates, he had to make sure that he had them on hand any time he traveled. In fact, even before he set out on a trip, he had to submit a detailed travel plan to the local authorities, along with letters of recommendation attesting to his good character. If the local authorities judged his paperwork to be in order, he would be issued a travel permit for that very specific trajec-tory, a trip that had to be accomplished in a set amount of time. If he traveled without such papers, or if he took too long a time on the road, he risked being arrested, caned, and defrocked.[34] Even abbots had to travel with this kind of paperwork in hand. Here, the state's goal was to minimize movement of the clergy and to keep very close tabs on their whereabouts at all times.

Obviously, once one realizes how this kind of state-control impinged on *all* monks and their basic freedoms, one has to rethink stock images in Song literature of the carefree monk who floated, from monastery to monastery, like a drifting cloud. Against that fantasy we have to see that to be a Buddhist monk, whether one was involved with Chan ideas or not, was to know and abide by a very clear set of state-given rules and regulations. To do otherwise was to put one's clerical career in jeopardy, while also potentially threatening one's superiors as well, since, in good Chinese fashion, they would be held responsible for the ethical lapses of their subordinates.

Despite the important similarities between Chan and non-Chan mon-asteries, Zongze's text does reveal some innovation regarding the process by which abbots were created and installed in their leadership roles. The

34. Ibid., 79.

first thing to see is that there were two tracks of authority at play in the making of an abbot. On the one track, it took a recognized abbot to begin to make another abbot. The way this worked was briefly mentioned above: during his years of service, an abbot would cultivate a group of younger monks to whom he would, in time, give dharma-transmission. This dharma-transmission, which came with a formal certificate of inheritance (*sishu*), signified that the recipient should now be considered a member of the Bodhidharma family.[35] Of course, receiving this transmission didn't in itself turn the younger monks into abbots—it merely made them legitimate candidates for some future posting as abbot.

When a monastery lost its abbot—to illness, old age, death, or his desire to move elsewhere—Zongze's handbook details the process by which his replacement was to be found.[36] It is in this process that we see the second track of authority in the making of an abbot. With the abbot gone, the senior monks at the monastery, in conjunction with local governmental officials and literati, were to gather together and, after careful consideration, draw up a list of candidates who, they felt, could take on the job of running the monastery. In effect, as this group of Buddhist and non-Buddhist leaders vetted prospective candidates, they functioned as an ad hoc board of directors for the monastery. While this sounds cordial enough, it is important to note that according to Song law, if the monastic officials moved to chose the next abbot without consulting government officials, they risked a caning of two to three hundred strokes; and, likewise, any official that allowed this breach in protocol risked the same punishment.[37] Clearly, the government was determined to prevent the larger monasteries from being taken over by self-perpetuating monk "families."

Once they settled on a candidate, the monastery's senior monks were to begin gathering up a range of official documents in order to

35. For more details on these documents, see Foulk, "Myth, Ritual, and Monasticism," 159ff.

36. For more details, see Yifa, *Origins*, 81–83, 212–17.

37. Ibid., 84.

formally invite the chosen candidate to assume the abbacy.[38] They then would organize a small coterie of senior monastic officials to travel to the candidate's monastery. A runner would be sent ahead of them to deliver a letter to the local governmental officials, petitioning them to release the selected master from his current position.[39] When the visiting entourage was on site at the candidate's monastery, they were to follow a complex set of ritual procedures for formally inviting the candidate to take over the role of abbot at their monastery. Throughout this visit, great attention was paid to hierarchy and rank, and many elaborate set phrases were used to punctuate steps in the ritual. Of course, the candidate could refuse the offer, but if he decided to accept it, another body of ritual action came to bear to choreograph the candidate's journey to his new monastery. If the invited monk was already serving as abbot, Zongze notes that he was allowed to bring with him his chosen attendants—those younger monks whom he had, presumably, been grooming so that one day they too could be invited to assume an abbacy somewhere.

Installed in his new position, the abbot was to serve as a representative of the buddha. Zongze explains the role thusly: "The abbot represents the Buddha in his propagation of the dharma, and he sets an example for the [monastic] administrators; he is therefore called 'Transmitter of the Dharma.' Abbots are spread across the land, each occupying his own place and continuing the Buddha's life of wisdom; they are therefore called 'Dwelling and Holding' [*zhuchi* – which is the title translated as "abbot"]."[40] In his capacity as resident buddha, he was to be relied upon for final explanations regarding the meaning of Buddhism and for the overall maintenance of the monastery and, of course, the moral purity of the monastery's trainees and officers.

In considering this arrangement whereby a monk graduated to this august status of in-house buddha, several structural matters are worth

38. Ibid., 212.
39. Ibid., 212–13.
40. Ibid., 216.

considering. First, as we've just seen, the selection of the new abbot was supposed to result from close consultation between senior monks and local officials, and it was conducted, in part, based on letters of recommendation from elite monks and literati who knew the potential candidates. What this meant is that while the new abbot was to be regarded as a living buddha, in another sense he was more or less *voted* into his buddhahood by local and national elites, Buddhist and non-Buddhist. Moreover, according to Song Chan rules, if a monk received dharma-transmission—taken to be proof of his enlightenment—but was never invited to be an abbot, he couldn't pass on his dharma-transmission. Consequently, the "fertility" of a monk who had received dharma-transmission was only actualized when he was chosen to be an abbot. Thus buddhahood, and its ongoing presence in real-time was, in a significant way, the result of decisions made by state officials and the local literati in their consultations with monastic officers.[41] Clearly, then, the Chinese state succeeded in turning the most perfect form of Buddhist authority into a bureaucratic office over which it had considerable control.

The office of the abbot and buddhahood overlapped in another way: a monk aspiring to join the Bodhidharma family didn't win dharma-transmission from the abbot based on intensive meditation or from some sudden spiritual realization. Instead, he won it from attending the abbot, day in and day out, and, in that way, figuring out how to perform in this role such that his master would begin to have confidence in one day sending him off to serve as an abbot in his own monastery. Looked at this way, it was, ironically, the young monk's Confucian diligence

41. Schlütter sums up the situation well: "*Only as an abbot at a public monastery could a Chan master give transmission to his students,* and Chan masters were very aware that they required the support of officials and local literati if they wished to obtain abbacies and continue their lineages." (Schlütter, *How Zen Became Zen,* 10; emphasis added). Juhn Y. Ahn offers a range of insightful perspectives on the work of being a Song-era abbot; see his "Buddhist Self-Cultivation Practice," in *Modern Chinese Religion I: Song-Liao-Jin-Yuan (960–1368 AD),* eds. John Lagerwey and Pierre Marsone (Leiden: Brill, 2015), 1160–86.

and filial devotion that was essential for his inclusion in the Bodhi-dharma family. Thus while becoming an abbot signaled one's buddha-hood within the system, training to become an abbot wasn't particu-larly focused on meditation or on other Buddhist practices, as one might expect, but rather on slowly gaining familiarity with all aspects of running a monastery by respectfully serving the current abbot and paying attention to how he handled the job. Given that abbots needed bureaucratic knowledge as much as enlightenment—however that term might be construed—there might not have been a better way to organ-ize the reproduction of these authority figures.[42]

This arrangement meant that any abbot who wished to reproduce his spiritual lineage needed a monastic site in order to effectively train his chosen disciples. The master obviously couldn't train these disci-ples in a secluded hermitage or cave, since no amount of Buddhist insight was going to prepare them for the rigors of running a monas-tery, and it was, of course, only in that capacity that they would be rec-ognized as buddhas capable of furthering the Bodhidharma lineage. In short, the future life of the abbot's spiritual family could only develop as he won and held abbot-level appointments and then arranged the same for his descendants. Put metaphorically, the successful abbot had to regularly nest in a monastery where he could instruct his fledgling disciples in the art of maintaining a monastic nest and reproducing therein.

This close dependency of the abbot and his dharma family on the monastic system shouldn't obscure a very basic tension between the abbot and the monastery where he resided. The problem was that the abbot presumably cared most about his dharma family—his own master, and his master's masters, along with his future descendants whom he was in the process of training. None of these figures, it should be noted, would necessarily have any future connection to the monastery in which they were currently residing. Thus, while an abbot had to take care of the

42. Schlütter, *How Zen Became Zen*, 60–77, develops this point.

monastery in order to preserve his public reputation—and the reputation of his lineage—he had no lasting interest in the future of any particular monastery where he might be "dwelling and holding," as his title speci-fied. Likewise, if he was interested in generating more of a reputation for himself and his lineage, then he would no doubt be considering the pos-sibility of future appointments to other monasteries, since it was by mov-ing around that abbots became better known. And yet, once installed in the new monastery, the dynamic would just repeat itself. In short, the abbot and his dharma family could never count any particular monastery as home, and this produced some interesting conflicts of interest.

In fact, there are at least three places in Zongze's handbook where ten-sions between the abbot and his monastery of residence are visible, and Zongze's straightforward treatment of these tensions suggests that these problems with the buddha-abbot system were widely understood.[43] First, Zongze makes it clear that when the abbot got ready to leave his post, a number of procedures should be carried out to ensure that he didn't take any of the monastery's wealth with him.[44] The anticipated avarice of the abbot is also visible in the admonition that the departing abbot shouldn't take much luggage with him, or a large retinue, or any gold, silver, or silk. In short, Zongze appears quite concerned that abbots might be inclined to steal from the monastery, especially when leaving to take up a new post. That Zongze was so worried about this possibility raises some important question about how he thought about abbots, in general.[45]

43. Yifa, *Origins,* 84, notes that the public monastic system, with its complex system for installing new abbots, was fragile and open to abuse; apparently by the second half of the Song there was a strong movement to abandon it.
44. Ibid., 219.
45. The *Baizhang Qinggui,* a very influential fourteenth-century monastic hand-book, includes a ghost story about a deceased abbot who returns from hell to explain to the current abbot the torture he is receiving for diverting donor funds (*Baizhang Zen Monastic Regulations,* trans. Ichimura Shōhei, 85–86). The story closes with a telling complaint: "Nowadays, the practice of ignoring moral retribution seems rampant in Chan temples. Not only are [funds and temple property] diverted for alternative pur-poses, but also, in extreme cases, temple possessions are stolen for personal use. What can be done about such people?" The *Baizhang Qinggui* gives more detailed directions

Likewise, since Zongze was writing his handbook for abbot-level readers, he seems intent on getting reigning abbots to submit to a set of checks and balances in the monastic system, and in that submission *to admit that this was, in fact, a necessary precaution.* He was, in effect, asking his readers qua abbots to understand that in order for the whole institution to survive, the abbot's supposed buddhahood needed to be offset with very strict rules governing his actual behavior.[46]

A second area of tension appears around the organization of the monastery's ancestors. Each public Chan monastery in the Song was supposed to maintain a hall filled with the portraits of all the abbots who had served there, along with portraits of more distant ancestral figures such as Bodhidharma and Baizhang. The problem here was that looking down this row of former abbots, men who were specifically called ancestors (*zu*), one might get the impression that they were all in one family. However, given that abbots couldn't appoint their dharma heirs as their replacements, each of these abbots was, by definition, in a different dharma subfamily from his predecessor and thus had no direct "family relations" with him. If there was any notion of family between the prior abbots, beyond the fact that they all supposedly were distant descendants of Bodhidharma, it was provided by the monastic entity itself, since the only thing that held these masters together was the fact

---

for controlling the retirement of the abbot in order to minimize the possibility of theft or corruption; see ibid., 116–17.

46. Schlütter has several insightful comments on the assumed venality of the Chan abbot; see his *How Zen Became Zen,* 40 and his note about the eleventh-century Chan master Zhenjing Kewen (1025–1102), who "is reported to have complained that in his day, people would praise an abbot for not appropriating monastic property, as if that were something extraordinary" (ibid., 194n60; his source is the *Chanlin baoxun, T* (no. 2022), 48.1021c). William Bodiford sums up the situation this way: "In a secular family, the economic power of the family head to spend the family property was unchecked. Buddhists, on the other hand, always were trying to come up with new ways to ensure that abbots of temples would not misappropriate temple funds or property"; see his "Dharma Transmission in Theory and Practice," in *Zen Ritual: Studies of Zen Buddhist Theory in Practice,* eds. Steve Heine and Dale S. Wright (New York: Oxford University Press, 2007), 266.

that they had each been chosen by the monastery and the local officials, and then served there. In this sense, we have to consider that this arrangement represented the creation of a new lineage: *the lineage of the monastery*, one that relied on the "private" lineages of the various masters for its staffing but, in the end, and in a very visible manner, celebrated the succession of Bodhidharma's family only insofar as these figures passed through the monastery as its leaders.[47]

The third area of tension is, arguably, the most interesting. At the very end of his handbook, Zongze details how the monastery was to treat an abbot who was retiring.[48] Somewhat shockingly, Zongze explains that the monastery should do what it can to get him to leave. Moreover, as mentioned above, he was to pack his bags in a way that allowed for close supervision by monastic officers in order to prevent him from taking items that were not his. Also, he was to apply for his travel permit well in advance of his exit, presumably so that there wouldn't be any cause for delay on that front. More shocking, he wasn't to interact with anyone in the monastery once he had tendered his letter of resignation; in fact, he was to head out without even leaving a forwarding address, thereby preventing anyone from contacting him and drawing him into any future power struggles at the monastery. In effect, once he announced his intention to retire, his buddhahood was for all practical purposes nullified and he was essentially pushed out of the monastery.[49]

47. For more discussion of the patriarchs' hall and its problematic structure, see Foulk, "Myth, Ritual and Monastic Practice," 172–76, esp. 175. See also Foulk and Robert H. Sharf, "On the Ritual Use of Ch'an Portraiture in Medieval China," *Cahiers d'Extrême-Asie* 7 (1993–94): 179–86; they conclude that "the patriarch hall came to represent not the genealogy of a particular individual, but *the genealogy of the monastery itself*" (ibid., 180; emphasis added).

48. Yifa, *Origins*, 219–20; this discussion is found at the end of chapter 7 of Zongze's text: *X* 63 (no. 1245), 63.543b.7. http://tripitaka.cbeta.org/X63n1245_007

49. If the abbot was very sick he was allowed to stay on at the monastery, but Zongze makes it clear that he was to be totally divested of his powers. However, in another passage it seems that retired abbots might be appointed as "chief seat emeritus," suggesting that some abbots stayed at their monasteries in some official capacity; see Yifa, *Origins*, 211–12.

What is most intriguing in this final passage of the handbook is that Zongze's comments suggest that he had a keen sense of what we might call a "sociology of authority." For instance, he appears quite aware of the dangers that come with having two functioning abbots on site, and provides rules to avoid just that disastrous situation. Writing with a kind of studied worldliness, he explains, "Once an abbot has retired from his post, it is not appropriate for him to be a constant presence or to take up residence in his former monastery. Relations among people are a highly unstable matter; it is best to be extremely cautious regarding the continuation of former relations."[50] Obviously, Zongze understood what kind of chaos could erupt if a monastery was hosting *two* working buddhas at one time. For Zongze, buddhahood was a good thing one could definitely have too much of.

On another level, we can see that Zongze, as a well-seasoned abbot, put his own wisdom about people and the world—a secular knowledge regarding the reality of institutional situations—above any kind of buddha-wisdom that any particular abbot might claim to have, and thus it was that he insisted that the buddha-abbots be carefully controlled in accordance with the rules he provided. Equally interesting, he seems to have understood the dangers that the abbots posed to the monastic system in a manner that might seem destined to ruin the sacrality of the Chan system, even as he *also* took great pains to explain how that system was to be maintained and reproduced. Coming to terms with just this kind of ironic commitment is, as I have been arguing, key to understanding the invention and management of the Chan system.

Summing up what Zongze's handbook implies about leadership, literature, and practical knowledge in Song Chan, it would seem clear that for Zongze, the abbot of a Chan monastery was responsible for mastering five kinds of language. He was to know the *vinaya* and all that it defined and prescribed; he was after all, in charge of interpreting and enforcing this extensive set of traditional monastic rules. Then he

50. Ibid., 220.

needed, naturally, to have mastered the language of the Mahāyāna sutras that were recited so regularly in the sangha hall. Then, on any given day he needed to be ready to perform as a Confucian gentleman in ritualized settings where he was expected to play his part in closely scripted exchanges—both with resident monks and visiting dignitaries. Fourth, whenever elite donors or governmental official showed up, the abbot was expected to have mastered literati conversation styles and the basics of traditional poetry, otherwise he would inspire little confidence in his lay supporters, and this could only hurt the monastery and its various businesses. Finally, he needed to know how to perform a kind of Chan-language, one that, by the Song, had become quite well established. In this zone of rhetoric, he had, on occasion, to sound wild and beyond the pale of normal logic, even while also lightly alluding to the high jinks of the Chan masters found in the massive Song compendiums. Here, a kind of Daoist-flavored rhetoric was the norm, one in which a resolute insouciance was joined with an attitude of completion: everything was always already perfect, even if the abbot was the only one who knew of this perfection. Thinking in Weberian terms, we might suppose that such performances were designed to put a little bit of charisma back into the otherwise overly formal office of the abbot. At any rate, we see that the Chan master and his required language skills existed at the end of a very long track of Buddhist and non-Buddhist literature, since he was that special place where the Buddhist tradition from India—with all its literature—was joined with the Confucian ritual texts and their set phrases, not to mention the Daoist classics and the poetic tradition. It was only with the mastery of *all this literature* that a Chan master could successfully occupy the office of abbot.

Before leaving Zongze's handbook, it is worth briefly mentioning what he had to say about meditation. As mentioned above, it seems clear that meditation was a key component in the daily monastic schedule. But how was that meditation thought of? To what extent was this really a Chan kind of meditation, different from more traditional forms of Buddhist meditation? While Chan writers had been notoriously silent on the details of practicing meditation, this changed shortly after the publication of Zongze's *Rules for Purity* when a short text called *The Meaning of Seated Meditation (Zuochan yi)* was appended to Zongze's handbook sometime in the middle of the twelfth century.[51] This text, which might or might not have been written by Zongze, explains in detail how a trainee was to meditate. What is most striking about these instructions is how traditional they seem. Thus, trainees were instructed in body posture, breathing techniques and so on, in a manner that seems reminiscent of much older discussions of the topic.

Actually, as Carl Bielefeldt has shown, much of *The Meaning of Seated Meditation* appears to have been taken from a manual written by the sixth-century Tiantai author Zhiyi.[52] Clearly, then, the author of *The Meaning of Seated Meditation* felt it completely acceptable to put in "Tiantai" teachings as the essence or meaning of Chan meditation. Such a confusion of origins and essences would have appeared all the more embarrassing given that the Song dynasty was one in which debates between the advocates of Chan and Tiantai raged decade after decade. Regardless of how we decide to frame this case of medieval plagiarism, we are again left with a sense that Chan authors were decidedly cavalier in recycling and rebranding the Buddhist tradition for their own benefit. One might even wonder if this self-serving approach to older versions of the Buddhist tradition wasn't of a piece with Zongze's fears that when it was time to move on to a new posting, abbots might very well "steal the silverware," as the saying has it.

CONCLUSIONS

Much more could be said about Zongze's handbook but for now let's draw out three conclusions. First, Zongze's text makes clear that he

---

51. See chapter 8 of Zongze's *Rules for Purity, X* (no. 1245), 63.544c.20.

52. See Carl Bielefeldt, "Tsung-tse's *Tso-Ch'an I* and the 'Secret' of Zen Meditation," in *Traditions of Meditation in Chinese Buddhism*, ed. Peter Gregory (Honolulu: University of Hawai'i Press, 1985), 129–61.

understood the slowness of everything. There is nothing sudden in Zongze's vision of the monastery. Everything is prepared for. Everything is ritualized.[53] Practically all important monastic acts had to be accompanied by elaborate set phrases and/or cumbersome form letters. Clearly, then, when we think of Chan literature and its fascination with the reproduction of tradition in moments of sudden enlightenment or instantaneous dharma-transmission, we have to remember that these stories came out of an institution that was committed to the opposite: the steady and painstaking maintenance and reproduction of all its elements, from top to bottom, with an emphasis on repeated ritual forms, carefully orchestrated negotiations, and closely monitored bureaucratic actions. Any account of Chan that ignores the cohabitation of the romantic and exhilarating Chan-of-literature with the legalism and bureaucracy of Chan monasteries is certainly missing the tensions and desires that structure Chan discourse. In fact, this pairing is probably far from accidental and instead likely resulted from a very perceptive assessment of how Buddhism existed in China, an overview that first took stock of the full complexity of the historical moment—both in and outside the monastery—and responded with a number of creative literary and ritual adaptions that were thought to best shelter and foster the Buddhist tradition.

The second conclusion is that Zongze's handbook calls forth a type of vision and wisdom that moves throughout every aspect of the monastery: from the need to beat defiant trainees, to organizing and disciplining the officer corps, to integrating fruitfully with the local economy, to remaining in the good graces of local government officials, and so on. Zongze's abbot is one who knows it all and, better, knows how to handle everything appropriately, regardless of what zone of society he

53. As Dale Wright put it, "virtually all life in a Zen monastery is predetermined, scripted, and taken out of the domain of human choice"; see his "Introduction: Rethinking Ritual Practice in Zen Buddhism," in *Zen Ritual: Studies of Zen Buddhist Theory in Practice,* eds. Steve Heine and Wright (New York: Oxford University Press, 2007), 3.

is functioning in. What becomes increasingly unnerving in Zongze's discussion, though, is that he expected abbots to understand that their supposed buddha status was far from being a foolproof reality, and that they, as a class of individuals, also needed to be carefully policed. That is, on top of all the practical and literary knowledge required of abbots, Zongze asked that they come to regard their position with a thorough-going irony—admitting that *even though the abbot was the spiritual leader of the community, he was also potentially one of the monastery's worst enemies.*

Congruent with this kind of irony regarding their status, Zongze's abbot appears as the consummate "company man," since he comes into his position knowing that it was the monastery (and the secular officials) that generated his status, just as he leaves apparently resigned to the fact that nothing he had been given in terms of spiritual authority was really ever his. Of course, Zongze's rules present an idealized version of Chan monasteries' practical and symbolic domination of their abbots, but it is a vision that is remarkable nonetheless for carefully arranging matters in order to keep the monasteries strong and intact as they hosted, one after another, these buddha-bureaucrats whom Zongze clearly understood to be a real threat to the well-being of the monasteries. In sum, Zongze demonstrates a global view of, and love for, Buddhist monasticism that is stunning for its breadth and depth, even as he also came up with precise procedures to prevent the most powerful figures in the system from acting on their not-so-buddha-like inclinations.

The final conclusion involves focusing on how the Chan system was situated at the national level. Zongze's stated goal was to normalize Chan monastic orders throughout the land and, of course, to establish and maintain a level of discipline that all members of the Bodhidharma family would see as their joint responsibility. While this was no doubt expected to solidify the Chan brand, Zongze's new system for sameness also seems designed to overcome regionalism in order to produce a Chan institution that, like the governmental offices throughout the empire, had a single set of procedures that guided its behavior. The abbot, then, ends up looking like a government official: he trained for his post by mastering a vast array of literature, and only assumed his office after having been investigated and approved by his peers— Buddhist and non-Buddhist—in a carefully orchestrated bureaucratic process designed to weed out all undesirables.[54] The Chan abbot was, in effect, supposed to be everybody's choice—that place of harmonious compromise between the state, Buddhism, and local literati.

Standing back from the details, it would seem that by the Song, the Chan monastery was a place where a plethora of Chinese values could be articulated and demonstrated for participants, and the general public, in a condensed and precise manner that would have been the envy of other sectors of society. In this, Chan Buddhism again looks like the state's Big Other, only now it has filled out that role such that the entire monastic system lends itself to the project of reflecting back to the throne an image of the perfect imperial state that is now purified, spiritualized, and wonderfully synchronized with itself and its surroundings. This symbolic service was inseparable from more obvious kinds of service that the Chan monastic system provided for the throne, including: generating merit to protect the state from enemies and ghosts, performing various kinds of ancestor worship for the royal family, praying for rain, and so on, while also inspiring ethical behavior among the locals. Zongze's handbook was, in sum, dedicated to using the newly bureaucratized form of the Bodhidharma family to better ground Buddhist monasticism on the landscape of the Chinese empire. That the Chan system slipped into near oblivion several times over the course of the following millennium in no way detracts from Zongze's

54. Based on a wide range of historical evidence, Schlütter, *How Zen Became Zen*, 70–73, also argues for this parallel between Chan abbots and secular officials, concluding that "[v]irtually all Chan masters for whom we have biographical information of any detail are said to *have been appointed to various public abbacies by secular authorities*, often at the recommendation of high-ranking officials and other members of the educated elite" (ibid., 72; emphasis added). However strict these formalities might appear to have been, Schlütter notes that state officials often demanded bribes; in some cases the abbacies were even auctioned off to the highest bidder; see ibid., 40–41.

sagely determination to set this intricate and refined form of Buddhism on the most secure foundation possible.

With a sense of the truly byzantine world of Chan monasticism during the Song dynasty, let us now turn to consider what is arguably the most developed form of Chan literature: koan commentary.

Koans and Being There

The English word "koan" comes from the Japanese pronunciation of the Chinese *gong'an,* which means "public case" in the sense of a legal precedent. The term *gong'an* begins to appear in Chan texts in the first half of the twelfth century as a technical term for a particular literary gesture that had already been in vogue in the eleventh century, one in which an author first selected a particular vignette or dialogue from some older strata of Chan literature and then offered commentary on it, or a poem about it, or often both.[1] Thus, it took at least *two* Chan masters to make a koan—the one who supposedly first said or did something that was recorded in a Chan text, and a later one who took

---

1. As T. Griffith Foulk points out in "The Koan: The Form and Function of Koan Literature," in *The Koan: Texts and Contexts in Zen Buddhism,* eds. Steve Heine and Dale S. Wright (New York: Oxford University Press, 2000), 15–18, the term *gong'an* seems directly related to an older term *ju gu,* which means, literally, "raising an old [case]," a practice in which someone would ask a master what he thought about an interesting story or discussion taken from the Chan literary tradition. The eleventh century texts that mention the practice of "raising an old case" give the impression that a master might be challenged in this way while giving a public sermon or in private discussions with his disciples, and in either situation, it provided an opening for him to discourse on truth and tradition. It also seems that the term was used as a strictly literary gesture in which a Song writer would "raise an old case" on the page and then write about it in the absence of any social interaction.

interest in just that account and developed it with his own commentary and/or poems.

Actually, it takes two Chan masters *and a reading audience* for the logic of koan writing to be fully established since, as we will see, the masters wrote about these older passages in a manner that sought to "speak" directly to their anticipated readers. Thus, as the Song master cleverly commented on the received words and deeds of prior patriarchs, he was establishing himself at the center of a one-man play in which his anticipated audience was invited to watch him read and evaluate the bits of Chan "history" that he found most interesting. To get a sense of recycling religious literature in this manner, one might imagine a modern Christian author picking out a debate between Jesus and the Pharisees from one of the gospels, and then offering a cheeky bit of commentary on their exchange, making it appear as though he really grasped what that ancient conversation had been all about, while also charming his readers with an incisive and artful critique of the whole encounter.

Since koan writing is enigmatic commentary on the equally enigmatic statements (or actions) of the Chan masters of yore, one might think that trying to explain them is next to impossible. And, yet, it turns out that one can say a number of reasonable things about koans *as literature,* and on several fronts. Among other things, it is important to see that the koan literature builds on themes and strategies that had appeared in the preceding centuries of Chan writing; in particular, rhetorics of negation, the insistence on innate buddhahood, and the claim that truth can't be put into language, again take up the lion's share of the discourse. What is new with koan writing is that sudden access to the essence of tradition is offered within a surprisingly impolite discourse, one replete with sarcasm, irony, and a general sassiness directed at older authority figures, the Buddha included.[2] For most readers, this cheekiness no doubt would have appeared as further

2. For a discussion of the role insults played in Chan writing, see Christoph Anderl, "Zen in the Art of Insult: Notes on the Syntax and Semantics of Abusive Speech in Late Middle Chinese," in *Studies in Chinese Language and Culture: Festschrift in*

enticement to find intimacy with the buddhas and patriarchs, and, of course, the author.

The excitement involved in writing this kind of commentary appears to have been infectious. In fact, once a master had built one of these peculiar literary museums of Chan moments, other masters often joined in the fray, writing their own comments on the selected koans and on the first master's commentary on those koans, thereby once again reinvigorating the literary tradition. Consequently, the writing process often extended over decades and, in some cases, even over centuries.[3] In a sense, then, a developed koan collection isn't all that different from what happens when someone posts an interesting photo on Facebook that draws commentary from friends and family who offer their opinions, not just on the photo, but on the commentaries that have already been posted. The result, of course, is a dense, multi-voice spectacle generated by that core spectacle that all commentators are referring to, even as they also engage each other.

The role that the koan literature played in daily life remains unclear. The problem here is that, unlike the situation that would develop later in Japan, Chan meditation manuals and monastic regulations from the Song era nowhere mention koans or any kind of practice connected with them. Although a Chan master named Dahui Zonggao (1089–1163) famously advised focusing meditations on just one crucial line in a koan, it seems that connecting koans with meditation was far from the norm in China; moreover, Dahui seems to have been addressing a lay audience, undermining the assumption that koans and meditation were linked in standard Chan monastic practice. Actually, when we look more closely at the koan collections, we see important evidence suggesting that the religious "payload" of this kind of literature was expect to be delivered to readers, not meditators. In the same vein,

---

Honour of Christoph Harbsmeier on the Occasion of His 60th Birthday, eds. Christoph Anderl and Halvor Eifring (Oslo: Hermes Academic, 2006), 377–93.

3. Foulk explains this layering process in detail in "The Koan: The Form and Function of Koan Literature"; see esp., 28ff.

it seems clear that reading koan collections could only be enjoyed by those with significant levels of literacy, which, presumably, wasn't the norm for run-of-the-mill monks and nuns, and thus again it isn't clear how "koan practice" could have been widespread.[4]

To begin making sense of this kind of writing, let's consider several koans from Wumen Huikai's (1183–1260) famous *Gateless Entrance* (*Wumen guan*), a fairly simple collection put together in 1228 that contains forty-eight koans, with an additional one added in slightly later. Koan #29 is built around that debate about the flag waving in the wind that had first appeared in the *Biography of the Great Master of Caoqi* in the late eighth century (see chapter 5), and was then recycled in the entries for Huineng in the *Ancestor Hall Compendium* and in the *Chuandeng lu*.[5] In the Tang text, and in the two flame histories, the debate had been presented as part of a "history" demonstrating how Huineng was naturally enlightened and thus could be trusted as a final authority on truth and tradition. In that narrative setting, Huineng's resolution of the debate—he claimed that it was neither the wind nor the flag that moved, but rather the mind that moved—was presented within the expectation that the reader could "see" for himself that Huineng really had the superior (and final) point of view, and that the other monks were both deluded and argumentative. In short, the dialogue had been an important spectacle supporting the claim that Huineng should be taken, by the reader, to be the sixth patriarch.

As Wumen builds the koan by first summarizing the older debate, Huineng and the issue of his buddha-status disappear, leaving just a

4. For Foulk's comments on the close connection between koans and reading, see ibid., 22–24. For a discussion of Dahui and his position on koans, see Morten Schlütter, *How Zen Became Zen: The Dispute over Enlightenment and the Formation of Chan Buddhism in Song-Dynasty China* (Honolulu: University of Hawai'i Press, 2008), 104–16.

5. Anderl's translation of this vignette in the *Ancestor Hall Compendium* is found in his *Studies in the Language of Zu-tang ji* (Oslo: Unipub, 2004), 2: 771; for a translation of the *Chuandeng lu* version, see Daoyuan, *Records of the Transmission of the Lamp*, trans. Randolph S. Whitfield, vol. 2 (Norderstedt Books on Demand, 2015), 84; *T* (no. 2076), 51.235c.3.

well-known moment of debate that Wumen wants, by bounding across the centuries, to join:

> The wind was flapping a temple flag, and two monks started an argument. One said the flag moved, the other said the wind moved; they argued back and forth but could not reach a conclusion.

Wumen's commentary:

> It is not the wind that moves; it is not the flag that moves; it is not the mind that moves. How do you see the patriarch [in this situation]? If you come to understand, intimately (*qinqie*), what just happened [in this exchange], then you will see that the two monks got gold when buying iron. On this occasion, the patriarch [Huineng] smiled and indulged [the monks' need for an explanation] which [lead on to] this regrettable affair.

Wumen's verse:

> Saying that it is "the wind," or "the flag" or "the mind" that moves —
> All [these explanations] lead into error.
> Only knowing how to open their mouths,
> They carelessly let [all these] words spill forth.[6]

Clearly Wumen is offering up a pretty challenging set of comments regarding this older conversation which, on its own, had been pretty readable and in fact *had to be readable* if it was to accomplish the goal of proving Huineng's natural mastery of tradition. Of the many interesting things going on here, let's first notice that with his commentary and poem, Wumen sets himself up as a perfect *reader* of this moment that had been preserved in the literary tradition. Thus, just as with Huineng's uncanny ability to understand the *Diamond Sūtra* at various points in the *Platform Sūtra*, Wumen likewise appears here to be a *sudden reader* of the Chan tradition, one who can penetrate effortlessly into the

---

6. *T* (no. 2005), 48.296c.17. For alternative translations, see Katsuki Sekida, *Two Zen Classics: The Gateless Gate and The Blue Cliff Records* (Boston: Shambhala, 2014), 96–97; and Thomas Cleary, *Unlocking the Zen Koan: A New Translation of the Zen Classic Wumenguan* (Berkeley, CA: North Atlantic Books, 1997), 141–42.

final zone of meaning that supposedly exists behind Huineng's pronouncements. Moreover, as Wumen critiques Huineng by asserting
that not even the mind moves, he has out-Huineng-ed Huineng. Consequently, for all the nostalgia at play in koan writing, it is also true that
here, and in other koan collections, the commenting master regularly
appears as the only buddha worth "listening" to, with the masters of
yesteryear coming in for ribbings and put-downs.[7]

In restaging the Huineng conversation, Wumen engages his reader
in two exciting ways. First, there is that sudden shift when Wumen
turns to ask the reader, "How do you see the patriarch [in this situa-
tion]?" This question appears to have nothing in particular to do with
the details of the wind-flag-mind debate or Wumen's parsing of it.
Rather it is a challenge to the reader, saying, in effect, "OK, that was the
event, now what do *you* make of it all?" This kind of direct "speaking" to
the reader—what is called "breaking the fourth wall" in theater jar-
gon—is then enhanced when Wumen, in a well-turned phrase, says
that the "the two monks got gold when buying iron" (*maitie dejin*), a
claim that would no doubt spur the reader to think that there was something of great value being transacted in this moment, if he could only
figure out what it was.[8] In effect, Wumen is saying to the reader: "I,
myself, know how great this exchange was and thus can see the value of
what the two monks received in Huineng's answer—even though they
could not—but now can *you*, dear reader, come along with me and turn
the iron of this exchange into gold?"

7. For more reflections on how Chan monks in the Song might have been reading
their literature, see Juhn Ahn's "Who Has the Last Word in Chan? Transmission,
Secrecy and Reading during the Northern Song Dynasty," *Journal of Chinese Religions* 37
(2009): 1–72.

8. This phrase, which I haven't seen elsewhere, seems to be an inversion of the stock
phrase "hanging up a sheep's head but selling dog meat," which Wumen uses in koan
#6. For more discussion of the I-you relationship and "the rhetoric of urgency" in
koan writing, see Christoph Anderl, "Zen Rhetoric: An Introduction," in *Zen Buddhist
Rhetoric in China, Korea, and Japan*, ed. Anderl (Leiden: Brill, 2012), 70–78; see also his
equally insightful discussion in "Coming to Terms with Terms: The Rhetorical Function of Technical Terms in Chan Buddhist Texts" in the same volume.

The second thing to see is that even as Wumen is provoking the reader with hints that the vast riches of tradition are right before him, he is doing so with a certain humorous disdain for tradition and its attempts at articulating truth. Thus, Wumen shifts the import of the conversation by including Huineng's original comment that it is "the mind that moves" in his critique, charging that "All [these explanations] lead into error." Similarly, in the concluding lines of the commentary, and in the poem, the whole affair is cast as an embarrassing moment of indiscretion. In satirizing Huineng and company in this manner, we see a style of discourse that is typical of the koan commentaries, one in which the standard Tang claim that "truth is ineffable" is joined with a taunting critique of anyone who ever tried to speak the truth of tradition. This of course makes Wumen and other Song commentators sound refreshingly free of tradition as they cast their darts of scorn at the older figures, and yet, obviously, this is yet another round of making meaning and value by negating older attempts to articulate meaning and value. Not surprisingly, even koan commentators could be manhandled in this way by later commentators who layered in their own style of philosophic abuse for all those who had written in the hope of communicating truth. Thus, although writing commentary was the weapon of choice for attacking the past, it also left one vulnerable to attack in the future.

In sum, in this koan, which is rather like others in the collection, Wumen's writing is fully performative in the sense that it makes him look like an absolute master of tradition—one who has even mastered the Chan masters of the Tang. From the reader's point of view, the koan is a spectacle about another spectacle, and both are presented as particularly worthy of the reader's attention. Moreover, as these two spectacles are blended together a certain timelessness results, with the commentator positioning himself as the pivot where the fullness of the past is, supposedly, made available in the living present.[9] That Wumen

9. David Schaberg finds a parallel commentorial gesture in pre-Han forms of writing history. See his *A Patterned Past: Form and Thought in Early Chinese Historiography* (Cambridge, MA: Harvard University Press, 2002), esp. 270ff.

closes out his treatment of the koan in careful verse again gives the impression of mastery since, after all, he has taken the prose version of events and poeticized it in a precise and stylish quatrain. In short, in Wumen's poem, as in the Tang poems, we see a fascination with rendering truth in ever more refined literary forms—a matter to which we will return in the Conclusion's assessment of Chan as a kind Buddhist beauty invented for (and by) Chinese readers.

To get a better sense of how authority, language, and aesthetics are combined in the *Gateless Entrance,* let's consider koan #41, which recycles the story of Huike sacrificing his arm in order to receive enlightenment from Bodhidharma:

> Bodhidharma [sat] facing the wall. The second patriarch [Huike] stood in the snow. He cut off his arm saying, "Your disciple's mind still has no peace! I beg you, master, please pacify my mind!" Bodhidharma said, "Bring your mind here and I'll pacify it for you." Huike replied, "I've searched for my mind and there is nothing to be had." Bodhidharma answered, "Then I have pacified your mind."

Wumen's commentary:

> That toothless old barbarian so self-importantly crossed over thousands of miles of ocean [to come to China]. You could call this [something as bizarre as] waves rising when there was no wind. It was only at the end of his life that he finally found a disciple; and, to make matters worse, the disciple was mentally deficient. Geez, the guy didn't even know four characters!

Wumen's verse:

> Coming from the West, and directly pointing,
> This gave rise to [Chan] instruction.
> [That we now] have that annoying clamor in the monasteries—
> It's all your fault.[10]

Two things seem clear in this new version of Huike's amputation of his arm, so carefully fabricated by Du Fei in the early eighth century (see

10. *T* (no. 2005), 48.298a.15. For Sekida's translation of this koan, see his *Two Zen Classics,* 118; for Cleary's, see *Unlocking the Zen Koan,* 181–82.

chapters 2 and 3). First, there is a noticeable shift in agenda. The original story focuses on demonstrating Huike's sincerity and the then radical claim that the totality of Indian enlightenment had passed into a Chinese body; the whole point of the Tang version is to convince the reader that this had in fact happened and under the most dramatic conditions—Huike traded his arm for the dharma, amazing! In Wumen's retelling of it, some five hundred years after Du Fei, the point of the vignette has shifted away from Huike's sacrifice to address a finer philosophical point regarding the reification of mind.[11] In accord with the standard Two Entrances doubling of tradition, Wumen has set up Huike to be the hardworking Buddhist attempting, in accord with the Second Entrance, to carry out the fundamental task of ordinary Buddhism: pacifying one's mind. Yet this approach isn't working since Huike doesn't seem to be making any progress. Bodhidharma then clarifies for him that it is impossible to find a mind to pacify and thus, by implication, standard Buddhism is mistaken in its teachings regarding the fundamentals of mind and practice. Thus, much like in the *Platform Sūtra* when Huineng upends Shenxiu's claim that enlightenment is won by the continuous purification of the mind, it is as though Bodhidharma is saying: "If only you could drop out of the (old) Buddhist paradigm, you would win all that Buddhism has to offer." Thus, when Bodhidharma concludes the interview saying "Then I have pacified your mind," the reader gets the impression that the (old) job of tradition has, in fact, been accomplished, *but only by denying the logic and structure of (old) tradition.*[12]

Clearly, in this retelling, the straightforward, logical, and serious historical claims of the original story have been overcome by Wumen's inter-

11. Actually, a version of this exchange about pacifying the mind is found in a Dunhuang text called the Second Record of "the Long Scroll of Bodhidharma." However, in that text the conversation isn't connected to Bodhidharma or Huike; for a translation, see Jeffrey L. Broughton, *The Bodhidharma Anthology: The Earliest Records of Zen* (Berkeley: University of California Press, 1999), 42.

12. Not to be overlooked, finding the value of tradition by rejecting all prior articulations of tradition is a repeating theme in the *Daode jing*. For more discussion of this issue, see my "Simplicity for the Sophisticated: Rereading the *Daode jing* for the Polemics of Ease and Innocence," *History of Religions* 46 (2006), esp. 10-12.

est in the antinomian side of Chan rhetoric. Put that way, this koan appears as a fine example of Chan *as genealogy* in the Tang being overtaken by Chan *as perplexing mind flip* in the Song, and, presumably, Wumen expects his reader to enjoy this shift in a personal way. That is, the account of Bodhidharma's supposed historical relationship to Huike, which had secured Huike's special ownership of tradition, has been transformed into a "teachable moment" potentially useful to all readers, one in which Wumen challenges his reader to drop through the floor of normal Buddhist logic to find some unthinkable way of being Buddhist that, despite its resistance to language and logic, is supposedly the real goal of Buddhism.

The second important point here is the way that Wumen teasingly disparages *both* the Buddhist institution and the former Chan masters. Thus, Bodhidharma is called "a toothless old barbarian" who seems to have needlessly troubled himself in making the journey from India to China. Likewise, Huike is portrayed as mentally deficient, out of control, and illiterate. Then, in the verse, what at first sounds like a good thing—Bodhidharma's "direct pointing"—turns out to be the source of trouble since he is supposedly to blame for the raucous and annoying monastic system.

With the former Chan masters now "blamed" for the meaningless chatter of normal monastic practice, Wumen's comments are basically doing to Chan what Chan authors had, during the Tang, done to the sutra traditions and the karmic form of traditional Buddhism, both of which were accused of being lost in language and fundamentally off-track, especially with regard to the reality of innate enlightenment. Wumen's playful sendup of the most crucial figures in the Chan lineage is a very normal, mid-Song, conceit, but no author in the Tang would have dared to write in such a flippant manner. And, yet, even as Wumen denounces the old Chan masters he is, in effect, revitalizing Chan by *performing* Chan's most basic gesture: negating and/or dismissing an earlier form of Buddhism in the confidence that real Buddhism is to be found in the wisdom-of-negation and in the "speaking" master himself, as he so easily flips Buddhism on its head.

Koan #37 from Wumen's collection seems to develop parallel themes:

A monk asked Zhaozhou, "What is the meaning of Bodhidharma's coming [to China] from the West?" Zhaozhou said, "The cypress tree in front of the monastery."

Wumen's commentary:

"If you understand Zhaozhou's answer intimately (*qinqie*), there is no Śākyamuni Buddha preceding you, and no Maitreya to come."

Wumen's verse:

Words cannot express things;
Speech does not convey the spirit.
Taking up words, one is doomed;
Stuck in sentences, one is lost.[13]

As Zhaozhou responds to the standard Chan question "Why did Bodhidharma come to China?" by calling attention to the cypress tree in front of the monastery, it would appear that the reader is invited to conclude that Bodhidharma's arrival is unimportant and superfluous, dwarfed by an immanent reality as big and solidly planted on the home ground of China as the cypress tree out front. This reality would seem to be none other than what the Chinese understood as (their own) innate enlightenment. Interpreting the exchange in this manner is supported by Wumen's commentary which links Zhaozhou's answer to the timeless presence of buddhas, past and future, clarifying thereby that with buddhahood, there should be no coming and going, just as one doesn't expect trees to move around. Asking about the meaning of Bodhidharma *coming* from the West is a question, then, that doesn't need to be answered; in fact, it shouldn't be answered if one wants to get at what real Buddhism is supposedly all about—from the master's point of view,

---

13. *T* (no. 2005), 48.297c.4. Based on Sekida's translation in *Two Zen Classics*, 110–12, with changes; for Cleary's rendering, see *Unlocking the Zen Koan*, 167–69.

that is. Wumen then closes out the koan with a poetic restatement of that standard claim that the truth of all this is beyond language.

Even with just these three koans in view, something else seems clear: Wumen is writing in something like the first-person voice, introducing each of his commentaries with the phrase "Wumen says" (*Wumen yue*). Thus it would seem that koan writing represents a critical moment in the history of Chan literature when Chinese authors no longer contented themselves with writing up speeches or poems to put in the mouths of the distant ancestors in order to generate the content of Chan literature, as we have seen in the preceding chapters. Instead, as Wumen writes out these lively and, at times, biting judgments of earlier statements-of-tradition, he appears to be directly addressing the reader, saying: "Can you take this? Are you enlightened enough and free enough to go along with me on this track? Can you see, in the end, why I, Wumen, have the right to write like this, and why you ought to keep on reading me?" This challenge is, in fact, what makes the koan literature so gripping, since without the reader's anticipated (and controlled) engagement in the "shakedown" of tradition, it is hard to see what's being gained.[14]

To put this kind of aggressive writing in context we should recall that in chapter 8, we saw that early Song accounts of the Tang masters showed a steady increase in their radical-sounding negations of traditional Buddhist values, practices, and points of view. Thus whether it was Mazu or Linji or some other master, they became progressively more "zenny" with each successive rewriting of their lives and teachings. Clearly, then, it was the Song *editors* who, ironically, were the masters of negation as they slid this bewildering language into the records of the long-dead

14. Where this more entertaining form of negation came from is hard to tell, but a parallel style of eloquent insult is displayed in the records of Buddhist-Daoist debates in the seventh century. For discussion, see Friederike Assandri, "Inter-religious Debate at the Court of the Early Tang: An Introduction to Daoxuan's *Ji gujin Fo Dao lunheng* (T2104)," in *From Early Tang Court Debates to China's Peaceful Rise*, eds. Assandri and Dora Martins (Amsterdam: Amsterdam University Press, 2009), 9–32. It is also worth noting the important role that the fly-whisk (*zhuwei*) plays in these early Tang encounters—a trope that would be prominent in Song Chan writing; see ibid., 25.

masters. At that point in the literary record, this kind of writing was only effective and acceptable when it was done *clandestinely:* each new editor handling Mazu's teaching, for instance, simply made some "silent changes" to the record and amped up the rhetorical power of Mazu's language.

With koan writing the emphasis on negative rhetoric continues to expand, but the voicing has shifted dramatically. In Wumen's text, the past masters are no longer given the good lines most likely to rile up the reader; instead, Wumen keeps those lines and attitudes *for himself.* In effect, then, the Chan verve for writing exciting negative rhetoric has been personalized: Wumen wants you, the reader, to appreciate *his* talent for writing like this. Presumably part of this shift was due to a kind of ripening of the rhetorical strategies of tradition—as a tradition becomes more at ease with its modes of making meaning, one naturally expects authors to experiment with bolder forms of proven rhetorical strategies. Another possibility is that this kind of writing that so highlights the current author's mastery of both negation *and* the essence of tradition emerged in response to new patterns of patronage. In this light, it obviously doesn't help a master's career to ghostwrite better lines for Bodhidharma or Mazu when he could brandish this rhetoric in his own name *and* apply it to older forms of tradition, making it appear that the final wisdom of tradition was even more powerfully installed in his own person.

Another possibility is worth considering. At the end of chapter 9 we saw the clear admission that part of being a Chan abbot in the Song involved admitting that abbots, though taken to be living buddhas, might very well also "steal the silverware" when given a chance, and thus there is an interesting parallel between the day-to-day irony demanded of the abbots and the kind of irony that is manifesting itself here in the koan commentator's "attack" on the supposedly perfect masters of the past. That is, as the living abbots of the Song were taken to be replicas of the hallowed masters of the Tang—and, after all, that's the central logic of the Chan genealogies in the Song—one could easily imagine that the holiness of the past became as suspect as the holiness of the present. Thus, an experienced master would have had a long career of negotiating the gap between the rites and rituals that treated him as a buddha and the bare-knuckle rules that governed his own actions and authority, rules which so clearly cast doubt on the integrity of his vision and conduct. In this sense one could easily imagine koan commentators thinking it appropriate to ridicule any claim to Chan perfection, given how they had seen "behind the curtain" of the whole setup and thereby understood such claims to buddhahood to be wild exaggerations. In this vein, I suppose that one could even imagine koan writers—presumably most of them having served as abbots—expressing a certain exhaustion with tradition, as though from a certain point of view, Bodhidharma *really did bring a lot of trouble to China,* as Wumen so directly charges.

As with prior cases of negative rhetoric, we have to ask how far Wumen's antinomianism went. Did Wumen expect to be taken literally—as many modern readers assume—or were there sturdy guardrails in place to keep his provocative dismissals of tradition on a meaningful track? The first thing to notice on this front is that Wumen dedicated his koan collection to the emperor. Thus, sitting at the front of his brazen sendup (and replication) of the Chan tradition, there is a short but very sincere sounding dedication to the emperor:

We respectfully greet the Imperial Commemoration Day of January 5, the second year of Zhao [1229]. Your humble servant, the monk Wumen, on November 5 of last year published a commentary on forty-eight cases of the spiritual activities of the Buddha and the patriarchs, dedicated to the eternal health and prosperity of Your Majesty.

I reverently express my desire that Your Majesty's wisdom may illuminate all as brightly as the sun, and that your life be as eternal as that of the universe, and that all the eight directions may sing and praise your virtue, and that the four seas enjoy happiness under your peaceful reign.

Written by Transmitter of the Dharma, your humble servant, the monk Wumen,
formerly abbot of Youci Chan Monastery, built to repay the merit of Empress Ciyi.[15]

The obsequious flattery so evident in this dedication raises questions
about how we should read the edgy and insulting antinomianism at
work in Wumen's koan commentaries. Should we assume that Wumen
understood that he could be as free and reckless as he liked with his in-
house Buddhist rhetoric as long as he was fastidiously Confucian in his
handling of matters external to Buddhism? That seems perfectly reasonable and, in that light, Wumen would be performing just as Huineng
did in the *Biography of the Great Master of Caoqi* where he was full of wild
negations *and* unerringly polite to the emperor's runner. In both cases,
negations of good and bad, and of all dualities, comfortably coexisted
with a deep and abiding concern that Confucian etiquette be maintained and, in particular, that one's dedication to the emperor be
exceedingly evident. That is, in practice, all distinctions and all dualities are rigorously maintained, but in rhetoric and fantasy, everything
can be obliterated and/or lambasted.

Another possibility is that Wumen is once again being ironic. Since
he had recently been the abbot at Youci Monastery, he surely knew
what it was like to be taken as a living buddha *and* a subject of the state's
exacting law. Likewise, he surely would have known of many other
Chan texts that were prefaced with dedications to the emperor. In
short, Wumen would have known the submissive role he was expected
to play vis-à-vis the emperor, and he played it perfectly. One might
quickly applaud this as a deep understanding of Buddhism's Two
Truths put into action, but I would argue for something a little less
uplifting. Chan monks submitted to imperial law for self-preservation
since any serious infraction could result in being defrocked, caned, or
even executed. In effect, then, there was the threat of violence holding
various kinds of rhetoric in place: speaking humorously about Bodhi-

---

15. Translation from Sekida, *Two Zen Classics*, 25, with changes; *T* (no. 2005),
48.292b.3.

dharma and Huike was all fine and good because they were dead and gone, if they ever existed in the first place, and anyway they never had any real world power. With the emperor and the state, everything was different, since there was the constant threat of reprisal and punishment, and thus Wumen and all other Chan writers produced nothing but traditional flattery and carefully formulated submissions when writing to, or about, governmental figures.

This submission to state power becomes even more interesting when we remember how often in the koan collections masters are made to appear impervious to pain and death, even though in the real world, Chan masters appear to have taken great care to stay on the right side of the law in order to avoid the pain and destruction that the state was so ready to deliver. Thus, if one wants to hold on to some version of the heroic Chan master, I would suggest that it is to be found in the courage to hold all of this together: to fulfill the contradictory demands of Buddhism, the state, and the literary tradition on a day-to-day basis and still have the courage to creatively explore one's relationship to truth and tradition in one's writing and public speeches. Of course, that this kind of mid-Song writing is often funny and idiosyncratic is just more proof of the courage involved since it announces a spirit of play and individuality precisely in a zone defined by real risks and corporate complexity.

POETRY: SELF AND OTHER, WHERE THERE IS NO TIME

Today I had the good fortune to read James Liu's classic essay "Time, Space, and Self in Chinese Poetry." Liu's main point is that the "time of utterance" of a poem has to be "understood as referring not to the historical moment when the poem was written but to the time when the reader, identifying with the speaker of the poem, or at least imagining the speaker as speaking, *revives that moment.* Thus ... the expression *ciri* [this day] in a poem should be taken as if it referred to our 'today,' not the day when the poem was written, even if the poet or some conscientious commentator tells us the exact date of composition."[16] This is a provocative claim, to be sure. And, though I am not sure this holds true for all Chan poems, his comments are nonetheless an excellent way to get at one of the key aspects of Wumen's writing.[17]

Above, I argued that Wumen's writing, and koan writing in general, developed a noticeably enhanced I–you relationship in the sense that Wumen is essentially calling out to the reader, "Hey, you, dear reader, can you see what I see?" Moreover, a certain kind of intimacy is also tendered since Wumen's commentaries and poems come across as timeless invitations to join him and all the buddhas and patriarchs, long after their deaths. Wumen makes this explicit in his unusually long commentary on the first koan, the one in which Zhaozhou famously answered "No" to the question "Does a dog have buddha-nature?" Wumen writes, "Those who pass through it [the koan], will not only see Zhaozhou in person, they will also go hand-in-hand with the successive patriarchs, entangling their eyebrows with theirs, seeing with the same eyes, hearing with the same ears. Isn't that a delightful prospect? Wouldn't you like to pass this barrier?"[18] Clearly, then, Wumen positioned his own language as both a barrier and a door: break through this, and you'll find yourself on the other side of time and history,

16. James Liu, "Time, Space, and Self in Chinese Poetry," *Chinese Literature: Essays, Articles, Reviews (CLEAR)* 1, no. 2 (July 1979): 137–56; the passage cited is on 137–38.

17. John R. McRae, *Seeing through Zen: Encounter, Transformation, and Genealogy in Chinese Chan Buddhism* (Berkeley: University of California Press, 2003), 130, also explores the issue of time-travel in koan commentary. However, McRae assumed that koans were "invariably taken from some transcription of encounter dialogue," although it is far from certain that these conversations were originally oral events that were then written down; for his position, see ibid., 128.

18. *T* (no. 2005), 48.292c.2. Translation from Sekida, *Two Zen Classics*, 28, with changes; Cleary, *Unlocking the Zen Koan*, 1–2. For an important discussion of how this koan was slowly edited down from a fairly complex debate to this single-word answer, "No!" see Ishii Shūdō, "The *Wu-men kuan* (J. *Mumonkan*): The Formation, Propagation, and Characteristics of a Classic Zen Kōan Text," in *The Zen Canon: Understanding the Classic Texts*, eds. Steven Heine and Dale S. Wright (New York: Oxford University Press, 2004), 207–44, esp. 227–31.

walking hand-in-hand with the patriarchs and even tangling eyebrows with them. The nature of this claim suggests that, for Wumen, Buddhist enlightenment has become inseparable from some basic Chinese notions about the timelessness of reading and writing poetry. That is, Wumen has located Buddhist enlightenment in that perpetual present where Chinese poets traditionally expected their readers to find them, and vice-versa. Once again, then, a Chan author appears to be bypassing meditation, and other practices, in favor of finding that trapdoor-like experience in which one drops out of normal language into something ineffable and yet full of meaning. And, of course, Wumen thinks poetry is a good way to make this trapdoor open.

Thinking more about these developments, it would seem obvious that Chan rhetoric is continuing to get more poetic and therefore less oral and spontaneous. Moreover, however one might think of the origins of the speaking voices in the stories, that supposed orality is being eclipsed by a more important kind of textual "orality" in which the magical conversation in koan writing isn't between the master and the disciple *in the story* but rather between Wumen and his reader, the "you" that he imagined working through his prose and poetry. Thus, above, we saw examples of how important this second-person is in Wumen's writing, and a careful look through the forty-eight koans would confirm that he is regularly "speaking" directly to the reader, whether or not he is using the Chinese character for "you" (*ru*).

The centrality of this universal "you" in these poems is matched by a kind of universality of the poems themselves: Wumen's poems, with their careful four-character quatrains, seem to be imbued with a life of their own, containing, as they do, a nascent power to call themselves into being. That is, once one knows the poem, it kind of *sings itself* due to its built-in cadences, rhymes, and order. Perhaps we should even say that the poems—with their balanced blend of negation, beauty, and order—threaten to occupy the reader, in both senses of the term "occupy." In sum, once again a Chan writer has shown a refined and even uncanny ability to employ various forms of language and desire in portraying truth beyond language and desire. Put that way, Wumen seems to live comfortably in both form and emptiness—he "speaks" so often of getting free of language, and, yet, with his finely wrought poetry and zippy commentaries, he proves he is a master of language.

This flexibility with language and emptiness is matched by a flexibility of character. Wumen's poems are presumably dedicated to just those people who literally don't know what he's talking about. And thus his poetry needs to give readers a sense of moving from a state of non-comprehension into some kind of comprehension, or the whole exercise would be a waste of time. Thus it is that Wumen has to play both sides of the conversation—he is both Wumen and "you"—and in this sense his intersubjective writing skills are quite parallel to those demonstrated in the *Diamond Sūtra*, the *Platform Sūtra*, and the many other Tang dialogues.

Wumen's practical mastery of the gap between writer and reader is then matched by his claim to have mastered the gap between himself and the buddhas and patriarchs. Thus, the promise of Wumen's poetry is mostly in line with Liu's estimation of how time and self work in Chinese poetry, except that, with Wumen, it is all explicitly set up as a challenge: *can* you make this Chan poem deliver what Chinese poetry has always promised—that fusion with the author in which self, other, and time collapse? And this challenge is put to the reader specifically in a context in which Wumen demonstrates that it is with just such a fusion with the past *that he reads tradition*. In short, Wumen is challenging the reader saying, "Can you read my poetry with that traditional Chinese form of 'poetic penetration,' so that we can read the Buddhist tradition *together, you and I,* and thereby confront the past patriarchs, eyebrow to eyebrow?"

In sum, staying true to the basic themes and strategies of Chan writing, Wumen's *Gateless Entrance* appears dedicated to providing a trapdoor into nirvana, with this trapdoor built around yet another improved version of the past that generates a hearty nostalgia for a lost era. Thus with his highly selective replaying of material from the flame histories, combined with his sly poetry and witty commentary, Wumen promises to transport the reader more convincingly to those original scenes in the Tang that supposedly generated all this writing in the first place.

CONCLUSIONS

Having considered just a few koans taken from the *Gateless Entrance*, it is true that this chapter represents but an initial and cursory effort to explain koan writing and its place in the larger history of Chan literature. Nevertheless, the above readings could easily be extended to other koans, both in Wumen's collection and elsewhere. For the moment, the most pressing conclusion to take away from this discussion is that koan writing *in China* appears to have been a thoroughly literary affair, with little or nothing to do with meditation. As noted at the outset of the discussion, a kind of koan-based meditation practice emerged in thirteenth-century Japan, but there is no clear evidence that anything similar developed in China. Once we let go of the assumption that koans were necessarily to be meditated on, we are in a much better position to appreciate the new styles of literary "orality" at work in this kind of writing. In particular, though many of the themes and rhetorical gestures had been explored in earlier strata of Chan writing, there is a whole new *voicing* of Chan "truths" in the koan literature, one that gives rise to a much more intense reading experience, and this is based precisely on the author's more developed capacity to "speak" directly to the reader, and in several registers. Naturally, this new literary voicing also supports a more lifelike presence of the author, giving the reader the sense of receiving a private tour of those chosen Chan moments deemed most revelatory, all within the larger promise that an "intimate" reading of the koan literature can take one to enlightenment, nirvana, and that zone where one can tangle eyebrows with the patriarchs.

It is this very heightened sense of the (writing) master's presence *in literature* that makes it likely that koan writing didn't emerge from day-to-day practices. What would have been the point of putting together these elaborate "guided tours" through Chan literature if daily monastic practice, based on oral instruction from the master, was already advancing just fine, independent of this dense and carefully constructed literary format? Moreover, knowing that the twelfth-century master Dahui advocated a kind of meditation on key phrases (*huatou*) taken from koans shouldn't be taken as proof that koans and meditation went hand in hand, but rather the opposite: Dahui had to find a way to make the koans amenable to meditation precisely because they were way too complex in terms of meaning and signification to be directly useful for meditation. No surprise, then, that tradition reports that Dahui supposedly burned the wood blocks for the koan collection called *The Blue Cliff Records*—written by his master!—because he thought the koans led one on to an unhealthy fascination with literary projects.[19] And, in this, his objections appear to have been quite on target.

One last thing to consider: koan writing seems to belong to an arc of literary developments that reflects the growing heartiness of the writing "I"—an "I" that confidently claims to know the Buddhist tradition through and through, and to know the reader well enough, too, to present comments about truth and tradition in a style that would reach audiences as intended. Such an "I" was crucial to Chan writing from the beginning, but in the Tang, it was an "I" that, though willfully rearranging and reinventing the words of past masters, never revealed itself to the reader. A more robust and visible writing "I" appeared in the *Ancestor Hall Compendium,* where Wendeng's poems were attached to the end of the masters' biographical entries. Those poems summed up the narratives in Wendeng's own voice and thereby demonstrated his confidence in having the last word about the past masters and their deeds, while also transforming prose narrative into crisp, catchy poetic summaries. Thus I argued in chapter 8 that in a sense Wendeng was blending his voice with the voice of tradition and "branding" it all as

19. For a brief account of this story, see Schlütter, *How Zen Became Zen,* 110.

his truth and tradition, with just this self-aggrandizement performed in full view of the reader. This surely prepared the ground for the emergence of koan writing, since the koan collections likewise present quick summaries of past "Chan" events, taken mainly from flame histories, that then were treated to commentary, critique, and poetic review—all in order to engage and delight the reader.

As the authors of the koan collections so carefully performed their creative and often idiosyncratic interpretations of tradition for the reading public, it is easy to understand what came next: autobiographical accounts in which Chan masters, writing in the first person, described their experiences struggling with truth, meditation, and enlightenment. Such writing is a rarity in the wider Buddhist world, but it is not hard to see how the possibility of such direct, intimate and *self-based* writing emerged in the late Song, since the trends in writing commentary on tradition were clearly headed in that direction from the late Tang onward. Thus when Xueyan (1216–87) writes in his "recorded saying" about the various problems he worked through as a monk, his readers would have been well prepared for this level of intimacy and audacity in which Buddhist experiences of truth were taken to be suitable topics for a developed "I" to explore and then share with the reading public.[20] Fuller exploration of this kind of "I-based" writing will have to wait for another day, but it is important to see how the development of

20. For more discussion of Chan autobiographies, see Pei-yi Wu, *The Confucian's Progress: Autobiographical Writings in Traditional China* (Princeton, NJ: Princeton University Press, 1990), 71–92. Jeffrey L. Broughton also considers early Chan autobiographical writing in his *The Chan Whip Anthology: A Companion to Zen Practice* (New York: Oxford University Press, 2014), 15–17. Miriam Levering argues that Chan autobiographic writing can be found even earlier than Xueyan, in the work of Dahui; see her "Was There Religious Autobiography in China before the Thirteenth Century?—The Ch'an Master Ta-hui Tsung-kao (1089–1163) as Autobiographer," *Journal of Chinese Religions* 30 (Sept. 2002): 97–122. Finally, for discussion of the emergence of a writing-I in China, see Christoph Harbsmeier's "Authorial Presence in Some Pre-Buddhist Chinese Texts," in *De l'un au multiple: Traductions du chinois vers les langues européennes*, eds. Viviane Alleton and Michael Lackner (Paris: Maison des sciences de l'homme, 1999), 221ff.

autobiography in late Song Chan reflects tendencies that had already been announced earlier in the Song and even back in the Tang. Ironically, then, the emergence of Chan's hard-hitting negation of everything has to be seen within the context of the parallel growth of charming and gripping literary techniques that gave Chan writing its distinctive Buddhist "voice," one that leaned ever more solidly on the idiosyncratic creations of authorial selves who no longer hid in the shadows of anonymity.

Conclusions

Chan, a Buddhist Beauty

Thinking back over the evidence in the preceding chapters, the most reasonable way to account for the composition of Chan texts—the inventive genealogies, the fictional conversations, the conspiracy theories, the poems of negation, the weighty compendiums, the "rules for purity," and the koan commentaries—is to assume that Chan authors were quite aware of the art of writing "religious literature," and were equally aware of how their efforts fit into a long tradition of reshaping tradition. Thus, though Chan authors no doubt wrote their texts for a variety of reasons, it remains altogether likely that their view of the Buddhist tradition and its ever-expanding body of literature was a particularly clear-eyed one, and that, based on that clarity, they felt entitled to continue the work of rewriting tradition in new and provocative terms.

In presenting this evidence, and treating it as I have, I hope to have cast doubt on the regrettably durable assumption that takes it as fact that ancient and medieval religious authors were, on the whole, simple people who straightforwardly wrote down what they thought about life and salvation, with little or no consideration for politics, personal gain, institutional longevity, state support, their place in history, and so on. This paradigm seems particularly unsuited for Chinese authors— Chan or otherwise—since from the earliest strata of Chinese writing, even back in the Warring States era, there is evidence of a steady and refined irony vis-à-vis truth claims, accompanied by a demonstrated will to shift historical claims around as need be.[1] Returning Chan writing to this wider context, it is hard to imagine that Chan authors were somehow strangers to the calculated intersubjectivity that was elemental in other kinds of Chinese literature.

To put it otherwise, seeing how Chan authors invented several kinds of literary snow globes in which one could watch terribly simple but engaging scenes of perfect tradition being reproduced, why should we assume that these authors lived in the snow globes they created? It doesn't seem likely or even possible that they could have done so. A better assessment would maintain that these authors easily moved in and out of these perfect set pieces—enjoying and developing these fetishized images of tradition while also continuing to participate productively in the workaday world of normal Chinese Buddhism, with all its political, economic, and sectarian struggles. In fact, it was probably due to a heightened sense of the challenges facing real-world Buddhism that Chan authors were so able to draw readers into their literary utopias in which imaginary but lovable forms of Buddhism proliferated.

As we have seen, the literary utopias created during the Tang and Song dynasties have quite a bit in common with each other; in fact, it seems there was a fairly stable set of ideas organizing their construction and it is this shared likeness that gives Chan literature its distinctive flavor. As I see it, these shared ideas circle around several fantasies of sameness. First, there was that brave assumption that the Chinese masters were essentially no different from the Indian Buddha. This equivalence took some getting used to, but it was supported by emphasizing an ontological sameness between buddhas and ordinary people—that

---

1. The debates over the writing of "history" in early China are rich and particularly useful for anyone interested in thinking about historiography in Chinese Buddhism. See, in particular, the work of Stephen Durrant, David Schaberg, and Mark Edward Lewis.

curious Chan claim that was repeated so reliably from the early Tang on. Then there was that Chan enthusiasm for Confucian idioms and rituals that, themselves, were dedicated to maintaining the image of an enduring sameness with the past. In particular, Chan authors took hold of the Confucian dream that the son could and should be the same as the father, which is, arguably, the fundamental fantasy that holds Chan ideology together. And finally, Chan authors reveled in the Daoist confidence that human consciousness could regain its original sameness with reality. Betting on a happy and sustaining cosmic wholeness seems to have been fundamental to Chan writing and thinking, and, in particular, appears to have served as a sanctuary from Buddhist anxieties about karmic retribution and endless rebirth.

Despite this steady commitment to several kinds of mythical sameness, there was one terribly important difference that also held Chan together: the difference of the master, the one who claimed, via "family inheritance," that he alone had confirmed his absolute sameness with the Indian Buddha and could, therefore, legitimately define the final truth/s of the Buddhist tradition. Ironically, then, from the beginning it was Chan's obsession with private, and even secret, "family" ties that made truth available to the Chinese public, or, rather, *partially* available. The Chan authors of the Song inherited this productive public-private arrangement from the Tang, but went on to formalize it by merging the often nebulous and mist-enshrouded figures of the Bodhidharma family with the very public office of the abbot, meaning that the sons of Bodhidharma would henceforth be responsible for maintaining, day by day, the ballet of order, repetition, and sameness that appears to have been one of the goals of monastic Buddhism in China.

Chan's resourceful blending of traditions seems to have culminated in two fundamental inventions: in the first, the dazzling and culturally sophisticated Indian Buddha was turned on his head such that Chinese buddhas—once they were invented in the late seventh century—appeared more like the simple but mysterious, all-natural sages of the *Daode jing,* the *Zhuangzi,* and the *Liezi.* Here, it would seem that just as buddha statues produced in various countries around Asia gradually took on the facial characteristics of the local adherents, so too did the Chinese buddhas of Chan literature begin to resemble the homegrown sages of China.

The second major Chan invention was the fantasy of "trapdoor Buddhism" in which the ultimate goal of Buddhism was brought into the present and redefined such that getting free of (traditional) Buddhism was taken to be essential to recovering a splendid, original wholeness. Thus, Chan authors regularly made clear that the best Buddhist masters were Daoist-looking sages who, at least in literature, appeared to no longer have any need for the Buddhist tradition, with its mountains of literature and complex institutions, and who also so regularly tempted readers with promises that they too could recover this original freedom, born of finally "tallying" with the dark principle of the Dao.

When this profile of the Daoist-styled Chan master first appeared in the Tang, it was pasted onto past masters, and hence it is hard to see how such claims would have influenced the actual practice of Buddhism in real-time. Thus, for instance, Huineng's instantaneous and literature-free accomplishment of buddhahood likely changed little or nothing in the practice of Buddhism in the Tang. And yet, in the world of literature, mining this gap between fantastic descriptions of the past Chan masters and the actual practice of Buddhism was enthusiastically continued into the Song, as the authors and editors of the Chan compendiums regularly overhauled the Tang figures to further highlight their Daoist-styled antinomianism. This gap also figured in the writing of koan commentaries since in that genre highly literate masters regularly demonstrated their mastery of tradition with quirky, Zhuangzian-sounding commentaries that condemned book-learning and the actual practice of Buddhism, even as Chan monasticism became even more rigid, Confucian, and imperial in style and focus. In sum, with Chan literature championing a Daoist-looking version of buddhahood and the fantasy of "trapdoor" Buddhism, it isn't clear to what degree Chan writing rearranged the day-to-day realities of lived tradition, even as enlightenment as an idea was written about in grittier, funnier, and more intimate terms.

And this brings us to the question that is perhaps the hardest to face: to what degree did Chan ever exist? Presumably, we can agree that the advent of new writing styles and the emergence of new literary genres represents a shift in ideological habitat, and thus proof of something new appearing in tradition. But what was this new thing? It certainly was never a separate Buddhist tradition. As we saw in chapter 9, monasteries designated as "Chan" institutions in the Song were basically run the same way as non-Chan monasteries. Likewise, it is clear that one could turn a monastery into a Chan monastery at the drop of a hat— one needed only to invite in an abbot who had the documents to "prove" that he belonged to a lineage of masters running back to Bodhidharma and the Buddha. What such a Chan abbot did, of course, was run the monastery as any abbot would, while also giving his dharma talks based on Chan literature and perhaps enlivening the daily routines with some well-rehearsed Chan theatrics.

If monastic practices across the various "schools" of Chinese Buddhism really had this much uniformity, then we need to understand Chan as largely dedicated to organizing durable leadership roles. In this view, Chan appears as the artful mystification of Chinese Buddhist leadership, a gradual development in which various literary, artistic, and even architectural forms blended images of buddhahood with older Chinese values—articulated in Daoist, Confucian, and imperial terms—while arguing that it was the "sons of Bodhidharma" who incarnated all these values.

Looked at this way, the charming simplicity and playful insouciance of the enlightened Chan master—as seen in literature or in ritualized performances—served to re-enchant a monastic reality that functioned in a completely opposite manner. More exactly, with Chan's various museums celebrating the perfectly enlightened masters, the daily grind of monastic practice was enlivened with images of the reproduction of Buddhist perfection in which total truth and enlightenment were glimpsed passing suddenly from master to disciple in inexplicable moments of dharma-transmission. These magical moments were, by definition, completely separate from real Buddhist practices such as meditation and monastic diligence; such moments were, of course, even more distant from the complex social and governmental formats relied upon to educate and authorize those select monks of the new generation who might, one day, assume the role of abbot and reproduce the system, including the maintenance of just this body of mythology regarding dharma-transmission.

Thus, while the Chan history of the Bodhidharma family appears to be the opposite of real Chinese Buddhism on the ground, these two form a pair, with the mythic version of the reproduction of tradition brightening up and invigorating the real means of reproducing tradition. Consequently, becoming a Chan master meant learning how to manage both the mythic version of Buddhist leadership and the real version, and understanding how the two fit together in such a way that both versions of tradition could be reproduced. One might even speculate that this task of fusing such disparate versions of tradition—mythic and real—into one tradition accounts for the powerful irony so abundant in Chan literature.

Actually, the role of irony in Chan warrants special consideration. Though many Mahāyāna Buddhist texts also have a kind of irony built into them, the irony of Chan literature is thicker and more demanding. This is probably because Chan masters had to regularly handle *so much literature, written from so many points of view,* including: the various layers of Chan literature (which often clashed with each other in terms of style), along with all the other kinds of Buddhist literature that were essential to Chan monasteries—the sutras and vinaya—and then there were all those other forms of Chinese literature that had to be mastered, including the classics from the Confucian, Daoist, and poetic traditions. But the circumstances demanding the rule of irony didn't stop there. In the final paragraphs of Zongze's *Rules for Purity,* we saw that being an abbot meant understanding that one's life as a buddha was to suddenly evaporate once that letter of resignation was handed in. From that moment on, the abbot was persona non grata within the very walls where he had formerly led the community as a living buddha. Surely knowing this at the beginning of one's career was a recipe for some pretty serious irony.

To read Zongze's *Rules for Purity* is to begin to glimpse how sophisticated and complicated the Chan habitat was, and how much talent and wherewithal was required of Chan abbots, who had to daily grapple with this gap between the utopia of perfectly simple Buddhism, produced in Chan writing, and the harsh realities of the monastic system. Understanding and managing that gap appears, then, as the fullest expression of the *practice of the Chan tradition,* and it was exactly that staggering talent that was expected of the Chinese Buddhist elite who aspired to be Chan masters. Arguably, then, it was just this practical awareness of the nature of their multilayered habitat that makes real-world Chan masters seem much like the old fish alluded to in the Preface to this book.

What matters most here at the end is that we recognize that medieval Chan was a bureaucratized form of lived nostalgia. The long line of masters were always supposed to be present, haunting the monastic grounds in a reliable and productive manner, even though they supposedly arrived from a distant and mysterious place where monasticism, governmental rules, rituals, practice, and literature were unnecessary, since Buddhist wisdom was so easily and reliably transmitted between masters and their disciples. These past masters were, literally, the soul of the institution, and they brought a kind of legitimacy to the Buddhist monasteries precisely because they seemed so free of real monasticism, with all its gritty politics. In a doubly ironic way, we might even say that they served to "selfify" the monasteries: as the soul of the monastery, the past patriarchs stood for the enduring identity of the entire institution—the one place where the monastery was, in good anti-Buddhist logic, really itself. The point of writing *Patriarchs on Paper* was to explore how and why these ancestral spirits were invented, and how they were so carefully, and lovingly, cared for generation after generation.

I realize that not everyone will want to trade the comforting, romantic version of Chan – findable only in literature—for a realistic account of Chan in which we have to imagine masters handling amazingly complex institutions, while *also* insisting in lectures, and in measured prose or poesy, on the complete non-existence of everything. Making this shift, however seems like a good idea, and not only for academic reasons, but also because it opens the door to a much more wholesome account of what happened. More exactly, it opens the door to understanding how rhetorics of simplicity, along with fantasies of gaining oneness with the Dao, were cultivated at the heart of complicated, confining, and exacting institutional situations. Reckoning this cohabitation of institutional complexity with the rhetorics of innocence and simplicity appears to me to be of enduring value, especially because it can be found in *so many* different religious and political settings. In short, if we still are claiming that the liberal arts tradition renders human experience more thinkable, then making sense of this human tendency to paper over complexity with rhetorics of simplicity needs to be put front and center in many types of analysis.

As the title of this chapter suggests, there is one last topic to mention before closing: Chan beauty. Just now, and in the preceding chapters, I have argued that Chan literature produced a sheen of lovability that was gradually added to Chinese monasticism and, in particular, to the abbots. To speak of beauty in this context, though, is to entertain some rather interesting and intricate philosophical ideas, ideas which are worth at least mentioning here at the end of the book.

For starters, I wonder if it isn't the case that we reserve the word "beautiful" for a thing or reality that, for reasons we hardly understand, seems to rise above the sum of its parts in order to "glow out" at us in some preternatural manner. Thus, a middle-period Beatles song is no longer a collection of chords, rhythm, melody and harmony, just as a face that stirs one to the core is no longer a constellation of eyes, cheeks, and a nose. A beautiful thing hardly seems to be a thing at all and, by definition, can't be explained in reference to its parts or its history, and thus it shimmers before us in a manner that resists analysis and calculation. In fact, the beautiful has to be reckoned as that which destroys our ability to reckon. What's more, in the presence of the beautiful, we seem ready to consent to the idea that a new reality has emerged: with the beautiful before us, all our old and dreary assumptions about life evaporate as we suddenly entertain the unbearable hope that this time it all could be different, and happiness and contentment will be ours. The beautiful Thing thus appears quasi-transcendental in its refusal to be the sum of its parts, just as it also promises a chance to transcend the causal, historical nature of our lives. In short, the beautiful is the place were the math of life is overcome and an inexplicable breeze of hope envelops us.[2]

Many moderns interested in Chan and Buddhism might be reluctant to focus on the role of aesthetics in the construction of the Chan tradition, but it nonetheless seems fair to say that Chan writing is designed to produce a transcendentalizing kind of Buddhist beauty since, with its heady rhetoric of negation, its soothing poetry, its Confucian probity, and its jolting accounts of the simple and immaculate transmission of truth, the reality of Chinese monasteries could be reimagined as the final fulfillment of everyone's dreams: that happy place where practically every Chinese value was articulated and respectfully lived out. Chan literature, in this reading, produced the fantasy of a perfect and beautiful form of Buddhism, a fantasy that, with careful pruning, blossomed like a rose in the imaginations of the masses, the literati, and state officials, not to mention the ardent Buddhist monks who lived with this language as part of their day-to-day habitat. It is for these reasons that I have been arguing that Chan was a utopic form of Buddhism that never existed; or, more exactly, existed only as the steady literary—and

---

2. By insisting on the role of desire and utopic thinking in the experience of beauty, I am obviously far from Kant's various discussions of beauty as the "disinterested" appreciation of objects and scenes. Looking back, I believe my ideas about beauty owe much to Roland Barthes's *Mythologies* (Paris: Seuil, 1957), where he explores numerous examples of how sculpted language and manicured images invite us to read the world along particular tracks of desire and meaning.

later, ritual—ability to produce convincing images of just this simple and pure form of Buddhism that never, and could never, exist.

While I'm altogether uninterested in judging the value of Chan as a cultural invention, I think we need to admit that if Chan literature is to be read as the means for steadily manufacturing this kind of Buddhist beauty, then it is precisely the opposite of old-style Buddhist wisdom that was *ostensibly* dedicated to destroying, not just beauty in its more fleshy forms, but also the philosophic possibility of beauty, since basic Buddhist notions of impermanence, suffering, and emptiness were supposed to prevent Buddhists from reifying any object, experience, or ideal into the promise of satisfaction and closure. Chan literature, on the other hand, fetishized Buddhism into forms that could be expected to enthrall and delight, while also grounding those fantasies in the familiarity of tried-and-true cultural icons and rituals from the past, Buddhist *and* non-Buddhist. Thus, in the world of Chan literature, all calculations and prior limitations seemed to slip away, and the perfect attainment of Buddhist wisdom appeared within reach. What could be more beautiful? Thus, the delicious end of Buddhist practice (and anxiety) was made to *appear* more and more present, even as the actual monastic system became increasingly complex and legalistic, and, in particular, increasingly sophisticated in building "tools"—such as the monastic handbooks—dedicated to securing its own longevity.

Getting a sense of the hard-won practical wisdom needed to handle just that combination of timelessness and history, enlightenment and duplicity, reality and rhetoric, freedom and the law, and so on, is, arguably, one of the more rewarding things to take away from this history of Chan literature. In sum, putting Chan patriarchs on paper might have seemed, at the outset, as a simple enough enterprise, but, in time, this practice gave rise to several forms of literature of rare complexity, while also shaping the lives of those who decided to nurture these spectral figures and build their institutions around them.

BIBLIOGRAPHY

Adamek, Wendi L. *The Mystique of Transmission: On an Early Chan History and Its Contents.* New York: Columbia University Press, 2007.

Ahn, Juhn Y. "Buddhist Self-Cultivation Practice." In *Modern Chinese Religion I: Song-Liao-Jin-Yuan (960–1368 AD),* eds. John Lagerwey and Pierre Marsone, 1160–86. Leiden: Brill, 2015.

———. "Who Has the Last Word in Chan? Transmission, Secrecy and Reading during the Northern Song Dynasty." *Journal of Chinese Religions* 37 (2009): 1–72.

Althusser, Louis. "Ideology and Ideological State Apparatuses." In *Lenin and Philosophy and Other Essays,* 127–86. New York: Monthly Review Press, 1972.

Anderl, Christoph. "Coming to Terms with Terms: The Rhetorical Function of Technical Terms in Chan Buddhist Texts." In *Zen Buddhist Rhetoric in China, Korea, and Japan,* ed. Anderl, 205–36. Leiden: Brill, 2012.

———. *Studies in the Language of Zu-tang ji.* 2 vols. Oslo: Unipub, 2004.

———. "Zen in the Art of Insult: Notes on the Syntax and Semantics of Abusive Speech in Late Middle Chinese." In *Studies in Chinese Language and Culture: Festschrift in Honour of Christoph Harbsmeier on the Occasion of His 60th Birthday,* eds. Anderl and Halvor Eifring, 377–393. Oslo: Hermes Academic, 2006.

———. "Zen Rhetoric: An Introduction." In *Zen Buddhist Rhetoric in China, Korea, and Japan,* ed. Anderl, 1–94. Leiden: Brill, 2012.

App, Urs. "*Mushinron* —Tonko shutsudo no ichi tekisuto." *Zenbunka Kenkyūjo kiyō* 21 (May 1995): 1–69.

———. "Treatise on No-Mind: A Chan Text from Dunhuang." *Eastern Buddhist*, n.s., 28, 1 (1995): 70–107.

Assandri, Friederike. *Beyond the Daode jing: Twofold Mystery Philosophy in Tang Daoism.* Magdalena, NM: Three Pines Press, 2009.

———. "Examples of Buddho-Daoist Interaction: Afterlife Conceptions in Early Medieval Epigraphic Sources." In *The e-Journal of East and Central Asian Religions* no. 1 (Dec. 2013): 1–38.

———. "Inter-religious Debate at the Court of the Early Tang: An Introduction to Daoxuan's *Ji gujin Fo Dao lunheng* (T2104)." In *From Early Tang Court Debates to China's Peaceful Rise,* eds. Assandri and Dora Martins, 9–32. Amsterdam: Amsterdam University Press, 2009.

Barrett, Timothy H. "The Date of the *Leng-chia shih-tzu chi.*" *Journal of the Royal Asiatic Society*, 3d ser., 1, no. 2 (1991): 255–59.

———. "The Emergence of the Taoist Papacy in the T'ang Dynasty." *Asia Major*, 3d ser., 7 (1994): 89–106.

———. "Kill the Patriarchs!" *Buddhist Forum* 1 (1990): 87–97.

———. *Taoism under the T'ang: Religion and Empire during the Golden Age of Chinese History.* London: Wellsweep, 1996.

———. *Li Ao: Buddhist, Taoist, or Neo-Confucian?* New York: Oxford University Press, 1992.

Barthes, Roland, *Mythologies.* Paris: Seuil, 1957.

Berling, Judith. "Bringing the Buddha Down to Earth: Notes on the Emergence of 'Yü-lu' as a Buddhist Genre." *History of Religions* 27, no. 1 (Aug. 1987): 56–88.

Bielefeldt, Carl. "Tsung-tse's *Tso-Ch'an I* and the 'Secret' of Zen Meditation." In *Traditions of Meditation in Chinese Buddhism*, ed. Peter Gregory, 129–61. Honolulu: University of Hawai'i Press, 1985.

Bourdieu, Pierre. *Language and Symbolic Power.* Cambridge, MA: Harvard University Press, 1991.

Brose, Benjamin. *Patrons and Patriarchs: Regional Rulers and Chan Monks during the Five Dynasties and Ten Kingdoms.* Honolulu: University of Hawai'i Press, 2015.

Broughton, Jeffrey L. *The Bodhidharma Anthology: The Earliest Records of Zen.* Berkeley: University of California Press, 1999.

———. *The Chan Whip Anthology: A Companion to Zen Practice.* New York: Oxford University Press, 2014.

———. *Zongmi on Chan.* New York: Columbia University Press, 2009.

Bumbacher, Stephan Peter. *Empowered Writing: Exorcistic and Apotropaic Rituals in Medieval China.* Magdalena, NM: Three Pines Press, 2012.

Chappell, David. "Hermeneutical Phases in Chinese Buddhism." In *Buddhist Hermeneutics,* ed. Donald S. Lopez Jr., 175–206. Honolulu: University of Hawai'i Press, 1992.

Chinese Buddhist Electronic Text Association [CBETA]. www.cbeta.org

Chu Dongwei. *The Wisdom of Huineng, Chinese Buddhist Philosopher: The Platform Sūtra and Other Translations.* Bloomington, IN: iUniverse, 2015.

Cleary, J.C. *Zen Dawn: Early Zen Texts from Tun Huang.* Boston: Shambhala, 1991.

Cleary, Thomas. *Unlocking the Zen Koan: A New Translation of the Zen Classic Wumenguan.* Berkeley, CA: North Atlantic Books, 1997.

Cole, Alan. "Conspiracy's Truth: The Zen of Narrative Cunning in the *Platform Sūtra*." *Asia Major,* 3d ser., 28, no. 1 (2015).

———. The Diamond Sūtra as Sublime Object: Negation, Narration, and Happy Endings." Paper presented to National University of Singapore's Philosophy Dept., Nov. 2013. www.academia.edu/8089546/The_Diamond_Sutra_as_Sublime_Object_Negation Narration_and_Happy_Endings. Accessed June 4, 2016.

———. *Fathering Your Father: The Zen of Fabrication in Tang Buddhism.* Berkeley: University of California Press, 2009.

———. *Fetishizing Tradition: Desire and Reinvention in Buddhist and Christian Narratives.* Albany: State University of New York Press, 2015.

———. "Homestyle Vinaya and Docile Boys in Medieval China." *positions: east asia cultures critique* 7, no. 1 (Spring 1999): 1–49.

———. *Mothers and Sons in Chinese Buddhism.* Stanford, CA: Stanford University Press, 1998.

———. "The Passion of Mulian's Mother: Narrative Sacrifices in Chinese Buddhism." In *Family in Buddhism: Buddhist Vows and Family Ties,* ed. Liz Wilson, 119–46. Albany: State University of New York Press, 2013.

———. "Simplicity for the Sophisticated: Rereading the *Daode jing* for the Polemics of Ease and Innocence." *History of Religions* 46 (2006): 1–49.

———. *Text as Father: Paternal Seductions in Early Mahāyāna Buddhist Literature.* Berkeley: University of California Press, 2005.

———. "Upside Down / Right Side Up: A Revisionist History of Buddhist Funerals in China." *History of Religions* 35, no. 4 (1996): 307–38.

Csikszentmihalyi, Mark, and Michael Nylan. "Constructing Lineages and Inventing Traditions through Exemplary Figures in Early China." *T'oung Pao* 89 (2003): 59–99.

Dai Nippon zokuzōkyō (Great Japanese Edition of the Buddhist Canon, Continued). 150 vols., eds. Maeda Eun and Nakano Tatsue, 1905-1912. Kyoto: Zōkyō shoin.

Daoyuan. *Records of the Transmission of the Lamp.* Vols. 1 and 2. Translated by Randolph S. Whitfield. Norderstedt Books on Demand, 2015.

Demiéville, Paul. *Choix d'études bouddhiques, 1929-1970.* Leiden: Brill, 1973.

———. "Deux documents de Touen-houang sur le Dhyāna chinois." In *Essays on the History of Buddhism Presented to Professor Zenryu Tsukamoto,* 1-27. Kyoto: Nagai Shuppansha, 1961. Reprinted in Demiéville, *Choix d'études bouddhiques, 1929-1970* (Leiden: Brill, 1973), 320-46.

———. "The Mirror of the Mind." In *Sudden and Gradual Approaches to Enlightenment in Chinese Thought,* ed. Peter Gregory, 13-40. Honolulu: University of Hawai'i Press, 1987.

Donner, Neal, and Daniel B. Stevenson. *The Great Calming and Contemplation.* Honolulu: University of Hawai'i Press, 1993.

The Encyclopedia of Taoism. Edited by Fabrizio Pregadio. 2 vols. London: Routledge, 2004.

Faure, Bernard. "Bodhidharma." In the *Encyclopedia of Religion,* 1st ed., 2: 263-65. Detroit: Macmillan Reference USA, 1986.

———. "Bodhidharma as Textual and Religious Paradigm." *History of Religions* 25, no. 3 (1986): 187-98.

———. *Le bouddhisme Ch'an en mal d'histoire: Genèse d'une tradition religieuse dans le Chine des T'ang.* Paris: École française d'Extrême-Orient, 1989.

———. *Chan: Insights and Oversights: An Epistemological Critique of the Chan Tradition.* Princeton, NJ: Princeton University Press, 1993.

———. "Relics and Flesh Bodies." In *Pilgrims and Sacred Sites in China,* eds. Susan Naquin and Chün-Fang Yü, 150-89. Berkeley: University of California Press, 1992.

———. *The Rhetoric of Immediacy: A Cultural Critique of Chan/Zen Buddhism.* Princeton, NJ: Princeton University Press, 1991.

———. *La volonté d'orthodoxie dans le bouddhisme chinois.* Paris: CNRS, 1988.

———. *The Will to Orthodoxy: A Critical Genealogy of Northern Chan Buddhism.* Translated by Phyllis Brooks. Stanford, CA: Stanford University Press, 1997.

Foulk, T. Griffith. "Chan Literature." In *Brill's Encyclopedia of Buddhism: Literature and Languages,* eds. Jonathan A. Silk and Oskar von Hinüber. Leiden: Brill, 2015.

———. "The Ch'an *Tsung* in Medieval China: School, Lineage, or What?" *Pacific World,* n.s., no. 8 (1992): 18-31.

———. "*Chanyuan qinggui* and Other 'Rules of Purity' in Chinese Buddhism." In *The Zen Canon: Understanding the Classic Texts,* eds. Steven Heine and Dale S. Wright, 275–312. New York: Oxford University Press, 2004.

———. "Daily Life in the Assembly." In *Buddhism in Practice,* ed. Donald S. Lopez Jr., 455–72. Princeton, NJ: Princeton University Press, 1995.

———. "The Koan: The Form and Function of Koan Literature: A Historical Overview." In *The Koan: Texts and Contexts in Zen Buddhism,* eds. Steve Heine and Dale S. Wright, 15–45. New York: Oxford University Press, 2000.

———. "Myth, Ritual, and Monastic Practice in Sung Ch'an Buddhism." In *Religion and Society in T'ang and Sung China,* eds. Patricia Buckley Ebrey and Peter N. Gregory, 147–208. Honolulu: University of Hawai'i Press, 1993.

———. "Ritual in Japanese Zen Buddhism." In *Zen Ritual: Studies of Zen Buddhist Theory in Practice,* eds. Steve Heine and Dale S. Wright, 21–82. New York: Oxford University Press, 2007.

———. "The Spread of Chan (Zen) Buddhism." In *The Spread of Buddhism,* eds. Ann Heirman and Stephan Peter Bumbacher: 433–56. Leiden: Brill, 2007.

———. "Sung Controversies Concerning the 'Separate Transmission' of Ch'an." In *Buddhism in the Sung,* eds. Peter N. Gregory and Daniel Getz Jr., 220–94. Honolulu: University of Hawai'i Press, 2002.

Foulk, T. Griffith, and Robert H. Sharf. "On the Ritual Use of Ch'an Portraiture in Medieval China." *Cahiers d'Extrême-Asie* 7 (1993–94): 149–219.

French, Rebecca French, and Mark A. Nathan, eds. *Buddhism and Law: An Introduction.* New York: Cambridge University Press, 2014.

Fukunaga Mitsuji, "'No-mind' in Chuang-tzu and Ch'an Buddhism." Translated by L. Hurvitz. *Zimbun* 12 (1969): 9–45.

Gernet, Jacques. "Biographie du maître Chen-houei du Ho-tsö." *Journal Asiatique* 239 (1951): 29–68.

———. *Buddhism in Chinese Society: An Economic History from the Fifth to the Tenth Centuries.* New York: Columbia University Press, 1995.

———. "Complément aux Entretiens du maître de dhyāna Chen-houei (668–760)." *Bulletin de l'École française d'Extrême-Orient* 44, no. 2 (1954): 453–66. www.persee.fr/doc/befeo_0336-1519_1951_num_44_2_5180.

———. *Entretiens du maître de dhyāna Chen-houei du Ho-tsö (668–760).* Paris: École française d'Extrême-Orient, 1949.

Gjerston, Donald. *Miraculous Retribution: A Study and Translation of T'anglin's Ming pao chi.* Berkeley, CA: Center for South and Southeast Asia Studies, 1989.

Greene, Eric. "Another Look at Early 'Chan': Daoxuan, Bodhidharma, and the Three Levels Movement." *T'oung Pao* 94 (2008): 49–114.

———. "Meditation, Repentance, and Visionary Experience in Early Medieval Chinese Buddhism." Diss., University of California, Berkeley 2012.

Gregory, Peter. "The Vitality of Buddhism in the Sung." In *Buddhism in the Sung,* eds. Peter Gregory and Daniel Getz Jr., 1–20. Honolulu: University of Hawai'i Press, 2002.

Groner, Paul. "The Ordination Ritual in the *Platform Sūtra* within the Context of the East Asian Buddhist Vinaya Tradition." In *Fo Kuang Shan Report of International Conference on Ch'an Buddhism,* 220–50. Gaoxiong, Taiwan: Foguang, 1990.

Hamlin, Edwin. "Discourse in the *Laṅkāvatāra Sūtra*." *Journal of Indian Philosophy* 11 (1983): 267–313.

Harbsmeier, Christoph. "Authorial Presence in Some Pre-Buddhist Chinese Texts." In *De l'un au multiple: Traductions du chinois vers les langues européennes,* eds. Viviane Alleton and Michael Lackner, 220–54. Paris: Maison des sciences de l'homme, 1999.

Heirman, Anne. "*Vinaya* from India to China." In *The Spread of Buddhism,* eds. Ann Heirman and Stephan Peter Bumbacher, 167–202. Leiden: Brill, 2007.

Hubbard, Jamie. *Absolute Delusion, Perfect Buddhahood: The Rise and Fall of a Chinese Heresy.* Honolulu: University of Hawai'i Press, 2001.

———. "Chinese Reliquary Inscriptions and the San-chieh-chiao." *Journal of the International Association of Buddhist Studies* 14 (1991): 253–80.

Hu Shi. *Hu Shi chanxue 'an.* Edited by Yanagida Seizan. Taipei: Zhengzhong shuzhu, 1975.

———. "Leng-ch'ieh tsung k'ao." In *Hu Shih wen-ts'un,* 3: 194–244. Taipei: Yuan-t'ung t'u shu kung-szu, 1953. Reprinted in *Ko Teki zengakuan,* ed. Yanagida Seizan, 154–95. Kyoto: Chūbun shuppan sha, 1975.

———. *Shenhui heshang yiji.* Shanghai: Oriental Book Co., 1930.

———. *Two Newly Edited Texts of the Chan Master Shen-hui from the Pelliot Collection of Tun-huang Manuscripts at the Bibliotheque Nationale in Paris.* Zhongyang yanjiuyuan lishi yuyan yanjiusuo jikan 29, no. 2 (1958). In Chinese. Reprinted in *Shenhui heshang yiji.* Taibei: Hu Shi jinian guan, 1968.

Ichimura Shōhei, trans. *The Baizhang Zen Monastic Regulations: Taishō volume 48, number 2025.* Berkeley, CA: Numata Center for Buddhist Translation and Research, 2006.

Ishii Shūdō. "The *Wu-men kuan* (J. *Mumonkan*): The Formation, Propagation, and Characteristics of a Classic Zen Kōan Text." In *The Zen Canon: Understanding the Classic Texts,* eds. Steven Heine and Dale S. Wright, 207–44. New York: Oxford University Press, 2004.

Jia, Jinhua. *The Hongzhou School of Chan Buddhism in Eighth- through Tenth-Century China.* Albany: State University of New York Press, 2006.

Jorgensen, John. *Inventing Hui-neng, the Sixth Patriarch: Hagiography and Biography in Early Ch'an.* Leiden: Brill, 2005.

———. "The 'Imperial' Lineage of Ch'an Buddhism: The Role of Confucian Ritual and Ancestor Worship in Ch'an's Search for Legitimation in the mid-T'ang Dynasty." *Papers on Far Eastern History* 35 (1987): 89–133.

Knaul, Livia [Livia Kohn]. "Chuang-tzu and the Chinese Ancestry of Ch'an Buddhism." *Journal of Chinese Philosophy* 13 (1986): 411–28.

Kohn, Livia. "Medieval Daoist Ordination." *Acta Orientalia Academiae Scientiarum Hungaricae* 56, nos. 2–4 (2003): 379–98.

———. *Sitting in Oblivion: The Heart of Daoist Meditation.* Dunedin, FL: Three Pines Press, 2010.

Kurz, Johannes. "On the Politics of Collecting Knowledge: Song Taizong's Compilation Projects." *T'oung Pao,* 87, fasc. 4/5 (2001): 289–316.

Lau, D. C., trans. *Mencius.* London: Penguin Books, 1970.

Levering, Miriam. "Was There Religious Autobiography in China before the Thirteenth Century?—The Ch'an Master Ta-hui Tsung-kao (1089–1163) as Autobiographer." *Journal of Chinese Religions* 30 (Sept. 2002): 97–122.

Lewis, Mark Edward. "The Suppression of the Three Stages Sect: Apocrypha as a Political Issue." In *Chinese Buddhist Apocrypha,* ed. Robert E. Buswell Jr., 207–38. Honolulu: University of Hawai'i Press, 1990.

———. *Writing and Authority in Early China.* Albany: State University of New York Press, 1999.

Liebenthal, Walter. "The Sermon of Shen-hui." *Asia Major,* n.s., 3, no. 2 (1953): 132–55.

Liezi. *The Book of Lieh-tzŭ.* Translated by A. C. Graham. New York: Columbia University Press, 1960.

Liu, James. "Time, Space, and Self in Chinese Poetry." *Chinese Literature: Essays, Articles, Reviews (CLEAR)* 1, no. 2 (July 1979): 137–56.

Low, Sor-Ching. "Seung Sahn: The Makeover of A Modern Zen Patriarch." In *Zen Masters,* eds. Steven Heine and Dale S. Wright, 267–85. New York: Oxford University Press, 2010.

Maraldo, John C. "Is There Historical Consciousness in Ch'an?" *Japanese Journal of Religious Studies* 12, nos. 2–3 (1985): 141–72.

Maspero, Henri. "Sur la date et l'authenticitè du *Fou fa tsang yin yuan tchouan*." In *Mélanges de'Indianisme (offerts à S. Lévi par ses élèves)*, 129–49. Paris: E. Leroux, 1911.

McRae, John R. "The Antecedents of Encounter Dialogue in Chinese Ch'an Buddhism." In *The Kōan: Texts and Contexts in Zen Buddhism*, eds. Steven Heine and Dale S. Wright, 46–74. New York: Oxford University Press, 2000.

———. "Daoxuan's Vision of Jetavana: The Ordination Platform Movement in Medieval Chinese Buddhism." In *Going Forth: Visions of Buddhist Vinaya*, ed. William M. Bodiford, 68–100. Honolulu: University of Hawai'i Press, 2005.

———. "The Hagiography of Bodhidharma: Reconstructing the Point of Origin of Chinese Chan Buddhism." In *India in the Chinese Imagination: Myth, Religion, and Thought*, eds. John Kieschnick and Meir Shahar, 125–38. University of Pennsylvania Press, 2014.

———. *The Northern School and the Formation of Early Ch'an Buddhism*. Honolulu: University of Hawai'i Press, 1986.

———. *Seeing through Zen: Encounter, Transformation, and Genealogy in Chinese Chan Buddhism*. Berkeley: University of California Press, 2003.

———. "Shen-hui and the Teaching of Sudden Enlightenment in Early Ch'an Buddhism." In *Sudden and Gradual Approaches to Enlightenment in Chinese Thought*, ed. Peter Gregory, 227–78. Honolulu: University of Hawai'i Press, 1987.

———. "Shenhui as Evangelist: Re-envisioning the Identity of a Chinese Buddhist Monk." *Journal of Chinese Religions* 30 (2002): 123–48.

———. "Shen-hui's Vocation on the Ordination Platform and Our Visualization of Medieval Ch'an Buddhism." *Zenbunka kenkyūjo kiyō* 24 (1998): 43–66.

Meinert, Carmen. "The Conjunction of Chinese Chan and Tibetan *Rdzogs chen* Thought: Reflections on the Tibetan Dunhuang Manuscripts IOL Tib J 689–1 and PT 699." In *Contributions to the Cultural History of Early Tibet*, eds. Matthew Kapstein and Brandon Dotson, 239–301. Leiden: Brill, 2007.

Morinaga Soko. *The Ceasing of Notions: An Early Zen Text from the Dunhuang Caves with Selected Comments*. Somerville, MA: Wisdom Publications, 2012.

Morrison, Elizabeth. "Contested Visions of the Buddhist Past and the Curious Fate of an Early Medieval Buddhist Text." Unpublished paper, Stanford University, 1996.

―――. *The Power of Patriarchs: Qisong and Lineage in Chinese Buddhism.* Leiden: Brill, 2010.

Nāgārjuna. *Le traité de la grande vertu de sagesse = Mahāprajñāpāramitāśāstra.* Translated and edited by Étienne Lamotte. Louvain, Belgium: Institut orientaliste, Bibliothèque de l'Université, 1966–.

Pelliot, Paul. "Notes sur quelques artistes des Six Dynasties et des T'ang." *T'oung Pao* 22 (1923): 215–91.

Penkower, Linda. "In the Beginning … Guanding (561–632) and the Creation of Early Tiantai." *Journal of the International Association of Buddhist Studies* 23, no. 2 (2000): 245–96.

Poceski, Mario. "*Mazu yulu* and the Creation of the Chan Record of Sayings." In *The Zen Canon: Understanding the Classic Texts,* eds. Steven Heine and Dale S. Wright, 53–80. New York: Oxford University Press, 2004.

―――. "Monastic Innovator, Iconoclast, and Teacher of Doctrine: The Varied Images of Chan Master Baizhang." In *Zen Masters,* eds. Steven Heine and Dale S. Wright, 3–32. New York: Oxford University Press, 2010.

―――. *Ordinary Mind as the Way: The Hongzhou School and the Growth of Chan Buddhism.* New York: Oxford University Press, 2007.

―――. *The Records of Mazu and the Making of Classical Chan Literature.* New York: Oxford University Press, 2015.

―――. "Xuefeng's Code and the Chan School's Participation in the Development of Monastic Regulations." *Asia Major,* 3d ser., 16, no. 2 (2003): 33–56

Robson, James. "Formation and Fabrication in the History and Historiography of Chan Buddhism." *Harvard Journal of Asiatic Studies* 71, no. 2 (Dec. 2011): 311–49.

Rorty, Richard. *Contingency, Irony, and Solidarity.* New York: Cambridge University Press, 1989.

Sartre, Jean-Paul. *What Is Literature? And Other Essays.* 1948. 3rd ed. Cambridge, MA: Harvard University Press, 1988.

Schaberg, David. *A Patterned Past: Form and Thought in Early Chinese Historiography.* Cambridge, MA: Harvard University Press, 2002.

Schlütter, Morten. *How Zen Became Zen: The Dispute over Enlightenment and the Formation of Chan Buddhism in Song-Dynasty China.* Honolulu: University of Hawai'i Press, 2008.

―――. "Vinaya Monasteries, Public Abbacies, and State Control of Buddhism under the Song (960–1279)." In *Going Forth: Visions of Buddhist Vinaya: Essays Presented in Honor of Professor Stanley Weinstein,* ed. William M. Bodiford, 136–60. Honolulu: University of Hawai'i Press, 2005.

Schlütter, Morten, and Stephen F. Teiser, eds. *Readings of the Platform Sūtra.* New York: Columbia University Press, 2012.

Sekida Katsuki. *Two Zen Classics: The Gateless Gate and The Blue Cliff Records.* Boston: Shambhala, 2014.

Shahar, Meir. "Epigraphy, Buddhist Historiography, and Fighting Monks: The Case of The Shaolin Monastery." *Asia Major,* 3d ser., 13, no. 2 (2000): 15–36.

———. *The Shaolin Monastery: History, Religion, and the Chinese Martial Arts.* Honolulu: University of Hawai'i Press, 2008.

Sharf, Robert H. "Buddhist Modernism and the Rhetoric of Meditative Experience." *Numen* 42, no. 3 (1995): 228–83.

———. *Coming to Terms with Chinese Buddhism: A Reading of the Treasure Store Treatise.* Honolulu: University of Hawai'i Press, 2005.

———. "D. T. Suzuki." In the *Encyclopedia of Religion,* 2nd ed., 13: 8884–87. Detroit: Macmillan Reference USA, 2005.

———. "Is Nirvāṇa the Same as Insentience? Chinese Struggles with an Indian Buddhist Ideal." In *India in the Chinese Imagination: Myth, Religion, and Thought,* eds. John Kieschnick and Meir Shahar, 141–70. Philadelphia: University of Pennsylvania Press, 2014.

———. "Mindfulness and Mindlessness in Early Chan." *Philosophy East & West* 64, no. 4 (Oct. 2014): 933–64.

———. "The Zen of Nationalism." 1993. *History of Religions* 33, no. 1 (1993): 1–43.

Shinohara Kōichi. "Guanding's Biography of Zhiyi, the Fourth Chinese Patriarch of the Tiantai Tradition." In *Speaking of Monks: Religious Biography in India and China,* eds. Phyllis Granoff and Kōichi Shinohara, 98–232. Oakville, Ont.: Mosaic Press, 1992.

———. "The Kaśāya Robe of the Past Buddha Kāśapa in the Miraculous Instruction Given to the Vinaya Master Daoxuan (596–667)." *Chung-Hwa Buddhist Journal* 13, no. 2 (2000): 299–367.

———. "From Local History to Universal History: The Construction of the Sung T'ien-t'ai Lineage." In *Buddhism in the Sung,* eds. Peter N. Gregory and Daniel Getz Jr., 524–76. Honolulu: University of Hawai'i Press, 2002.

Smith, Jonathan Z. *Imagining Religion: From Babylon to Jonestown.* Chicago: University of Chicago Press, 1988.

Sørensen, Henrik H. "Observations on the Characteristics of the Chinese Chan Manuscripts from Dunhuang." *Studies in Central & East Asian Religions* 2 (1989): 115–39.

————. "Perspectives on Buddhism in Dunhuang during the Tang and Five Dynasties Period." In *The Silk Roads: Highways of Culture and Commerce,* ed. Vadime Elisseeff, 27–48. New York: Berghahn Books, 2000.

Suzuki, D. T. *An Introduction to Zen Buddhism.* 1934. New York: Grove Press, 1964.

Taishō shinshū daizōkyō. 100 vols. Edited by Takakusa Junjirō and Watanabe Kaigyoku. Tokyo: Taishō issaikyō kankōkai, 1924–32.

Teiser, Stephen F., and Jacqueline I. Stone, eds. *Readings of the Lotus Sūtra.* New York: Columbia University Press, 2009.

Tokiwa Gishin. *A Dialogue on the Contemplation-Extinguished: A Translation Based on Professor Seizan Yanagida's Modern Japanese Translation and Consultations with Professor Yoshitaka Iriya.* Kyoto: Institute for Zen Studies, 1973.

Tonami Mamoru. *The Shaolin Monastery Stele on Mount Song.* Translated and annotated by P. A. Herbert. Edited by Antonino Forte. Kyoto: Italian School of East Asian Studies, 1990.

Wallace, David Foster. Commencement speech. Kenyon College, Ohio, 2005.

Van Schaik, Sam. *Tibetan Zen: Discovering a Lost Tradition.* Boston: Snow Lion, 2015.

The Vimalakīrti Sūtra. Translated by Burton Watson. New York: Columbia University Press, 1997.

Walker, Rob. "Can a Dead Brand Live Again?" *New York Times Magazine,* May 18, 2008.

Ware, James R., *Alchemy, Medicine and Religion in the China of A.D. 320: The Nei Pien of Ko Hung.* 1967. New York: Dover, 1981.

Weinstein, Stanley. *Buddhism under the T'ang.* Cambridge: Cambridge University Press, 1987.

Welter, Albert. "Contested Identities in Chan/Zen Buddhism: The 'Lost' Fragments of Mazu Daoyi in the *Zongjing lu.*" In *Buddhism without Borders: Proceedings of the International Conference on Globalized Buddhism, Bumthang, Bhutan, May 21–23, 2012,* eds. Dasho Karma Ura and Dendup Chophel, 268–83. Thimphu, Bhutan: Center for Bhutan Studies, 2012.

————. "Lineage and Context in the Patriarch's Hall Collection and the Transmission of the Lamp." In *The Zen Canon: Understanding the Classic Texts,* eds. Steve Heine and Dale S. Wright, 137–80. New York: Oxford University Press, 2004.

————. *The Linji Lu and the Creation of Chan Orthodoxy.* New York: Oxford University Press, 2008.

————. "Mahākāśyapa's Smile: Silent Transmission and Kung-an (Kōan) Tradition." In *The Koan: Texts and Contexts in Zen Buddhism*, eds. Steve Heine and Dale S. Wright, 75–109. New York: Oxford University Press, 2000.

————. *Monks, Rulers, and Literati: The Political Ascendancy of Chan Buddhism.* New York: New York: Oxford University Press, 2006.

Wright, Dale S. "The Discourse of Awakening: Rhetorical Practice in Classic Ch'an Buddhism." *Journal of the American Academy of Religion* 61, no. 1 (Spring 1993): 23–24.

————. "Humanizing the Image of a Zen Master: Taizan Maezumi Roshi." In *Zen Masters*, eds. Steven Heine and Dale S. Wright, 239–65. New York: Oxford University Press, 2010.

————. "Introduction: Rethinking Ritual Practice in Zen Buddhism." In *Zen Ritual: Studies of Zen Buddhist Theory in Practice*, eds. Steve Heine and Dale S. Wright, 3–20. New York: Oxford University Press, 2007.

————. *Philosophical Meditations on Zen Buddhism.* Cambridge: Cambridge University Press, 1998.

Wu, Jiang. *Enlightenment in Dispute: The Reinvention of Chan Buddhism in Seventeenth-Century China.* New York: Oxford University Press, 2008.

Wu, Pei-yi. *The Confucian's Progress: Autobiographical Writings in Traditional China.* Princeton, NJ: Princeton University Press, 1990.

Xu zangjing. Reprint edition of the *Dai Nippon zokuzōkyō.* Taipei: Hsin-wen-feng, 1968–70.

Yampolsky, Philip. *The Platform Sūtra of the Sixth Patriarch: The Text of the Tun-huang Manuscript with Translation, Introduction, and Notes.* New York: Columbia University Press, 1967.

Yanagida Seizan, ed. *Hu Shi chanxue 'an.* Taibei : Zhengzhong shuzhu, 1975.

————. *Shoki no Zenshi, I: Ryōga shijiki; Denhōbō ki.* Tokyo: Chikuma shobō, 1971.

————. *Shoki Zenshū shisho no kenkyū.* Kyoto: Hōzōkan, 1967.

Yang Zengwen, ed. *Shenhui heshang chanyu lu* [Records of the Chan Talks of the Venerable Shenhui]. Beijing: Zhonghua shuju, 1996.

Ye Derong. "'Ancestral Transmission' in Chinese Buddhist Monasteries: The Example of the Shaolin Temple." In *India in the Chinese Imagination: Myth, Religion and Thought*, eds. John Kieschnick and Meir Shahar, 110–24. Philadelphia: University of Pennsylvania Press, 2014.

Yifa. *The Origins of Buddhist Monastic Codes in China: An Annotated Translation and Study of the "Chanyuan qinggui"* [Rules of Purity for the Chan Monastery]. Honolulu: University of Hawaii Press, 2002.

————. "From the Chinese Vinaya Tradition to Chan Regulations." In *Going Forth: Visions of Buddhist Vinaya,* ed. William M. Bodiford, 124–35. Honolulu: University of Hawai'i Press, 2005.

Young, Stuart. *Conceiving the Indian Buddhist Patriarchs in China.* Honolulu: University of Hawai'i Press, 2015.

Zeuschner, Robert. "The *Hsien Tsung Chi* (An Early Ch'an [Zen] Buddhist Text)." *Journal of Chinese Philosophy* 3 (1976): 253–68.

Zhuangzi [Zhuang Zhou]. *The Complete Works of Chuang Tzu.* Translated by Burton Watson. New York: Columbia University Press, 1968.

————. *Chuang-Tzu: The Inner Chapters.* Translated by A.C. Graham. London: Mandala, 1991.

Ziporyn, Brook. "Anti-Chan Polemics in Post-Tang Tiantai." *Journal of the International Association of Buddhist Studies* 17, no. 1 (1994): 26–63.

————. "Tiantai School." In *Encyclopedia of Buddhism,* ed. Robert E. Buswell Jr., 845–51. Detroit: Macmillan Reference USA, 2003.

————. "Tiantai Buddhism." In The Stanford Encyclopedia of Philosophy Archive (Winter 2014 ed.), ed. Edward N. Zalta. http://plato.stanford.edu/archives/win2014/entries/buddhism-tiantai. Accessed June 4, 2016.

Zürcher, Erik. *The Buddhist Conquest of China: The Spread and Adaptation Buddhism in Early Medieval China.* Leiden: Brill, 1959.

GLOSSARY

ANXIN 安心

BAIGUWU 柏谷塢
BAIGUZHUANG 柏谷裝
BAIZHANG HUAIHAI 百丈懷海
BAOLINSI 寶林寺
BAOLIN ZHUAN 寶林傳
BAOPUZI 抱朴子
BENXIN 本心
BIGUAN 壁觀
BINCHENG 稟承
BOSI GUO 波斯国
BU SHI WUQING 不是無情

CAOQI DASHI ZHUAN 曹溪大師傳
CHANFA 禪法
CHANLIN BAOXUN 禪林寶訓
CHANSHI NA 禪師那
CHANSHI 禪師
CHANYUAN QINGGUI 禪院清規
CHANZONG 禪宗
CHAOWU 超悟
CHENGKEN 誠懇

CHENHOU 沈厚
CHIXIU BAIZHANG QINGGUI 敕修百丈清規
CHONGYUAN 崇遠
CHONGYUE 重曰
CHUAN FABAO JI 傳法寶紀
CHUJI 處寂
CIRI 此曰

DACHENG WUSHENG FANGBIAN MEN 大乘無生方便門
DADE 大德
DAFANSI 大梵寺
DAHUI ZONGGAO 大慧宗杲
DAMO 達摩
DAMOLUN 達摩論
DAODE JING 道德經
DAOHENG 道恆
DAOXIN 道信
DAOXUAN 道宣
DAOYING 道英
DAOYU 道育
DAOYUAN 道原
DAYUE 答曰
DENGLU 燈碌
DENGSHI 燈史
DICHUANFA 遞傳法
DIDAI 帝代
DU FEI 杜朏
DUGU PEI 獨孤沛
DUNJIAN FOXING 頓見佛性
DUNJIAO 頓教
DUNRU 頓入
DUNWU 頓悟

ERRU SIXING LUN 二入四行論

FABAO 法寶
FACHONG 法沖
FANGBIAN 方便

FAQI 法棄
FARU 法如
FATAN 法壇
FOMIYI 佛密義
FOTUO 佛陀 (ALSO WRITTEN 跋陀)
FOXING 佛性
FU 符
FU FAZANG YINYUAN ZHUAN 付法藏因緣傳
FUZHU 付囑

GAOSENG ZHUAN 高僧傳
GAOZONG 高宗
GE HONG 葛洪
GENG BU SUIYU WENJIAO 更不隨於文教
GONG'AN 公案
GUANDING 灌頂
GUIZHEN 歸真
GUOQING BAILU 國清百錄
GUOQINGSI 國清寺
GUOSHI 國師

HEZE SI 荷澤寺
HONGREN 弘忍
HUAIRANG 懷讓
HUANGMEI 黃梅
HUATAISI 滑臺寺
HUATOU 話頭
HUICHAO 惠超
HUIKE 惠可
HUIMAN 慧滿
HUINENG 慧能, ALSO WRITTEN 惠能
HUISI 慧思
HUIWEN 慧文
HUIYUAN 慧遠

JIETAN 戒檀
JIJIAO WUZONG 藉教悟宗
JINGCHENG 精誠

JINGDE CHUANDENG LU 景德傳燈錄
JINGJUE 淨覺
JINGXIN 淨心
JINGXIU 淨修
JINGZHOU 荊州
JISHEN CHAOWU 機神超悟
JISHOU QIDAO 即授其道
JUEGUAN LUN 絕觀論
JUEZHAO 覺照
JUGU 舉古

LAO'AN 老安
LENGQIE SHIZI JI 楞伽師資記
LI 里
LI ZUNXU 李遵勗
LIDAI FABAO JI 曆代法寶記
LIEZI 列子
LINGBAO DINGGUAN LUN 靈寶定觀經
LIUCHENG 劉澄
LIUZU TANJING 六祖壇經
LONGXINGSI 龍興寺
LUOYANG QIELAN JI 洛陽伽藍記

MAITIE DEJIN 買鐵得金
MAZU 馬祖
MINGBAO JI 冥報記
MINGQI YUXI 冥契於昔
MINGXIN XUJI 冥心虛寂
MOHEZHIGUAN 摩訶止觀

NA CHANSHI 那禪師
NAI 乃
NANYANG HESHANG DUNJIAO CHANMEN ZHILIAOXING TANYU 南陽和上頓教解脫禪直了性檀語
NINGZHU BIGUAN 凝住壁觀
NINGZHU JUEGUAN 凝住覺觀

PU 樸

PUJI 普寂
PUTI DAMO NANZONG DING SHIFEI LUN 菩提達摩南宗定是非論

QINGGUI 清規
QINQIE 親切
QISHEN YOUGU 栖神幽谷
QIZUTANG 七祖堂
QUANPU 全朴
QUANZHOU 泉州
QUANZHOU QIANFO XINZHU ZHU ZUSHI SONG 泉州千佛新著諸祖師頌

RU 汝
RULI 入理
SANJIEJIAO 三階教
SANWEI 三昧
SENGCAN 僧璨
SHAOLINSI 少林寺
SHAOLINSIBEI 少林寺碑
SHAOZHOU 韶州
SHENHUA YOUZE 神化幽賾
SHENHUI 神會
SHENXIN HANSHENG TONGYI ZHENXING 深信含生同一真性
SHENXIU 神秀
SHEWANG GUIZHEN 捨妄歸真
SHI DADE 十大德
SHIJI 史記
SHIREN 世人
SHOUBEN 守本
SHOUCHUAN 授傳
SHOUQIDAO 授其道
SHUANGFENG 雙峰
SISHU 嗣書
SONGSHAN 嵩山
SONGYUESI 嵩嶽寺

TAI SHANG 太上
TAN 檀
TANFA YIZE 壇法儀則

TANGGUO 唐國

TANGLIN 唐林

TANLIN 曇林

TIANSHENG GUANGDENG LU 天聖廣燈錄

TIANTAI ZONG 天台宗

WANG WEI 王維

WANG XIANG 妄想

WANGXIN ZHISHI 亡心之士

WANGXIN 妄心

WANGYAN WANGNIAN WUDE ZHENGGUAN WEIZONG 忘言忘念無得正觀爲宗

WEIJING 惟勁

WENDAZA ZHENGYI 問答雜證議

WENDENG 文(人+登)

WO SUO XIN 我所心

WU FANGBIAN 五方便

WULIANGSHOU GUANJING 無量壽觀經

WUMEN GUAN 無門關

WUMEN HUIKAI 無門慧開

WUMEN YUE 無門曰

WUNIAN 無念

WUQING 無情

WUWEI 無爲

WUWENZI 無文字

WUXIANG 無相

WUXIN LUN 無心論

WUYOU FENBIE JIRAN WUWEI 無有分別 寂然 無爲

WUZHU 無住

WUZI WUTA FANSHENG DENG YI 無自無他 凡聖等一

XIANG JUSHI 向居士

XIANGCHENG CHUANFA 相承傳法

XIANGCHENG 相承

XIANGCHUAN 相傳

XIANYOU FUZHU 先有付囑

XIANZONG JI 顯宗記

XIAOZI 孝子

XICHAN LUN 習禪論

XIFASI 希法嗣
XINDI 心地
XINGZHUANG 行狀
XINMU LUN 心目論
XINRU FOXIN 心如佛心
XINSHEN XIANGJI 心神向寂
XINTONG RULAIXIN 心同如來心
XINXING 信行
XINYAO 心要
XINYI 信衣
XINYUANXIANG 心緣相
XINZHI DUDE 心知獨得
XIUDAO ZHI BENTI 修道之本體
XIUXI ZHIGUAN ZUOCHAN FAYAO 修習止觀坐禪法要
XIUXIN YAOLUN 修心要論
XU BAOLIN ZHUAN 續寶林傳
XU GAOSENG ZHUAN 續高僧傳
XUANGAO 玄高
XUANGONG 玄功
XUANLI 玄理
XUANWANG 玄網
XUANZE 玄賾
XUEFENG YICUN 雪峰義存
XUEJIAN 薛簡
XUEYAN 雪巖

YANG XUANZHI 楊衒之
YANG YI 楊億
YANGXING SHANZHONG 養性山中
YAOSHOUJI 遙授記
YIFU 義福
YIJIAN ZHONGZHI 一見重之
YINKE 印可
YINZONG 印宗
YIWEI FAXIN 以爲法信
YIWEI XINYAO 以爲心要
YIXING SANMEI 一行三昧
YIXING 一行

YIYIN ZHENGXIN 以印證心
YIYIN ZHIFA 一印之法
YOUGU 幽谷
YOUGUAN 幽關
YUANMEN 緣門
YULI MINGFU 與理冥符
YULU 語錄
YUQUANSI 玉泉寺

ZHAOQING 招慶
ZHEN YOULI 真幽理
ZHENDAO 真道
ZHENGXIN 證心
ZHENJING KEWEN 真淨克文
ZHENRU 真如
ZHENRUMEN 真如門
ZHENTANG 真堂
ZHENXIN 真心
ZHENZONG 真宗
ZHILUN 至論
ZHIRU 直入
ZHISHEN 智詵
ZHIYAO 智藥
ZHIYI 智顗
ZHIZHE 智者
ZHUAN 傳
ZHUANGYAN 莊嚴
ZHUANGZI 莊子
ZHUCHI 住持
ZHUFA DUN GU 諸法鈍故
ZHUWEI 麈尾
ZHUXIN RUDING 住心入定
ZI CHONGJING 自崇敬
ZI SHOU YU XIN 自守於心
ZIJUE 自覺
ZIRAN 自然
ZIZAI 自在
ZONGJI 宗極

ZONGMI 宗密
ZONGZE 宗賾
ZONGZHI 宗旨
ZU 祖
ZUNSHI 遵式
ZUOCHAN 坐禪
ZUOCHAN YI 坐禪義
ZUOWANG LUN 坐忘論
ZUOZHUAN 左傳
ZUSHI 祖師
ZUTANGJI 祖堂集

INDEX

absolute master, the, 25–26, 61–62, 258
abbots (of Chan monasteries), 196,
    220–22, 224, 239, 245–51; as akin to
    government officials, 249–50; as
    chief executives, 227–28, 235,
    245–46, 248–49; funerals of, 229–30,
    233; and literature, 234, 245–46;
    morality of, 222, 242–43, 245, 247;
    reproduction of, 229–31, 234–48
    passim; retirement of, 244–45;
    selection of, 221, 225–26, 229,
    238–40
Adamek, Wendi, 24n10, 32n24, 86n3,
    87n5, 159n32, 161n36, 169n2
aesthetics: of Chan, x, 259, 283–84
alchemy, 11, 16, 72
all-natural buddhas (free of
    Buddhism), 7, 100, 115, 122–23, 277
Analects, 99–100, 149
Ānanda, 62–63, 110, 124, 209–10
ancestor hall, 88, 88n, 111, 201, 232
Ancestor Hall Compendium, 202–14, 255,
    272
ancestors, 2, 14–15, 52, chap. 3, 86, 92,
    101, 197, 199, 201–2, 232, 236, 243, 250,
    263; the Buddha's, 4; Confucian, 17,
    199

Anderl, Christoph, 138n2, 197n6, 203n13,
    205n16, 207n17, 210n24, 211n27, 213n32,
    223n7, 253n2, 255n5, 257n8
Ahn, Juhn Y., 240n41, 257n7
anti-literature literature, 7, 93. *See also*
    literature: celebrating nature,
    simplicity, and orality
antinomianism, 133, 265–66, 278;
    introduced by later editors, 15,
    214–19
App, Urs, 183n30, 188n46
arm-offering (Huike's), 75–76, 115, 260
art: of rewriting tradition, xiv, 159; of
    writing religious literature, 275
artful mystification of Chinese
    Buddhist leaders, 173–74, 278–79, 281
asceticism, 43–46, 49, 122–23
Assandri, Friederike, 263n14
authenticity, images of, 4, 9, 79, 86, 119
authority, 4–7; final voice of, 29, 38, 39,
    106, 135, 159, 193–94, 235, 255
autobiography, 137, 147n16, 273, 273n20,
    274

Baigu Estate (*Baigu zhuang*), 59–60
Baizhang, 217, 233–34, 243
Baizhang qinggui, 229n17, 242n45

Baofu (supposed master of Wendeng), 213
Baolin Monastery, 120–21, 128, 130, 135, 155
Baolin zhuan, 202n12
barbarians, 99, 139, 259, 261
Barrett, T. H., 36n29, 89n12, 187n47
Barthes, Roland, 283n2
Berling, Judith, 193n51
Bielefeldt, Carl, 247
Big Other(s), 22, 22n4, 44, 250
Biography of the Great Master of Caoqi (Caoqi dashi biezhuan), chap. 5, 139, 151–52, 155, 162, 166, 210, 266
blind dragon: in the *Ancestor Hall Compendium*, 207
Bodhidharma: arrival in China, 1, 20, 29–30, 73, 156, 262; as Big Other to China, 43–44; as brand name, 54–57, 68, 74, 78, 82, 85, 88, 98; death of, 40, 41; earliest mention of, 27–30; as one hundred and fifty years old, 28, 38; sons of, 222, 277, 279; transmission to Huike, 1, 20, 29, 39–40, 43–45, 47, 49–51, 57, 64, 73–77, 78n22, 82, 93–95, 111, 115, 124, 156, 259–61
Bodhidharma family: in the Tang, 1–6, 55, 66, 68, 71–72, 76, 81–89, 96–98, 101–2, 104, 109, 115, 117–18, 140–41, 152, 158, 160, 169, 277; in the Song, 198, 204, 211, 221, 228–33, 238–41, 249–50, 277, 280
Bodhidharma's Treatises (Damo lun), 73–74
Bokenkamp, Stephen, 34n26
brand equity, 54–57, 68, 74, 78, 82, 85, 88; and brand names, 98, 200, 247; and Chan, 232, 234, 247, 249; and monasteries, 226, 232, 272; and Wendeng, 212
Brose, Benjamin, 195n1
Broughton, Jeffrey, 28n18, 30n19, 31n21, 35n27,28, 40n33, 41n35,36, 42n40, 43n41,42, 78n22, 168n1, 173n10, 260n11, 273n20

Buddhism: freedom from, 11, 162, 169, 205, 278, 282; normal version of, xi, 11, 42, 34, 96, 144, 148, 150, 162, 173–74, 179, 183, 205, 230, 261, 276. *See also* Daoist-styled forms of Buddhism
Buddhabhadra, 30, 30n20
Buddha, the, 1, 4, 100, 104–5, 112, 118, 130; enlightenment in *Ancestor Hall Compendium*, 206–9; as origin of the Chan lineage, 1, 4, 17, 24, 61–63, 67, 71, 110, 115, 124–25; and Zhiyi, 22–24
buddha-mind, 176–79, 181–82
buddha-nature, 121–23, 133, 138, 147, 175–76, 179, 268
Bumbacher, Stephan Peter, 34n26, 53n49, 221n4

cakravartin (emperor model for Buddhist legitimacy), 108
Carus, Paul, 8
Chan: birth of, 1–3; definitions of, 1, 6, 12–13, 19, 37, 38, 196, 223–24, 275–84; as "fantasy Buddhism," 7, 11, 115–16, 198, 237, 277–79, 283; as habitat, x, xi, 233, 279, 281, 283; as philosophy, 13, 69, 119, 136; as supplement to Chinese Buddhism, 196, 196n2, 223, 279; as theory of authority and leadership, 57, 67, 109, 111, 115, 196, 202, 222, 231, 233, 237, 245, 279–80
Chan masters: image of, in the Tang, 12, 13, 46, 52–53, 75–76, 97, 198, 200–201, 278; in the Song, 214–15, 217–18, 222–24, 246, 253, 261, 267, 273, 278–79; one per generation, 107–12
Chan studies, xiii, xiv, 2, 7, 27, 58, 197
Chappell, David, 215n34
Chinese buddhas, 2, 6, 90, 222, 277–78
Chinese Buddhism, as decadent, 29, 73–76, 95
Chinese Buddhist Electronic Text Association [CBETA], xv, xvii
Chinese law, 227n15, 233–34, 266

Fu fazang yinyuan zhuan. See *History of
the Transmission of the
Dharma-Treasury*
Fukunaga Mitsuji, 184n32
funerals: the Buddha's, 209–10; in
Chan, 230, 230n18, 233

Gaozong (emperor), 60, 128–34, 129n20,
155
Gateless Entrance (Wumen guan), chap. 10
genealogies. *See* Bodhidharma family.
See also Buddha, the, as origin of the
Chan lineage
genre, 25, 72, 168, 196, 196n, 220, 278–79
Gernet, Jacques, 102n33, 104n35,36,
105n38, 106n40, 221n4
Gjerston, Donald, 26n16, 80n24
God (as a Big Other), 22
Gómez, Luis O., xiii
"gouge out the mind," 99
gradual vs. sudden enlightenment, 36,
153. *See also* sudden enlightenment
*Great Calming and Contemplation (Mohe
zhiguan)*, 23–24
Great Cloud Monastery, 103, 107
Greene, Eric, 13n2, 25n14
Gregory, Peter, 202n
Guanding, 21–25, 25n12, 52, 60, 62, 68
Guṇabhadra, 32n22, 47, 91, 94–95
"guarding the true mind," 176–83
passim
Guoqing si. See Nation Purified
Monastery
*Guoqing bailu (One Hundred Letters from
Nation Purified Monastery)*, 21n3

Hall of Seven Patriarchs, 88, 111
Harbsmeier, Christoph, 273n20
Heirman, Anne, 221n4
hierarchy, 8, 38, 80–81, 115, 123, 131,
141–42, 162, 239
historians, xiii, 2, 7, 210, 214; inventing
the masters, 15
history, x–xi, xiii, xiiin3, 1–10, chap. 1,
23–27, 49, 58, 60, 67–73, 88n10, 109,

111, 117, 124–27, 135, 137, 143–45, 161,
165–66, 199–202, 210n23, 228, 231,
276n1, 280, 284; bad versions of, 118,
140, 143, 146; and koans, 253, 255, 258,
258n9, 268; and meta-history, 159. *See
also* fictionalizing process
*History of the Masters and Disciples of
Laṅkāvatāra Sūtra (Lengqie shizi ji)*,
30n19, 86n2, 89–98. *See also* Jingjue
History of the South (Nanshi), 99
*History of the Transmission of the
Dharma-Treasury (Fu fazang yinyuan
zhuan)*, 23–24, 52, 69, 72n15, 124
Hongren, 7, 15n4, 27, 85; his Daoist
ways, 79–82, 96–97, 115, 121; with
Daoxin, 57–59; death of, 64, 100;
with Faru, 58, 61–64, 66–67, 69–70,
76; with Huineng, 98–101, 122–29, 137,
139–52; with Shenxiu, 70, 78–79, 81,
109, 111; with ten descendants, 85–86,
89–90, 98, 108; and zany language,
96
Hopkins, Jeffrey, xiii
Hu Shih, 40, 40n32, 102n33, 104n35,
105n38, 106n40, 108n41, 111n44,
113n47, 147n16
Hubbard, Jamie, 26n15, 27n17
Huichao (disciple of Faru), 88n10
Huike, 1, 20, 29, 39–54, chaps. 5 and 6;
arm auto-amputated, 44, 74–76, 115,
259; arm cut off by bandits, 43–44,
74; attempt to assassinate, 41; letter
from, 42; as only good son in
China, 76; receiving the
Laṅkāvatāra Sūtra, 76–77; standing
in the snow, 44, 93–94, 115, 259
Huiman, 44–46; standing in the snow,
44, 46
Huineng, 7, 27, 86, 98–101, 278; in
Ancestor Hall Compendium, 210–12, 214;
autobiography in *Platform Sūtra*,
137–41; as composite Confucian,
Daoist, Buddhist sage, 101; in
Gateless Entrance, 255–58, 260, 266; as
illiterate, 121–22, 145–46, 148, 150;